THE NEW HOME BUYING STRATEGY

Solve Your Cash Crunch with Team Buying Power

Marilyn D. Sullivan

Venture
2000 · Publishers
LARKSPUR, CALIFORNIA

The New Home Buying Strategy: Solve Your Cash Crunch with Team Buying Power
Copyright ©1997 Marilyn D. Sullivan

Library of Congress Cataloging-in-Publication Data
Sullivan, Marilyn D.
   The New Home Buying Strategy: Solve Your Cash Crunch with Team Buying Power/Marilyn D. Sullivan, p. cm., Includes Appendix, Glossary, Index.
   1. House buying - United States.   2. Residential real estate - United States - Purchasing. 3. Real estate investment - United States. 4. Joint tenancy - United States. 5. Real property and taxation - United States. I. Title.
CIP 96-20702
ISBN 0-9629239-1-5

---

10   9   8   7   6   5   4   3   2   1

Acknowledgments

As with all worthwhile endeavors, this book is the product of cooperative effort. While the final product is my own, a team of legal, tax, real estate and literary experts contributed their talents — Jean Howard, chief editor and master wordsmith, as the polish behind the print, Charles Lewis, C.P.A., as tax and accounting consultant, Lawrence Scancarelli, Esq., as legal consultant, Maryann Diluzio as real estate consultant, and Cathy Baehler as copy editor. I thank them heartily for their valuable contributions and support.

Dedication

This book is dedicated to the spirit of democracy in home ownership, one of our most valuable American rights.

Gender Notice

Throughout this book general references are primarily to *he* and *his*. This choice of format is merely for readability and continuity. As a female attorney/real estate broker, it is the author's position that property ownership, buying and selling real estate, and professionalism have nothing whatever to do with gender. You are earnestly invited to bear with us throughout this chosen format.

Limits of Liability

About the Author

Combining her expertise as award-winning attorney, real estate broker, and instructor for the California Department of Real Estate, Marilyn D. Sullivan is the national authority on joint ownership, having successfully assisted thousands across the nation to buy real estate by joint ownership. An attorney practicing real estate law in Larkspur, Marin County, California, Ms. Sullivan also directs Real Estate & Construction Dispute Resolution Forum, which provides arbitration and mediation services for real estate and construction disputes. As Director of Real Estate Dynamics Institute, she heads an organization which presents certified educational programs throughout the State of California. Ms. Sullivan has authored three books on real estate investments.

For inquiries about the author's services contact:
Law Office of Marilyn D. Sullivan
100 Larkspur Landing Circle, Suite 112
Larkspur, California 94939
415-461-2311

For books, forms, and software:
See Order Form or contact:
Venture 2000 Publishers
P. O. Box 625
Larkspur, California 94977
1-800-843-6700/415-461-1470

For trade distribution:
National Book Network
4720 Boston Way
Lanham, Maryland 20706
1-800-462-6420

TABLE OF CONTENTS

· Fixed Rate Loans · Adjustable Rate Mortgage (ARM) · Which Is Better – ARM or Fixed Rate? · The Annual Percentage Rate Is Important · Pre-Payment and Assumption Features · Negative Amortization · More on Private Mortgage Insurance (PMI) · FHA-Backed Loans · VA Guaranteed Loans · The Quick Qualifier · A Closing Comment

INTRODUCTION

$\mathscr{I}$f you've picked up this book . . . you're probably having a problem buying or selling a home. You have lots of company. The American Dream – to own your home – seems more elusive with each passing day. If you're looking to buy, you may not have the steep down payment funds. What's more, if you're trying to sell, you may not find a qualified buyer in today's expensive, cash-poor market.

How can you solve both problems? With *joint ownership*. Joint ownership is the new home buying strategy that uses the Internal Revenue Code to team up buyer with seller or investor for profit.

What Can This Book Do for You?

The New Home Buying Strategy is your ticket to the lucrative real estate market anywhere in the United States. It takes the joint venture – so successful in the commercial market – and, with the blessings of the Internal Revenue Code, transforms it into a buying strategy for *homes*. It answers the profit needs of the Investor co-owner and the occupancy and privacy needs of the Occupier. It produces optimum tax use of the property for the co-owners, and a windfall of tax benefits.

1

Why Is Home Ownership So Desirable?

In the past 20 years average home prices have nearly tripled, as reported by the National Association of Realtors. The house worth $44,000 twenty years ago is now worth $121,000. This represents a national average appreciation rate of 8.75% per year. The average owner received profit of $77,000 and tax deductions of $89,000, and realized $30,000 in after-tax cash. By comparison, the homeowner's counterpart who rented for the same 20 year period paid $78,000 in rent. The result – the home buyer accumulated $107,000 of profit while the renter accumulated none and paid out $78,000.

By this national average, you can see that real estate proves itself to be a most valuable asset. It not only provides us with comfort, security and tax shelter, but it increases substantially in value at the same time. No other asset can claim such multiple benefits. Is it any wonder Americans are clamoring to get their foot in the home ownership door?

Why Is a New Home Buying Strategy Needed?

The American Dream has a downside, now showing up in the residential market. The seller's benefits have resulted in a big burden for the first-time buyer, who is obliged to pay his seller's increased price tag. Our average first-time buyer faces a down payment of $25,000, plus nearly $4,000 in closing costs. Buyers are finding it tougher and tougher to come up with these door opening funds. Most Americans just don't have that kind of cash. To meet these times of downsizing and belt tightening in the wake of rapidly rising real estate values, new strategies are needed to buy properties – especially homes. Joint ownership does just that.

Why Is This Book Unique?

It's the Blueprint for Residential Joint Ownerships

Here is the *first* standard model of a residential joint ownership – created by a real estate attorney and broker. For the first time, *The New Home Buying Strategy* establishes residential joint ownership as a *formal discipline* – it presents a blueprint for the residential joint ownership transaction which gives it validity for all participants. With its universal definitions it will be understood by all in the same way, legitimizing joint ownership as a new and reliable means to acquire, sell and retain homes.

The Author Is an Expert

The New Home Buying Strategy brings the author's three fields of expertise to you, the reader, so you will succeed in joint ownership. The author – an award-winning real estate attorney, broker and educator – is the recognized joint ownership authority, having developed what has now become the uniform Joint Ownership Agreement, which she has herself successfully applied to thousands of transactions.

...And There's More Practical Information

Other strategies: Although joint ownership is the focus of this book, all other reliable home buying strategies are presented – lease option, seller financing, loan assumption, and a full array of low down payment loan programs including VA and FHA.

How to qualify as a buyer: This book is chock full of facts about loans – from qualifying criteria to charts showing you how much of a home you can afford, how much income you'll have to make and whether you'll have to pay for mortgage insurance.

First-time buyer coach: The first-time buyer, typically overwhelmed by his first purchase, is coached on all the basics of buying a home alone *or* with a co-owner. The reference materials available through the Order Form give you additional aids to walk you through your first purchase.

Uses of your living trust: The living trust is ideal for relatives to invest as a co-owner and gift their interest away at death in one easy step. When the Investor is alive, he earns his profit. When he dies, his interest goes to his co-owner.

Solution for distressed times: Joint ownership as the solution for divorce, foreclosure or relocation.

At last – understand the tax benefits of home ownership: Home ownership's tax benefits are some of the primary reasons that buying a home is the American Dream. This book about home ownership would not be complete without discussing this important issue. "Taxes" have always been a topic to be avoided. Americans tend to think they are complicated and beyond their understanding. But in this book, they are not.

The New Home Buying Strategy weaves short-term and long-term tax benefits into each sample, presenting each tax benefit in a simple, easy-to-understand manner. Investor and Occupier are shown how to defer taxes on gain they have made by rolling out of the joint ownership under Internal Revenue Code §1034 or by exchanging out under Internal Revenue Code §1031.

What Tools Do You Get?

Sample transactions clearly illustrate a joint ownership transaction from offer to buyout, refinance, and sale. You get all documents necessary to develop the transaction – also available through the Order Form at the end of this book by fax, mail order, on line or as user-friendly software. Handy charts, also available as math-based software, help you evaluate your transaction, including ownership splits, Investor return, tax deductions, and the figures at buyout and sale. Finally, the Joint Ownership Checklist carefully steps you through your transaction.

You'll learn all the strategies you'll need to solve the proverbial Cash Crunch and realize *your* American Dream – whether by joint *or* sole ownership. This book is indeed the result of these well-tested strategies that make home ownership accessible to you, the reader, and that make joint ownership The Great Equalizer as we move into the 21st Century.

Chapter One

JOINT OWNERSHIP: THE GREAT EQUALIZER

You are the real estate consumer. As such, you are entitled to the many rights and powers that come with owning property. Now, here's your ticket: *joint ownership*. This chapter explains joint ownership and answers your questions: How does it work? Is this something new – or is it tried and true? Were new rules created for joint ownership as your home buying strategy? Can you and your co-owner truly enjoy equal benefits and burdens, and maximum tax use? And most importantly: How will it work for *you*? Discover why *joint ownership* is The Great Equalizer – and your best buying strategy for real estate – as we enter the 21st century.

*T*he value, accessibility, and tax benefits associated with real estate make it far and away the most desirable of assets. This distinction endows real estate ownership with decisive influence over human events. For the many reasons presented throughout this book, we predict that shared purchases will become more popular during this decade, giving the joint ownership concept increasing influence on our lives.

We believe in joint ownership as The Great Equalizer. As team structures and buying strategies gain popularity, co-owners in increasing numbers receive the rights and powers of property ownership – a more equitable distribution of those rights and powers.

Here, then, is our blueprint for the joint ownership transaction: a blending of tax definitions, obligations, and rights that creates home ownership. Through this book, we hope to bring the goal of property ownership within your reach.

Joint Ownership: A History

The history of joint ownership is no mystery. Its rules and regulations have been around for a long time: joint ownership has been used for maximum profit in the commercial real estate market for decades. Consumers of commercial real estate realized that they could sweeten the purchase pot if they combined resources from more than one party. With joint buying power, they could successfully purchase properties and share in the ownership benefits and burdens.

Joint Ownership – A Boon from the Internal Revenue Service

In fact, joint ownership in the commercial market became so popular that in 1981 the Internal Revenue Service extended its tax benefits to the residential marketplace by enacting Internal Revenue Code ("IRC") §280A. That section, to be found in its complete form in the *Appendix*, permits one individual to assist another in buying a principal residence to be occupied by just one of the co-owners, while substantial tax benefits are reaped by all.

Note: IRC §280A specifically offers the dual advantages of (1) making home ownership possible in otherwise difficult situations and (2) permitting one of the owners (the Investor) to claim expenses associated with rental property. It applies to the purchase where two or more acquire an ownership interest in a dwelling and one person is entitled to occupy the unit as a principal residence. For example, this section provides a means for a parent to help a child purchase an otherwise unaffordable home, while protecting the parent's investment with an ownership interest in the property.

Why Joint Ownership Now?

Because the residential real estate market was on the upswing through most of the 80s, there was really no need to take tax advantage of IRC §280A through joint ownership of homes. Now, however, there *is* a reason for residential joint ownership: a rise in real estate values, coupled with a lasting downturn in the economy. The resulting changed financial climate mixes sluggish home sales with unaffordable property and lack of capital. It could be discouraging – but wait a minute. These are the *ideal conditions* for a team buying strategy like joint ownership!

Qualified buyers are still plentiful, but their cash resources have dwindled. Properties are available, but the market has slowed down. The residential market is ripe for a solution. Enter: joint ownership. It fills the bill by teaming up qualified buyers who need a down payment with payment-heavy sellers who need buyers or profit-seeking Investors.

Enter Residential Joint Ownership

In prior times, the residential market did not really lend itself to partnership. Demand for home co-ownership did not exist. Although real estate has always been expensive, homes were affordable enough for the single-family purchaser to buy alone. Also, the financial climate was such that the purchaser could squeeze out a down payment.

But appreciation of residential property crested in the mid-80's, and recession followed. Now, times have changed. Residential property has become outpriced for the average buyer, and down payment funds are hard to come by. Coming into the 21st century we have a lot of credit-worthy buyers without down payment cash. We also have a surplus of owners who can't sell their properties. There's an elegant solution here: team up for joint ownership.

The Down Payment That Wasn't...

In the mid-1990s in the United States the median salary for a male in his early 30s was $28,500, and for his female counterpart, $23,500. The median price of a first home was $121,000. With two wage earners to a family, a mortgage payment could be met. But there is no reserve: that elusive $25,000 down payment is still out of reach. In an economy marked by recession and vastly appreciated real estate prices, the down payment becomes a deal breaker as it never was before.

...And How to Create It

There are two ways to go to solve this problem: either reduce down payment requirements, or add to the down payment pot. The former is highly unlikely. The goal, then, is to add to the virtually empty down payment pot. The pot sweetener is an Investor wearing the hat of seller, family member, friend, or interested outside party.

Is Home Ownership Really So Valuable?

Joint ownership boosts the Occupier's economic status – advancing property ownership and creating substantial tax deductions. The Occupier's greatest advantage is his becoming an owner of property. His participation in the joint ownership transaction transforms him from a renter into a home owner. The Occupier converts what was once a monthly rental payment into a tax deduction. Instead of paying rent each month, he makes a mortgage payment and claims a large part of it as tax-deductible interest.

Note: Gender references throughout are made for readability and continuity only.

His cash outlay becomes an investment in the property and a series of valuable tax deductions. These deductions provide the Occupier with his most valuable tax break – and his most significant reason for entering into joint ownership. The Occupier ends up with about a third of his payments as an after-tax cash return. On top of that, his equity in his home grows — all the while earning his title as a home owner with its ample bundle of rights.

With the joint ownership, the Occupier jumps on the ownership bandwagon despite his lack of funds for the proverbial down payment. After the Occupier-Investor team qualifies for a mortgage loan, the Investor provides the down payment. In this way the Occupier can acquire property about five years earlier than he could have otherwise. Should the Occupier wait the five years and lose valuable tax deductions in the interim – or does he choose to join with an Investor now and share property appreciation with his co-owner? Personally, I'd prefer to give a share to the Investor instead of the government, and enjoy exclusive occupancy of my home.

Some Real-Life Examples

They say a picture is worth a thousand words. My philosophy is that a true-life example is worth a million bucks. The example I use here is truly a representative one. It involves a property I selected solely because I bought it recently myself, and therefore I had personal access to all the numbers. I was as shocked by its statistics as you may be. This is an average California home in an above-average California town.

Example 1: The $51,000 Property

22 years ago Doris and Bill were married and decided to purchase their first home. The cost in high-priced California was $51,000. Over the course of ownership they made minimal capital repairs and installed additional landscaping at $2,200. Now, 22 years later, they are selling their home for $411,000! In addition, in their 22 years of ownership, they have claimed a total of $288,000 in tax deductions: $225,000 for mortgage interest and $63,000 for property taxes. Their home appreciated 32% per year, amounting to a profit of $360,000. By comparison, had they rented a comparable home they would have paid $224,000 in rent over the 22-year period, and on top of that would have lost $288,000 in tax deductions (amounting generally to $95,000 in after-tax dollars), and $360,000 in appreciation.

Are you shocked by this example? In California, it reflects the norm. But nationally it is not. So let's pull the national average referenced in the introduction and compare it.

Example 2: The $44,000 Property

As reported by the National Association of Realtors, twenty years ago the average price of an American's first home was $44,000. Now, twenty years later, that same home is worth $121,000. That amounts to simple appreciation of 8.75% per year, earning the first time home buyer $77,000. Tax benefits over the twenty years were $89,000: $72,000 in mortgage interest and $17,000 in property taxes. (After-tax realization amounts to about $30,000.) Had this person rented a similar home for the same period, he would have paid $78,000 in rent instead of accumulating wealth of $107,000 – $30,000 after-tax cash and $77,000 in property appreciation.

Thus, computations using the national average for first-time home ownership reveal nearly 9% simple annual appreciation over a twenty-year ownership. This proves the adage that the longer you own, the more you make. The reason for *the longer the better* is that every five to seven years the market generally experiences a down cycle. Longer ownership allows the down cycles and up cycles to balance out into a consistent appreciation rate. For this reason, we suggest that it may be best to begin your joint ownership transaction with a term of seven to ten years. In reality, we find that neither Occupier nor Investor wants to be tied into an ownership that long. But for appreciation purposes, the longer the better. The above examples prove this point.

Now that the advantages of home ownership have been demonstrated, let's focus on joint ownership as the means to get your foot in this valuable home ownership door.

Joint Ownership: The New Home Buying Strategy

As we discussed above, joint ownership is not new to real estate. This structure of ownership has been well-tested in its commercial form. What *is* so new is its use in the residential market. Joint purchases of commercial property have been popular for decades: recall the joint ventures and limited partnerships so popular in the 70s and 80s. Groups joined and purchased commercial real estate, operated it, and jointly profited. By 1985, the limited partnership achieved widespread recognition as a highly profitable way to buy commercial property.

Joint ownership in the residential market may be new, but it has withstood the test of time in its commercial form. In fact, it has proven itself to be a highly profitable use of shared resources. While new strategies are often needed in changing times, consumers hesitate to use them until they are proven. Here, we have the best of both worlds — a new strategy for the residential market that has already been vigorously tested in the commercial forum.

How We've Created This New Home Buying Strategy

The key to a successful residential joint ownership transaction is the customized Joint Ownership Agreement and its accompanying documents. Here, created for this book, we present this package for your use. It blends the needs of the co-owners with the requirements of the Internal Revenue codes in a structure appropriate for residential real estate.

The Joint Ownership Agreement uses the proven model of the commercial joint ownership, but carefully tailors it to the unique needs of residential co-owners. The sister joint ventures in the commercial market consist of co-owners, but the structure is vastly different from that called for in the residential market. The transactions modeled in this book have been structured correctly and with the right documents – that is what we have done for you. After testing our model with thousands of transactions, we present you with a uniform Joint Ownership Agreement to fit your own residential transaction in any state of the union. It works. In fact, it works very well.

The Return of Teamwork

Prior to the 70s and 80s, teamwork was a commonplace strategy. Families worked together to realize important goals, including home ownership by its members. Typically, a child lived at home, and the family members all saved together to buy a home. When the child matured into adulthood, the family pot provided that essential down payment and entry into home ownership. In those days economic "graduation" was a move from family to new family, usually by marriage.

A few decades ago, team effort also gained importance outside of the family. Teaming up became a valuable way of solving community problems. Teams met at church, at neighbors' homes, at school, and at social functions. Cooperative efforts utilized resources efficiently and got results. Team contribution was a natural problem-solving strategy.

The Me Generation – The 70s and 80s

The 70s and 80s transformed team effort into individual enterprise. Independence became more important than results. It became essential to know yourself and get what you needed. Achievement of goals became a personal issue. Some called it the "me generation." What began as "independence" transformed into isolation.

Times Have Changed

But the world's economy has changed. The days of financial independence are over – especially in the residential real estate market. In the wake of recession we have a burgeoning number of buyers who are qualified to own, but can't come up with that down payment. In many parts of the United States, where the real estate recession still lurks, we have a growing number of sellers who can't get relief from their mortgages. For them, foreclosures have more than tripled.

Family members and friends look on, not knowing how to assist. Sellers feel burdened, unable to sell their properties. Outside investors still believe in real estate as the best investment, but don't want to manage the property. It's time for these individuals to join together for mutual benefit. The answer is to team up for mutual profit. The joint ownership transaction allows them to solve their problems together – conferring most tax deductions on the Occupier and most profit on the Investor.

Joint Ownership Is the Teamwork Solution

Joint ownership has proven itself in the current market to be an extremely practical and workable way to buy residential real estate and defer tax on profit for all co-owners. Let's take a look at why this is true. The residential joint ownership is a direct response to the high cost of residential property and the average buyer's inability to afford a house on his own.

The 90s were bench marked by restriction in our economy. Everywhere you looked, paring down and tightening budgets were the mode of the day. This same restriction has filtered to the buyer real estate market, leaving sellers with a very select group of buyers and a surplus of qualified buyers who don't have the down payment cash. Times have changed. Financing structures now need to change to meet real estate needs — and to solve the buyer's and seller's problems.

Teaming Up to Solve Buyer's and Seller's Problem

The buyer's problem: lack of down payment cash. The seller's problem: he's saddled with expenses he'd rather not meet or can't meet. They can team together and solve one another's problems, or invite a third party to help do so. The seller joins with his credit-worthy buyer, they get a new loan, the seller cashes out with all but the down payment amount, and stays on title for the rest.

The buyer moves into the property, exclusively occupies and pays all the property expenses. The seller stays on title since he still has an investment in the property. The buyer cashes him out in five years – and the seller has the opportunity to earn far more than the down payment funds if the property appreciates. In their agreement they make appreciation a condition. If the required appreciation is not met, co-ownership continues until it does. It's a win-win in every sense of the word.

This is just one example of joint ownership with the seller. There are many Investor sources other than the seller. But before we examine the Investor and his many faces, let's look at the overall anatomy of the joint ownership.

Anatomy of a Joint Ownership

There are three basic ingredients to a successful joint ownership: a qualified Occupier, a willing Investor and a good property. Who are the players? Here are the profiles of Occupier and Investor as they function in the working joint ownership. Later, in Chapter Two, we'll examine these team members in more depth.

The Occupier Profile

For joint ownership to work in the residential market, full uninterrupted occupancy of the property must be given to the Occupier, who uses the property as his principal residence. This feature qualifies the residential joint ownership as an *arms-length* transaction; hence, it meets Internal Revenue Code requirements. Of course, the Occupier also pays the price for full occupancy – he pays all the expenses.

The Investor Profile

The Investor to the joint ownership can wear many faces. He can be the home seller. The Investor can be a member of the Occupier's family or friendship group who wants to assist the Occupier, but also wants to make a profit. Or, the Investor may be someone the Occupier doesn't know, but someone who wants to invest in real estate.

The Investor provides all or part of the down payment – or defers it as retained equity, in the case where the Investor is the seller – and co-signs with the Occupier for a loan. After that, the Investor basically walks away, leaving exclusive occupancy and all obligations to the Occupier. In return, Investor receives an ownership interest, a good share of the property's appreciation, and tax benefits including deferred capital gains.

Creating Security for the Investor

In the family situation, the predecessor to the Joint Ownership Agreement was a *handshake* cash contribution by a family member – rarely to be repaid. And was that contribution documented by a note and mortgage? Usually not. By conveyance of an ownership interest? Typically not. By a clear agreement as to repayment and terms? On the contrary. Most often the lender required a *gift letter* by which the lending relative declared that the loan was a gift. The lending relative received a copy of a gift letter with no promise to repay – much less any secured interest in the property.

Joint ownership is a system that has matured far beyond the gift letter transaction. A carefully constructed Joint Ownership Agreement provides security to the contributing party – including proof of co-ownership and a mortgage. The lending party is designated the Investor, and the obligated party is the Occupier. Both parties are identified as co-owners by title vesting in their names.

For the Investor who is a relative, the joint ownership transaction clearly documents his down payment contribution as an *ownership interest* in the property. The terms and conditions of that ownership interest are specified in the Joint Ownership Agreement, for which a memorandum is formally recorded on the property. The Investor is also granted a Deed of Trust/Mortgage by the Occupier. This secures the Occupier's performance promised in the Joint Ownership Agreement. In contrast to the gift letter transaction, the joint ownership Investor is in a far more secured and desirable position. He is there on title to make a profit, secure that the occupier will pay all expenses.

Investor's Dream – No Management Duties or Carrying Costs

The well-planned Joint Ownership Agreement is the Investor's dream. His investment bears no carrying costs since the Occupier pays all expenses. The Occupier has agreed to be responsible for all ownership duties and obligations, including payments and capital improvements. Even better, our joint ownership Investor doesn't have tenant headaches since his team member is exclusively occupying and maintaining the property. Thus, the Investor is on title and secured by a Deed of Trust/Mortgage accompanying the Joint Ownership Agreement. In this position, the Investor can basically sit back and await his profit, fully secured, while all cash requirements are met by the Occupier.

When the Seller Is the Investor

The joint ownership transaction can be the seller's best strategy for selling his property and beginning or adding to his investment portfolio. By offering joint ownership he expands his pool of buyers. In a slow market, the seller gets financial relief through co-owning with the Occupier. He gets relief from the mortgage, property taxes, and insurance. The occupying co-owner takes over those obligations. From the loan he and the Occupier obtain together, the seller immediately cashes out with at least 80% of value. He can then move on to his next home while at the same time co-owning his old property, earning a good profit for the equity he has left in. In this way, the seller gets the best of both worlds – selling and investing at the same time. With this diversification, the seller reduces his basis for tax purposes through his partial sale. Finally, he adds impressively to his investment portfolio through his joint ownership interest.

Equal Benefits to Investor and Occupier

The joint ownership scenario is designed to be equally beneficial to both Occupier and Investor. Let's tally the pluses and minuses, benefits and burdens. Are they fairly allocated?

If not, is there a balancing feature elsewhere? In the ideal joint ownership, the Occupier and Investor reap mutual benefits from the highest possible tax use of their property. Although the joint ownership transaction gives the Occupier the majority of the tax deductions, the equities are balanced with the Investor's receipt of an equity interest that matches his profit requirements over the term of the Joint Ownership Agreement.

In the joint ownership, the Investor and Occupier decide how long the agreement will last. Past trends are used to project future property appreciation — for a projected return to the Investor in line with the parties' expectations. The Occupier and Investor can project any return they wish to the Investor. It all depends on these parties' mutual agreement.

They can also agree that if the property's appreciation has not reached a certain point by term, the agreement will automatically be extended. This ensures that if the market takes a downturn during their ownership, term will not be greeted with loss. It will defer cashout or buyout of the co-owners until the market has recovered.

Occupier's Share of Benefits

In the examples recited earlier in this chapter, the Occupier's tax deductions during his joint ownership begin his wealth-building foundation. Aside from his abundant mortgage interest and property tax deductions, another formidable benefit to the Occupier reveals itself in his long-term tax portfolio. The Occupier can shelter all profit he has earned through his co-ownership. He is entitled to cash out of the joint ownership and roll into another property of like value.

Internal Revenue Code §1034, included in the *Appendix,* authorizes the Occupier to continue his investment in another property without having to declare capital gains. Tax-free continuation of investment is the Occupier's prime long-term benefit. So once the Occupier attains the rank of home owner, all profit he earns in his home becomes his tax-free bank roll. It's a right no American should be without.

Thus, the Occupier's cumulative tax deductions and tax deferral options are clearly substantial. When you read Chapters Nine and Ten, you'll see just how much the two Occupiers mentioned therein were able to claim in tax deductions. In Chapter Eleven the Occupier's long-term savings are highlighted. These tax benefits alone point to home ownership as the most lucrative investment a taxpayer can make. But for the Occupier, these hefty benefits are only a part of the privileges the Occupier derives from the joint ownership. Armed with his newfound co-ownership of property and his share of profits to come, the Occupier co-owner attains a sound and respected financial position and the beginning of his financial empire.

Investor's Share of Benefits

The joint ownership transaction confers its share of benefits on the Investor as well. First, there is profit. The typical joint ownership projects a higher return on investment to the Investor than he could expect from any marketplace. Although the future cannot be predicted, joint ownership profits depend on appreciation of real estate — a proven trend over time.

The second benefit to the Investor arises from the depreciation deduction. Since his property interest is defined in the Joint Ownership Agreement as an *investment holding,* the Investor is entitled to claim a depreciation deduction — if his portfolio otherwise allows it. The Occupier creates the Investor's investment holding by exclusively occupying the property and paying rent. Without this legal proof of investment holding, such a deduction would not be available to the Investor. The Investor can also make property payments and claim their deductions if he so chooses.

Even more significant are the joint ownership Investor's long-term tax options. Under the exchange provisions of Internal Revenue Code §1031, included in the *Appendix,* the Investor is entitled to defer tax on all profits he has earned in the joint ownership transaction. He qualifies for a tax-deferred exchange because he is an *owner,* not a *lender.* This is the key to the Investor's tax deferral benefits.

A seller or third party who merely *lends* must recognize and pay tax on *all profit* he makes. He cashes out; he pays tax. Not with the joint ownership. The sound Joint Ownership Agreement clearly defines the Investor as an owner. The only true lender in the entire transaction is the financing institution. Thus, the Investor co-owner can safely defer all tax on his profit by utilizing the exchange provisions of Internal Revenue Code §1031. By contrast, the seller agreeing to seller financing or the Investor making a loan cannot defer tax since he is a lender, not an owner.

Joint Ownership Is the Great Equalizer

Joint ownership, therefore, is equally attractive to Occupier and Investor. Their risks of ownership are equally minimized when they carefully analyze appreciation factors and wisely claim optimum tax treatment. Using the ownership split method (later explained and available on software) and the uniform agreement, these important factors are fully incorporated into the joint ownership structure. They also prevent loss with automatic extension of their co-ownership if required property appreciation is not met.

Blueprint for the Joint Ownership Transaction

Thanks to this legally sound Joint Ownership Agreement, woven throughout with essential tax definitions, obligations, and rights, the joint ownership transaction creates a clear, legal ownership interest in residential real estate for all parties. Some of the requirements met by our uniform Joint Ownership Agreement are:

Tax benefits must be defined and preserved: The Joint Ownership Agreement must adequately protect the interests of both Investor and Occupier, specifically meeting Internal Revenue Code requirements.

Complete documentation: Agreements ignoring many of the parties' rights and obligations result in lightweight documentation of transactions. The uniform Joint Ownership Agreement must include all components, including the Deed of Trust/Mortgage and lease between the co-owners.

Exclusive occupancy to Occupier: This creates the necessary arms-length transaction in accordance with IRC §280A.

Exclusive Occupier obligations: The joint ownership assigns exclusive obligations to the Occupier. Tax considerations are carefully met so only one set of tax deductions is claimed by these co-owners. The Occupier claims all property expenses, including mortgage and property taxes.

Returns cannot be guaranteed: Projected return to the Investor cannot be guaranteed. The tax benefits flow to these co-owners because they are owners, not lenders. Return guaranteed to the Investor jeopardizes his ownership status and exposes him to characterization as a lender. Thus, the uniform Joint Ownership Agreement does not guarantee any return – it projects return based on realistic assumptions. With its required appreciation rate, the joint ownership does end up guaranteeing returns – but in a way that preserves ownership and tax status.

Default options must be recorded: The Investor must have a way of gaining title to the property in the unfortunate event of Occupier default. The uniform Joint Ownership Agreement includes a Joint Ownership Note and Deed of Trust/Mortgage to the Investor backing up the Occupier's obligations, so if the Occupier does not perform, the Investor forecloses and gets title in his sole name.

Investor must charge rent to Occupier: If the Investor is to claim tax deductions on the co-ownership he must receive rent from the exclusively occupying Occupier per Internal Revenue Code §280A. The uniform Joint Ownership Agreement covers this essential aspect.

This book legitimizes the uniform Joint Ownership Agreement as the standard blueprint for the residential co-owner transaction across the United States. Joint ownership means Team Purchase Power – The Great Equalizer for home ownership.

What Does This Mean for You?

Did it once seem impossible for you to own real estate? Joint ownership can be your solution. You need two basic components: a team and a superior plan. With this book, you'll create the team and the strategy to make it happen.

Now that we've reviewed the evolution of joint ownership, its entry into the residential market, and why it is the home buying solution now, let's move on to Chapter Two — *The Joint Ownership Team* — so you can put your own team together.

Chapter Two

THE JOINT OWNERSHIP TEAM

Just how do you create your joint ownership package? Let's begin by putting the team members together. How do an Investor and Occupier find each other? How is a suitable property chosen? An ideal joint ownership is a satisfying mix of well-matched co-owners, planned profit, optimum tax use of property, and equal benefits. How does such a package come to be?

In Chapter One, equal benefits and optimum tax use were explored. This chapter creates the basic ingredients of a successful joint ownership – a qualified Occupier, a willing Investor, and a good property. The *Joint Ownership Checklist* featured in Chapter Three, a favorite for the first-timer, walks you step by step into the joint ownership transaction.

$\mathcal{W}$e set the ground work for joint ownership in Chapter One by analyzing its rules, regulations, and structure. Now for the hands-on part: assisting you in creating your joint ownership team. This chapter profiles the Occupier and Investor. We will begin our inventory with the Occupier – the most essential party in the creation of the joint ownership. But first, let's review the reasons why the residential joint ownership works so well to assure the Occupier a home – and privacy in his ownership.

The Logistics of Joint Ownership

Joint ownership in the residential market depends upon its meeting the requirements of Internal Revenue Code §280A. The uniform Joint Ownership Agreement and accompanying documents developed for this book fulfill these requirements. Its provisions set up a true arms-length transaction between the co-owners. This is accomplished by giving full, uninterrupted occupancy of the property to the Occupier, who uses the property as his principal residence. Thus, the Investor providing the down payment or the seller deferring a down payment walks away from management of the property for the agreement term, conferring full responsibility upon the Occupier. That responsibility carries a price – the Occupier pays all the expenses of the property. Considering the Occupier's ownership interest and tax deductions, that price is well worth it.

Why Is Joint Ownership Called for Now?

The concepts behind what we now call residential joint ownership have been authorized by real estate tax law for quite some time. But unlike the commercial real estate market, the residential market just did not have the need or the opportunity to apply joint venturing to workable arms-length relationships between co-owners of homes.

Now, joint ownership is a home buying strategy whose time has come. It solves buyer's cash crunch, seller's search for qualified buyers, and Investor's return and security needs.

Joint ownership for homes has achieved its arms-length characteristic by legally defining the parties as Occupier and Investor in the Joint Ownership Agreement. This legal definition includes an important separation of rights and powers inherent in a true arms-length relationship. This separateness is necessary for the home occupier who requires undisturbed occupancy of his principal residence.

The *Investor* who provides all or a part of the down payment funds is otherwise uninvolved in the day to day responsibilities and enjoyment of the property. He's truly the money man or woman. The *Occupier* has exclusive occupancy of the property and assumes all obligations of property ownership. He fits into his role as the property resident. This separation of ownership rights and occupancy obligations achieves the required arms-length relationship between the co-owners. It is through the distanced role of the Investor that the Occupier's necessary privacy is conferred and preserved.

Who Is the Ideal Occupier?

What are the qualities of a suitable joint ownership Occupier? An ideal Occupier would be someone with a good rental history for the past five years. Good credit qualifies him to join with the Investor for an 80% loan on the property. The Occupier's past rent should approximate 65% of the anticipated costs of mortgage, insurance, and property tax. Employment history should reflect stability for at least five years.

Monthly income should be about three times the amount of total property-related expenses, excluding utilities.

The *ideal* Occupier has available cash equal to at least 5% of the property's purchase price. Usually this amount will in large part go to closing costs – not reimbursable under the Joint Ownership Agreement, but largely deductible to the Occupier.

Interviewing the Occupier

Choosing a reliable Occupier is as important as choosing a joint ownership property with value and potential. The Occupier must be proven stable and responsible in order to ensure performance of his promises under the Joint Ownership Agreement. The Occupier will make the mortgage and property tax payments. He will exclusively occupy the property, maintaining and repairing it.

The Investor applies qualifying strategies even more stringent than any financing institution. He should interview the Occupier at length to assure himself that the Occupier is reliable, and follow up the interview with a complete reference check. This interview serves the interests of both Investor and Occupier, as it gives the Occupier a chance to present his best credentials and establish the trust necessary for both parties to enter into a formal Joint Ownership Agreement.

Where to Find Qualified Occupiers

There are a number of ways to locate qualified Occupiers. First, if a seller intends to be the joint ownership Investor, he can locate his counterpart by targeting qualified buyers – through his real estate agent or by advertising the joint ownership feature on his own. If he is represented by a real estate agent, the agent will market the joint ownership feature in the multiple listing book and by other specialized means. If unrepresented by an agent, the resourceful seller will advertise the joint ownership feature to qualified buyers himself. These selling strategies are detailed later in this chapter under *Matching Up Seller and Occupier.*

In some transactions the Investor is a *third party.* This means that the seller (the first party) is only involved in the transaction by selling property to the Occupier and Investor (second and third parties). A third-party Investor's best marketing choice is a real estate agent, who should be able to find him a suitable property and a qualified Occupier. He may also want to advertise in the newspaper for a qualified team member. The *Seller-Investor Checklist* and *Outside Investor Checklist* in Chapter Three provides step-by-step guides for locating an Occupier.

Sellers Make Excellent Investors

A joint ownership is an excellent marketing device for a seller. In particular, sellers can create a competitive edge for themselves in a buyer's market by becoming joint ownership Investors in their own properties. For a qualified Seller-Investor, joint ownership may *triple* his pool of potential buyers while generating future profits from his own property.

In a slow market, buyers tend to call the shots. Many sellers must compromise on the purchase price and other issues. In a joint ownership, a seller can be firm on his property's appraised value. Further, a joint ownership transforms him into an Investor – and his property into a lucrative business investment. He is then entitled to liberal tax breaks and deferral of gain, and continues to own an interest in his property's appreciation after selling it to the new co-owners – his Occupier and himself.

Buyers Should Suggest Joint Ownership to the Seller

The joint ownership feature is not exclusively reserved to the seller. Buyers, too can initiate a joint ownership offer. Qualified buyers lacking down payment funds should solicit sellers for a joint ownership sale. Once a seller understands the concept, joint ownership benefits become attractive. In a sluggish market like the one that ushered in the 1990s, many sellers were able to conquer unfavorable market conditions by joint ownership of their properties. Shrewd buyers with a good grasp of joint ownership can bring about similar results, even in a strong market.

Seller-Investor: Do You Qualify?

We have developed criteria to qualify a seller as a joint ownership Investor. There are others, but these provide a useful starting point.

First, the seller must be willing to defer all or most of the buyer's cash down payment. This means that the seller must have sufficient cash from a new loan or another source for the down payment on a replacement property. Second, the seller must be prepared to wait out the term of the Joint Ownership Agreement before receiving the deferred down payment and his accompanying ownership interest. Third, he must rely on appreciation over time for his return. Fourth, he must make arrangements with the buyer or another party for payment of the agent's commission, if necessary.

Joint Ownership vs. Seller Financing

Joint ownerships are sometimes compared with seller financing, but are actually quite different. In conventional seller financing the seller becomes a *lender*, receiving the down payment and a straight note for the rest of the purchase price, plus interest. The seller is then paid on a monthly basis with final pay-off sometime down the line. As a lender, the seller must pay tax on all profit from the sale. Further, he gives up all subsequent appreciation of the property. It will belong to the buyer. See Chapter Fifteen for more on seller financing.

In a joint ownership transfer, the seller defers the same down payment. He waits until the agreement expires to receive his return. But on top of that, he shares the property's appreciation with the Occupier. At the end of the joint ownership term, he collects the down payment he deferred and his share of the profit. Of course, the seller looks solely to the property's appreciation for return of the down payment he deferred and his additional ownership interest. But the transaction is structured so it doesn't terminate until the property *has* appreciated. This way, he protects against loss: the parties agree that if the required appreciation has not occurred, the joint ownership will automatically be extended.

A joint ownership's potential return will far outdistance interest earned on a conventional seller-financed note. Moreover, the seller's joint ownership risks – reduced by the Occupier's assumption of all ownership duties and costs – are nominal when compared with profit potential.

But the *major* inducements for sellers to sell their properties by joint ownership are ownership tax benefits, including depreciation and exchange-based shelter of gain. The joint ownership seller receives a generous tax break when it comes to recognizing gain. The joint ownership seller defers all tax on his profit by exchanging under Internal Revenue Code §1031 while the *lending* seller must recognize and pay tax on all profit he makes. Thus, this distinction between lender and owner can mean substantial tax savings to the joint ownership Seller-Investor.

Since the team ownership structure suits market and consumer needs so well, joint ownership will continue to increase in popularity, stimulating the residential market. Sellers who can leave about 20% of value in the property should offer the attractive joint ownership option. There is an ever-increasing surplus of qualified first-time buyers without down payment funds. The joint ownership seller has no problem drawing from this pool of qualified buyers if the joint ownership feature is marketed correctly. This is fairly straightforward. Refer to the *Seller-Investor Checklist* in Chapter Three for an easy marketing guide.

Occupier's Research of the Residential Market

Before looking for a third-party Investor, the Occupier should do his homework. First, he should investigate the real estate market and spend time previewing properties. Go to open houses. Open houses are listed in the real estate section of the newspaper. Anyone is welcome at an open house. Many of the people you will see there are just doing investigation, as you are. Working up to making the most important investment of your life doesn't come overnight. It takes time and patience. But don't think of this process as work. Searching for your dream home should be fun and exciting. The time you invest in researching the market will be well worth your while. In this way the Occupier will have a realistic idea of the value of the property he wants to acquire – and becomes quite knowledgeable about the real estate market in the process.

Loan Pre-Qualification by Occupier

Research loan qualification. Find out all you can about the criteria for loan qualification. The Occupier who has qualified for an 80% loan on his own attracts potential Investors as well as lenders. Get a complimentary copy of your credit report. TRW, Inc., P. O. Box 2350, Chatworth, California 91313-2350 is the leading credit reporting agency. Send them a request with your full name, date of birth, social security number, spouse's name, current address, and prior five years' addresses. They also need a copy of your driver's license or some other identifying document to verify your identity.

You always have the right to review your credit report. If there are mistakes on your report, ask to have them corrected. If your request is denied, you have the right to have your version of the facts included in your report. Lenders will pay attention to the explanation you give. Work on your report and get as many items as you can cleared up. If you need help, contact Consumer Credit Counseling Service at 800-388-3337. They have offices across the country and provide an excellent service for a nominal fee. If you have no credit history, deposit one to three thousand dollars in a savings account and use that as collateral for loans. With prompt payments, your good credit history will begin.

When your credit history is in order, you will be ready to pre-qualify for a loan – assuming you have the required down payment funds. You will have these funds from your Investor. The lender should be given a target price based on the properties you have previewed. If you feel that your application is weak, look for a lender that doesn't sell its mortgages in the secondary market. Most lenders do trade mortgages. These lenders have strict requirements and do not bend much because their loan packages must conform to specific standards. A lender that keeps some of its mortgages or sells them to private investors is likely to be more lenient. A mortgage broker should be able to place your loan with the right lender as long as the broker deals with this unconventional type of lender.

If you cannot pre-qualify, there is no blemish against you. Failure to pre-qualify is not recorded anywhere. In the application process you will have discovered where your weaknesses lie; now you can work to strengthen those areas. If you have found your team member, you may find that submitting loan applications with a qualified co-owner, your Investor, will make the difference. A willing Investor with a strong financial statement can often tip the scales in favor of loan approval.

Looking for an Investor

Whether you've qualified for the loan or not, move forward with your search for an Investor. If you have not loan-qualified, your mission will be twofold – improving your credit profile and seeking an Investor. The search for an Investor begins with the current pool of property sellers, explored above. The next source of Investors is the intended Occupier's roster of relatives and close friends. He should also post notices at the meeting places of his social and cultural organizations.

Another valuable source is the intended Occupier's employer. As an incentive, the employer may be willing to assist his employee in obtaining suitable housing while sharing in the profit to come from appreciation. If a job relocation is involved, the employer may be particularly motivated toward joint ownership. Refer to Chapter Thirteen for valuable information on employer-assisted plans.

Finally, the intended Occupier should consult his real estate agent, loan broker, and banker for Investors. These professionals usually have good Investor sources of their own. Some charge a separate transaction fee for matching up Investors and Occupiers. A fee is appropriate as long as its nature and extent is fully disclosed.

The Occupier can also advertise the joint ownership to the general public by placing an ad in the real estate section, specifying:

JOINT OWNERSHIP: Highly qualified buyer seeking investor interested in no risk co-ownership of owner-occupied residential property. [Optional: Buyer willing to contribute sweat equity.]

Sample Ad Seeking an Investor

The classified section you select should be targeted toward investment. Select a section heading such as *Real Estate Investments/Joint Ventures,* if available. Refer to the *Outside Investor Checklist* in the next chapter for a step-by-step guide to locate your outside Investor.

Investor Groups

Investors and Occupiers alike are alerted to the following conditions. In the last decade, several companies have been set up around the United States to assist buyers in acquiring their first properties. Be wary. Oftentimes, the amounts these groups charge to assist the first-time buyer can be excessive and disproportionate to the investment through hidden charges such as management fees, transaction fees, carrying charges, and the like. However, these lenders will provide most of the down payment funds at a high premium. The premium either lies in these lavish setup fees or disproportionately high ownership percentages to the Investor.

If you look into one of these Investor groups, be sure to review their package with a fine tooth comb and a well-energized calculator. Tally their start up, management, and termination fees. Calculate all property interests running to both the individual Investor and to the Investor group. Review the proposed co-ownership or loan agreement well. Make sure that you are not *guaranteeing* the Investor's return. As is examined in Chapter Six in *Guarantees: The Defeat of a Joint Ownership*, guarantees to the Investor jeopardize his own tax benefits, while making the Occupier a target for personal liability. Review all buyout options. Only through this level of scrutiny will you know whether the funds offered are worth what you are giving up.

Finding the Right Joint Ownership Property

You should begin looking for your property once you have completed your market research and loan analysis. You may already have your Investor or you may be planning to make the seller your Investor. Now that you have conducted your preliminary investigation of the residential real estate market, it's time to hone in on the home of your choice.

Finding the right joint ownership property is as vital to a successful joint ownership as finding the right co-owner. The aim in getting into this venture is to make a profit through appreciation. Hence, the right property is chosen for its appreciation factors as well as its price.

You can't read the future – but you can come close. Perform your own independent investigation of property values in your area. Talk to savvy real estate agents. Review classified ads. Go to open houses. Previewing and tracking sales of properties will give you a good idea of fair market value.

Housing markets reflect local and national conditions, such as inflation, the job market, new construction, and many other variables. These factors influence supply and demand, which in turn dictate the strength of the real estate market. You will have to investigate and review these factors and make your own judgment as to market durability – which will ultimately determine your property's appreciation over time.

Of course, if your intention is to transform the seller into your Investor, the seller's Investor-qualification characteristics will be about as important as the property's appreciation history. You will want to locate a seller who can leave up to 20% of value in the property. The amount will be determined by the amount of down payment and closing costs you are missing. The seller will have to fill in that blank.

After spending a reasonable period educating yourself about the market, you will most likely choose to hire a real estate agent to find the best property. The real estate agent's role in the joint ownership is explored in Chapter Four. If you are the Occupier, you will also want to choose a property you expect to live in for the next five to seven years. If you are the Investor, you will necessarily be more objective than the Occupier for the sake of your investment. Both parties should strive to base their analysis and resulting decisions purely on mathematics.

Matching Up Seller and Occupier

Seller Seeking Occupier

Once a seller has decided to sell his property by joint ownership, he should clearly market it as a joint ownership deal. The joint ownership feature summons up an entirely different group of potential buyers – the ones that have good income and credit, but little cash.

The seller can advertise in the real estate classified ads, stating the detailed parameters of his proposed joint ownership. For example, if he is willing to defer the full 20% down payment, he should state:

JOINT OWNERSHIP: Seller willing to defer 20% down payment to good income, good credit Occupier to co-own and exclusively occupy residential property.

Sample Ad Seeking Occupier

An even *more* catchy ad would read:

NOTHING DOWN. You live in house and make payments for co-ownership.

Sample Ad Seeking Occupier

If the seller needs more cash out of the transaction, he should offer to defer only a part of the down payment. The wise joint ownership seller also circulates flyers through his social, cultural, religious, and employment circles.

Occupier Seeking Seller

The intended Occupier should watch the real estate classifieds for joint ownership offers. For his own advertisement, he should target a category titled *Joint Venture*. Ask yourself: If I were a seller interested in joint ownership-selling my property, where would I place such an ad?

The Occupier can also place his own ad, which would read something like this:

TO JOINT OWNERSHIP SELLER: Occupier with good income and credit desires to co-own and exclusively occupy residential property with seller willing to defer down payment.

Sample Ad Seeking Seller-Investor, "Real Estate" Section

Another way to phrase such an ad is:

I'LL PAY, YOU OWN: Buyer willing to take over your payment for occupancy and ownership interest.

Another Ad Seeking Seller-Investor, "Real Estate" Section

Local real estate Investor groups offer another market-ing tool. Most cosmopolitan areas have groups that meet regularly, giving members and visitors an opportunity to market real estate. Usually, this method of open marketing is not limited to the Seller-Investor, but is available to potential Buyer-Occupiers as well. To locate these groups, consult the real estate section or the real estate and business events calen-dars of your newspaper.

Last, but not least, the most powerful ingredient for marketing a property is a real estate agent. Resources are available to an agent that no consumer can access on his own – such as the multiple listing service. And the agent has the knowledge and experience necessary to attain maximum exposure.

Now let's move on to Chapter Three, *The Joint Ownership Checklist:* your easy step-by-step guide for assembling your valuable team and acquiring a property.

Chapter Three

THE JOINT OWNERSHIP CHECKLIST

Here is the *Joint Ownership Checklist* for your use in developing your own transaction. There is a separate checklist for each of the three types of co-owners – Occupier, Seller-Investor, and outside Investor. The joint ownership checklist steps you through your transaction – from marketing and research to funding and signing the documents. It's a proven formula for success of your joint ownership, no matter which role you play.

Occupier Checklist

1. Submit loan documents to pre-qualify for a loan through your loan broker or bank.

Your joint ownership choices become more meaningful if you know from the start the maximum loan for which you qualify. Most lenders have pre-qualification packages. This process will define the value of the joint ownership property you can afford and how much Investor participation you need.

Even if you cannot pre-qualify, you will know where you come up short – so you can intelligently address your short-coming with your potential Investor. By identifying where your financial profile is weak, you can concentrate on strengthening or correcting the problem. Sometimes it only takes clearing up a few lingering items on your credit report. You may be able to correct these items and submit an amended package for pre-qualification after all.

2. Go to advertised open houses; investigate the residential real estate market and properties available.

3. Advertise for an outside Investor.

4. Advertise for a joint ownership seller.

5. Enlist the services of a real estate agent to access the local index of properties for sale, especially those featuring creative financing options.

6. Explore your own resources for Investor funds – from relatives to friends, employers, and co-workers.

7. Give a copy of this book to all prospective team members.

8. Find an attorney who is well-versed in preparing Joint Ownership Agreements. If you use the form agreement or you are in a state that utilizes escrow companies, we suggest that you hire an attorney, at least to review your documents.

9. Enter into the Joint Ownership Preliminary Commitment (see Chapter Five) with an Investor you select.

10. Locate a suitable property if you have not already done so.

11. Make an offer on a property.

If no Investor has been located, make an offer contingent upon the seller's participation as Investor.

12. Retry the same sources for an Investor.

If the joint ownership participation offer has been rejected and you have not found an Investor, retry the same sources. Now that you have a specific property in mind, you will have an additional selling point – the property itself. Use the approach that appeals to potential Investors – work up past appreciation figures on the property and present your statistics in business format.

13. Retry advertising.

If you still haven't located an Investor, advertise again. This time, feature your intended investment – the joint ownership property. You may want to include a *projected* annual return to the Investor – but be careful to stress that there are *no guarantees.*

14. Open escrow with an attorney or escrow company, depending upon which state you are located in, after the offer is accepted.

15. Fund the loan.

Once the offer is accepted and the Investor is located, go back to your loan broker or lender and request that the purchase be funded. Advise your consultant that the purchase will be a co-ownership and the Investor will also sign on the loan. Submit Investor loan applications and advise that a Deed of Trust/Mortgage will issue from Occupier to Investor for the Occupier's interest in the property. Advise that this co-owner security instrument will be subordinated to the lender's and will be recorded within the escrow, but after the lender's senior security interest.

If the lender is adamant that no other security interest be recorded at closing, consider recording the Occupier-Investor Deed of Trust/Mortgage after closing. (See Chapter Four, *Putting the Joint Ownership Together, Reassuring the Lender.*)

16. Contact your attorney for preparation of the joint ownership documents or review of the form documents you have prepared.

The ideal time to have the documents prepared or reviewed is after loan approval comes through. Before that, you'll be paying for a review that may not result in a sale. Thus, we suggest setting up the attorney appointment for after the loan contingency is to be removed.

17. Contact your accountant.

Submit the Joint Ownership Agreement to your accountant for allocation and confirmation of tax deductions and other tax-related issues.

Seller-Investor Checklist

When not using a real estate agent:

1. In the real estate classifieds advertise the property for sale, offering joint ownership participation.

2. Post a sign outside advertising the property for sale and offering seller joint ownership participation.

3. Advise relatives, friends, and co-workers of your willingness to sell by joint ownership.

4. Attend real estate networking groups to market your property and the joint ownership feature.

If selling through a real estate agent:

If the above methods do not produce results, you will most likely choose to hire a real estate agent to market your property for sale.

5. Hire a real estate agent.

Advise your agent of your willingness to sell by joint ownership. Be sure to select an agent who understands joint ownership. If they do not, give them a copy of this book.

6. Have your agent list the property as "Seller willing to co-own with qualified buyer who will occupy and pay expenses."

With or without an agent:

7. When you accept any joint ownership offer, specify that it be subject to a two to three week period for approval of Occupier suitability.

8. Consider the following criteria to determine Occupier suitability:

· The maximum loan for which he pre-qualifies. He should be able to qualify for the loan on his own or with minimal assistance from you.

He should have:

· A good credit rating and history.

· A good five-year rental history.

· A good employment history for the past five years.

· A history of reliability and pride, especially when it comes to taking care of the contemplated joint ownership property.

9. Accept the offer subject to the parties' entering into a mutually agreeable Joint Ownership Agreement within the next 30 days.

At this point it is also wise to enter into the Joint Ownership Preliminary Commitment (see Chapter Five), establishing the primary terms that will be incorporated into the formal Joint Ownership Agreement. The commitment should be attached to the offer as an addendum.

10. If a real estate agent is involved, determine how the agent's commission will be paid.

Through joint ownership participation, the seller may not always cash out with enough to pay the agent's commission. Payment of the real estate commission can be a major obstacle to a joint ownership by the seller. Thus, the seller should make sure he will be able to pay the commission, either alone or with participation by the Occupier, before he seriously explores joint ownership sale through his agent. If the seller is depending upon contribution to commission payment by the Occupier, he should discuss this with the intended Occupier at the beginning.

11. Fund the loan.

Once the offer is accepted, the seller should begin loan application – beginning with his current lender if their loan package is attractive. Advise the lender that the purchase will be a joint ownership, and the seller will stay on title and bring in a co-owner. Both parties will be signing on the loan. Advise the lender that a Deed of Trust/Mortgage will issue from Occupier to Seller-Investor pledging the Occupier's interest in the property. Their security instrument will be subordinated to the lender's and will be recorded within the escrow, but after the lender's senior security interest.

If the lender is adamant that no other security interest be recorded at closing, consider recording the Occupier-Investor Deed of Trust/Mortgage after closing. (See Chapter Four, *Putting the Joint Ownership Together, Reassuring the Lender.*)

12. Contact your attorney for preparation or review of the Joint Ownership Agreement and related documents.

13. Contact your accountant.

Submit the Joint Ownership Agreement to your accountant for allocation and confirmation of tax deductions and other tax-related issues.

Outside Investor Checklist

1. Advertise in the real estate classifieds offering to participate as Investor in a residential joint ownership with a qualified Occupier.

2. Advise relatives, friends, and co-workers of your willingness to joint ownership invest.

3. Advise real estate agents of your willingness to joint ownership invest.

4. Attend real estate networking groups to announce your willingness to jointly own properties.

5. When you locate a potential Occupier, determine suitability by the following criteria:

· The maximum loan for which he pre-qualifies. He should be able to qualify for the loan on his own or with minimal assistance from you. He should have:

· A good credit rating and history.

· A good five-year rental history.

· A good employment history for the past five years.

· A history of reliability and pride, especially when it comes to taking care of the contemplated joint ownership property.

6. Have the Occupier pre-qualify for a loan. If he comes up short, submit your team application, which may shift the lender toward approval.

7. Enter into a Joint Ownership Preliminary Commitment with the Occupier you select (see Chapter Five).

8. Search for a joint ownership property.

When you have selected the Occupier, you and/or the Occupier should search for a suitable joint ownership property based on the following criteria:

· Price at or below fair market value.

· Past appreciation shows upward consistent trend.

· Geographical area expecting appreciation in the next five years.

· General desirable physical property traits.

9. Jointly make an offer on the property desired.

10. Fund the loan.

Once the offer is accepted, go back to the loan broker or lender who pre-qualified the Occupier and request that the purchase be funded. Advise your consultant that the purchase will be a joint ownership, and both Investor and Occupier will be signing on the loan. Submit Investor applications and advise that a Deed of Trust/Mortgage will issue from Occupier to Investor pledging the Occupier's interest in the property. Their security instrument will be subordinated to the lender's and will be recorded within the escrow, but after the lender's senior security interest.

If the lender is adamant that no other security interest be recorded at closing, consider recording the Occupier-Investor Deed of Trust/Mortgage after closing. (See Chapter Four, *Putting the Joint Ownership Together, Reassuring the Lender.*)

11. Contact your attorney for preparation or review of the Joint Ownership Agreement.

After loan approval comes through for the purchase agreement, contact your attorney for preparation or review of the Joint Ownership Agreement and related documents.

12. Contact your accountant.

Submit the Joint Ownership Agreement to your accountant for allocation and confirmation of tax deductions and other tax issues.

If you've followed the recommendations of this chapter, joint ownership is nearly a reality. You've found a co-owner and property – or are clearly on your way. Chapter Four guides you through the next step – choosing your team of professionals.

Chapter Four

PUTTING THE JOINT OWNERSHIP TOGETHER

The cast of a play – as well as the script – determine its success. The joint ownership production is no exception. Investor and Occupier must cast a qualified team of professionals to launch their joint ownership. Documents are generated, lenders approached, and cash obtained. Whether you are a potential Investor or Occupier, the team you choose for your joint ownership is vital – for its success and for your peace of mind. Who are the players? How do you find them? How do they best contribute to the successful joint ownership? Once the team is chosen, how does the ideal joint ownership get started? This chapter presents the cast and program for your own successful joint ownership.

$\mathcal{W}$ho are the professional players in a typical real estate purchase? In most western states, including California, the usual participants are the buyer, real estate agent, mortgage broker, and title company. In other areas, including most eastern states, an attorney must participate in the real estate transaction. Exactly who will your team members be?

Your Team Members

The real estate agent handles purchase and sale. The mortgage broker obtains financing. The title company provides title insurance. Depending upon your geographical location, the title company or attorney provides escrow services. Let's begin then with the first team member you will typically be hiring – the all-important real estate agent.

The Real Estate Agent's Role

Clearly, the real estate agent is the key to starting up a successful joint ownership. Finding the right property and an appropriate Occupier – or Investor – are decisive, and the real estate agent versed in joint ownership can do both. Buyers and sellers who hire savvy agents are taken directly into the joint ownership market – the ideal place for them to find each other.

A seller hires a real estate agent to produce a buyer for the property. This agent performs all marketing activities necessary to achieve that goal. The seller signs a listing agreement and pays a commission, but cost is usually well worth the result – heightened exposure to a targeted market. Fortunately, the commission is not payable until sale proceeds come in.

The real estate agent begins marketing the property with direct inter-office techniques, then places the property on the multiple listing service. This service makes the listing available to all member real estate agents within that county or sector. The enterprising agent may advertise the property and hold open houses on the premises. Because of the agent's access to these valuable marketing tools, the seller's property attracts qualified buyers – a result far better than the seller could achieve on his own.

The Joint Ownership Seller's Agent

The real estate agent who knows joint ownership not only attracts qualified Occupiers – but can also turn prospective buyers into Occupiers, providing he can explain joint ownership with accuracy. The joint ownership seller finds an agent who fully understands the joint ownership concept and who will present it to qualified buyers as an option. Ask your potential agent some questions about his or her understanding of joint ownership. Assure yourself that your candidate fully comprehends the structure. The agent who does not understand or believe in joint ownership will make a poor presentation on your behalf.

If you do not feel assured, ask your agent if he would be willing to become better acquainted with the transaction. If he does, give him a copy of this book and then set up a meeting to discuss the concept and sign the listing agreement. Some agents are open to learning and some are unwilling to educate themselves about the joint ownership feature. This agent will have to understand residential joint ownership in order to obtain your listing.

The joint ownership agent's strategy can be effective at any time – but its special value to sellers becomes apparent in a buyer's market. In a slow market, when other sellers are forced to cut prices and wait for offers, the joint ownership seller may not have to bring the price down. Even more rewarding is the seller's participation in the joint ownership itself. He continues to share in the appreciation of his property while receiving generous tax breaks.

The savvy real estate agent can explain these and other joint ownership features to both sellers *and* buyers, often creating real estate transactions in the process. You and your agent will already have discussed the commission and the way the joint ownership transaction will generate the agent's commission. (See *Sale Commission*, this chapter.)

The Joint Ownership Buyer's Agent

Agents hired to find joint ownership sellers are a special breed. They know what joint ownership is. They know its pros and cons for both seller and buyer – Investor and Occupier. Their skill in explaining joint ownership to sellers actually generates a new market of joint ownership Investors. To develop this market further, some agents have recommended that the multiple listing book for their locality allocate a special section exclusively to joint ownership listings.

The buyer who wants to be an Occupier is wise to hire a real estate agent to produce a joint ownership property and an Investor. But the Occupier must select an agent who truly understands the residential joint ownership. If he does not understand, but wants to learn, give him this book and tell him you will sign an agency agreement once he learns about joint ownership. Before signing, make sure your agent candidate can intelligently converse with you about joint ownership. It cannot be stressed enough how important it is that your agent is well versed in joint ownership. Without these credentials, your agent will not be able to sell anyone on your deal.

If you cannot locate an agent who has joint ownership expertise, tap the commercial market. Realtors with a CAM designation, meaning certified commercial investment member, have a special knowledge of finance and investment that other realtors typically do not share. A national list of agents designated CAM may be obtained from the National Association of Realtors in Chicago, Illinois. Although these specially designated realtors are most often found in the commercial marketplace, they may very well be willing to represent you in the residential market. These agents are far more likely to understand the joint ownership arrangement. What's so good about it is they don't charge any more than the residential agent.

The services of your agent are usually cost-free to the buyer as sellers typically bear the agent's expense. The agent can quickly search the multiple listings for all joint ownership properties. If there are no acceptable joint ownership listings, a golden opportunity presents itself to the agent who under-stands the joint ownership concept.

This agent begins to generate a market of joint owner-ship sellers. How? By making joint ownership offers to sellers. It's not a trick – it's education. This agent must be able to explain to sellers exactly how they can become Investors in their own properties. The agent presents the complete scenario to those sellers. The worst the seller can do is reject the offer. In a *buyer's market*, sellers need all the leverage they can get. A joint ownership offer from a qualified Occupier may be the solution.

The Title Company

Title to the property – and its transfer – are insured, guaranteed, and recorded by the title company. How the co-owners hold title to the property determines their entitlement to tax deductions and deferral options, and sets up a defense to protect the property from judgment creditors. Joint ownership documents featured in this book have been designed to move a transaction smoothly through the title vesting process.

Title Company Instructions

The joint ownership attorney assures title vesting and document recording for Occupier and Investor. Depending upon the laws of your state, the attorney either personally performs these services or gives instructions to the title company. In particular, two escrow instructions arise from preparation of the Joint Ownership Agreement. First, a title vesting instruction indicates co-ownership. The title company will prepare the grant deed using this instruction. Second, a recording instruction to the title company requires recording of the Investor's joint ownership Deed of Trust/Mortgage, depending on which is used in your state, if applicable, and a Memorandum of Joint Ownership Agreement at close of escrow, allowing title insurance guarantees to take effect.

The Importance of Recording

Since title insurance guarantees only apply to recorded documents, recording the Investor's Deed of Trust/Mortgage at closing is the best guarantee the Investor can obtain. This recordation ensures the Investor's option to foreclose in the future. Extended coverage can later be obtained, but holding an unrecorded Deed of Trust/Mortgage is discouraged. Such unrecorded documents – which are also known as silent Deeds of Trust/Mortgages – don't qualify for title insurance coverage.

Once a document is recorded it becomes accessible to the public, and can later serve to enforce the rights of the parties who signed it. Therefore, the Memorandum of Joint

Ownership Agreement is recorded to give *public notice* of joint ownership of property, should this issue ever come into question. Since the Joint Ownership Agreement is far too private and lengthy for recordation, the brief memorandum serves this purpose.

Record After Closing

The co-owners may find that they have selected a lender who frowns upon recording a second mortgage or deed of trust at closing. If the lender refuses to close if recording of these documents is requested, the alternative is to record the Deed of Trust/Mortgage after escrow has closed. The Investor's security instrument will not receive title insurance guarantees, but it will be recorded.

The Loan and the Lender

Without financing there would be no joint ownership property. Since the lender controls financing, the joint ownership parties must guide their transaction carefully through the lender's loan application process, doing what they can to enhance their chances of approval.

Getting Approval

Loan approval for a joint ownership proceeds more effectively when the lender knows it is a joint ownership transaction. When applying for a loan, the parties advise the lender of their intent – first, that the purchase will be a co-ownership with one party exclusively occupying, and second, that the Occupier will be executing a Deed of Trust/Mortgage to the Investor pledging his interest in the property if he fails to abide by the terms of the joint ownership.

As with all things, simplicity is the answer. Explain it to the lender or your loan broker in these simple concise terms. A lender never wants to think the transaction is complicated by other security interests. If the lender asks questions about the Deed of Trust/Mortgage to the Investor, be sure to point out that it is not for a loan; its sole purpose is to allow the co-owner Investor a way to foreclose on his co-owner if the Occupier fails to meet his obligations.

The Second Deed of Trust/Mortgage

Some states call security devices *mortgages,* while others use *deeds of trust.* Generally, the states in the West use deeds of trust while states in the East use mortgages. The difference is in enforcing them if there is default. Mortgages must be foreclosed through the courts, which generally takes seven months. Deeds of trust are easier and faster by allowing foreclosure sale in four months through a trustee instead of by court order.

In either jurisdiction, the inquiring lender should be told that the Joint Ownership Agreement assigns numerous ownership obligations to the Occupier, whose Deed of Trust/Mortgage to the Investor secures performance by pledging his property interest to the Investor. The Occupier's Deed of Trust/Mortgage to the Investor is clearly labeled a *subordinate* deed of trust because the primary lender's trust deed takes precedence over it. In fact, the parties' obligations to the primary lender are repeated in the second Deed of Trust/Mortgage. As long as the lender is informed of these features, it should not object to the transaction.

Handling Lender Objection

If the lender does object, it is only because of a misunderstanding. But with rigid lender requirements sometimes objection will occur. The only way around lender objection, if you want the loan, is to record the Memorandum of Joint Ownership Agreement and the Investor's Deed of Trust/Mortgage from Occupier *after* close of escrow. The lender's "due on sale" clause in its Deed of Trust/Mortgage will not be triggered because the lender's security interest is not impaired. Contrary to popular belief, recording another security interest is not by itself sufficient to trigger the lender's calling the loan due for violation of its due on sale clause. In addition, the lender must prove that its security is otherwise impaired. Thus, the security instrument between the Occupier/Investor should not be a problem – except possibly in the eyes of the lender at closing. It will not be a problem thereafter unless there exists a breach of the lender's loan agreement other than the mere existence of the Occupier-Investor Deed of Trust/Mortgage.

Joint Loan Responsibility

With joint ownership the lender typically treats the co-owners separately, as if they were each applying individually for the loan. It doesn't matter to the lender that the Occupier has agreed with his co-owner to make all the payments. Since all co-owners on title must sign on the loan, each assumes full liability for loan repayment. Even if the lender did not require both parties to be obliged on the loan, these co-owners each want to be on the loan in order to acquire reinstatement and other valuable loan rights.

Reassuring the Lender

Again, simplicity is the answer. Don't rock the boat if the water is calm. The only reason to recite the intimate details of the joint ownership is if the lender asks. The lender will inquire if they are concerned that their first security interest may be impaired.

Actually, the lender is twice blessed in a joint ownership. First, the lender's repayment source is doubled when two fully responsible parties sign on the loan, instead of just one. Second, the joint ownership Deed of Trust/Mortgage repeats all of the lender's primary loan obligations, reinforcing them further. The lender is given *more security* in a joint ownership than in a single owner real estate purchase.

If the lender is concerned, and *only* if they voice concern, provide them with a brief summary of the purpose of the Deed of Trust/Mortgage from the Occupier to the Investor. In most situations, that will suffice. If they further inquire, give them a copy of the joint ownership documents. The Deed of Trust/Mortgage will be the recipient of the lender's attention.

The joint ownership Deed of Trust/Mortgage featured in the *Appendix* has been tailored to pass lender tests. By reviewing the Joint Ownership Agreement and the Investor's Deed of Trust/Mortgage, the lender is reassured. As long as the parties' interests are clearly defined in the documents and subordinated to the lender's interest, the lender's security remains unimpaired.

The all-inclusive feature of the Joint Ownership Note and Deed of Trust/Mortgage can, at first glance, present a problem to the lender. Once the lender understands the all-inclusive feature, hesitation disappears. It all began decades ago when the all-inclusive Deed of Trust/Mortgage earned a bad reputation – which lingers on in the minds of lenders. In the early 80s, interest rates were high. Instead of obtaining new loans, properties were transferred with existing financing in place by use of the all-inclusive feature. This resulted in a practice of lender-qualified borrowers selling their properties to unqualified purchasers inclusive of the lender's financing. Foreclosure and litigation followed.

The concerned lender should be reassured that the joint ownership security feature is quite different. No unqualified buyer enters the picture – both Occupier and Investor are on their loan. This should make all the difference. The purpose of the co-owners' security document is merely to confirm the Occupier's promise to the Investor to be primarily responsible for the loan. Once this is made clear, lender resistance will vanish.

Lender Requirements

The majority of lenders process the joint ownership transaction as any other, treating the co-owners as a unified purchasing team. Some lenders apply different rules to the joint ownership transaction, requiring proof that 5% of purchase price comes from the Occupier. This can be in the form of closing costs.

Typically, the lender prefers not to be involved in the joint ownership feature and generally treats the parties as co-borrowers. A few lenders will want to understand the relationship between the co-borrowers. Leave it to them to ask. Generally, a simple oral description will suffice. It is uncommon for a lender to ask to review the joint ownership documents, but there have been a few isolated instances when lenders have over-processed a joint ownership, directing their legal staff to pore over the Joint Ownership Agreement and related documents.

Where a seller is involved as the Investor, some lenders categorize this transaction as *a refinance with a partner*. Although the lender may choose to look at it that way, the tax treatment selected by the parties remains valid. The lender's characterization of the transaction will have no effect on the parties' tax status. In a refinance with an existing lender the procedures are often less stringent, and qualifying for the loan is easier. An Occupier who nearly qualifies can tip the scales by seeking a Seller-Investor for such a refinance.

In sum, lenders will not object to your residential joint ownership and will generally treat you as co-borrowers. Your rule of thumb: keep it simple. The lender wants to fit you into a recognized category called "co-ownership." Any lender who hesitates can be encouraged by the issues explained in *Reassuring the Lender*, above.

The AAAs: Attorneys, Accountants, Appraisers

A joint ownership can expand the team to include the joint ownership co-owner, attorneys, and accountants for each Occupier and Investor, and an appraiser. Why call in an attorney or two and two accountants? The attorney steps in to identify, sort out, and incorporate the legal, tax, and personal requirements into the all-important Joint Ownership Agreement. The accountants establish the joint ownership's special tax designations and tax issues arising from shared ownership. Let's take a look at each of these professionals to ascertain their place in your joint ownership transaction.

Attorney Roles

In every joint ownership, each party's unique needs and requirements are met by a hand-tailored Joint Ownership Agreement. It takes far more than simply filling in blanks to adequately structure a joint ownership transaction. Although sample forms are included in this book and available on disk, you are cautioned against using them as substitutes for legal counsel – your only guarantee for a sound, legally valid agreement.

The joint ownership transaction is a tapestry of complex rights, obligations, and calculations that must pass the tests of law, taxation, and lending institutions – all of which may vary from state to state. Although the form agreement is a complete model, the attorney can best coordinate and weave the co-owners' unique needs into the finished package: the Joint Ownership Agreement and its related documents.

Most often, the attorney follows the real estate agent as the next professional consultant for the joint ownership. Often, because of the added complexity of the joint ownership feature, the attorney will also be required to facilitate the transaction. This includes joint ownership approval, shepherding the transaction past your chosen co-owner, the escrow agent, and the lender or other necessary party. This coordination by the attorney gives the joint ownership transaction an excellent start and a good chance to close. Often times, your co-owner receives the assurance needed with the presence of an attorney on your team to bless the transaction. Until joint ownership becomes mainstream in the residential marketplace, a versed attorney is the best team member to guide the transaction through to successful conclusion.

The reason for this is that the joint ownership transaction's joint characteristic makes it more technical and complex than the sole owner transaction. It presents a challenge for even the most skilled practitioner. To name just a few complexities, the agreement imposes payment, occupancy, and maintenance obligations on the Occupier. It calculates valuations of each party's interest at buyout or sale. It determines and allocates tax deductions and deferral options to each party. It mandates the procedures to be followed in making an improvement. It specifies each party's remedies upon breach by the other.

An attorney with skillful knowledge of joint ownership – as described in this book – has already mastered these challenges. The ideal attorney for the joint ownership must be well versed in real estate law, joint ownership concepts, and real estate taxation. An attorney inexperienced in these areas may not address all of the necessary issues. If something is left out, the resulting agreement might fail its taxation and legal tests.

Bearing all of this in mind, it may be that you are savvy enough, with the use of this book and its forms, to set up the transaction yourself and select the appropriate legal and tax designations. That is the intent of this book – to guide you through your transaction. But we do strongly suggest that you hire an attorney and accountant to review the structure and forms you have set up. An attorney well versed in joint ownership should review the Joint Ownership Agreement to ensure that it dovetails the co-owners' unique tax and co-ownership issues. In states that require attorneys to act as escrow, make sure you hire an attorney who knows about residential joint ownership. At the very least, fax your documents to the author for review.

Accountant Roles

Investor and Occupier alike should confer with their accountants to confirm the ownership tax deductions, prorations, and calculations best suited for their joint ownership. The parties' accountants are key participants in a joint ownership. They know their clients' tax profiles, the tax aspects of joint ownership, and how to plan accordingly. The tax aspects of joint ownership are as vital to its success as the legal issues. Extreme consequences may result if the parties fail to properly set up the tax deductions on the property. Only one set of deductions exists for a joint ownership property, and they must not be duplicated. Moreover, these deductions must be accurately claimed in conformity with the Internal Revenue Code.

Proper tax planning of a joint ownership gleans many tax benefits. By carefully defining their ownership, the parties become entitled to defer tax on their gains. Given the magnitude of property ownership deductions available to the individual taxpayer – ranging from interest and property tax to depreciation – adequate tax planning for the joint ownership is crucial.

Even more important to a party is an accountant's knowledge of the client's current personal tax profile. With that knowledge, the accountant can tailor the available joint ownership deductions to the client's tax portfolio for optimum tax benefits. For example, one party may not need to claim full interest, while the other may have lots of room for such a deduction. If the Investor's tax package deems depreciation inappropriate, the co-owners modify their rental obligations under Internal Revenue Code §280A (see Chapter Eight).

The parties' accountants can recommend payments under the Joint Ownership Agreement that best accommodate their financial and tax profiles. For these reasons, the accountant is a valuable resource to both Occupier and Investor. If you are tax wise, go ahead and plan your deductions and allocations. But please do take the time to obtain the stamp of approval of your accountant, at the very least. Again, you can do most of this yourself if you have that level of knowledge, but getting the licensed professionals' blessing is one step you must not miss.

When You Should Hire an Independent Appraiser

If the seller is participating in the joint ownership as an Investor, and if the seller has enlisted the services of a real estate agent to list the property, you will want to confirm the comparables the agent has chosen to establish the value of the property. But if there is no agent involvement, you will need to hire an independent party to place a value on the property. The seller will have his idea and you will have yours, but if no real estate agent is involved, the property's comparables have not been checked. The Seller-Investor and Occupier must then take steps to confirm value.

If either of you has a real estate agent with whom you are familiar, that agent can establish value for you in a short period of time. Usually this is done free of charge. You can also offer to pay a nominal amount to give you a suggested listing price for the property. I usually offer a fee since I have a lot banking on the purchase price, and I therefore want the agent to spend some quality time arriving at value. The amount the agent will charge will be far less than your licensed appraiser, and the agent's value will probably be quite accurate.

You may say to yourself, "We are taking out a loan and the lender will require an appraisal. We'll just use that appraisal." There are two problems with this: first, you and the seller need to establish value in order to enter into a purchase agreement, long before the loan is obtained. Second, the lender's appraisal is for loan purposes and is obtained in order to justify the loan amount. Often it is not an accurate valuation of the property.

The Joint Ownership's Program

Now that your joint ownership team is chosen, how is the transaction itself created? The joint ownership transaction often begins with a listing agreement. It proceeds with loan and title documents, and culminates in the Joint Ownership Agreement and its accompanying documents. How does a Seller-Investor set his joint ownership deal in motion? Suppose an Investor and Occupier buy a property together from someone else. How do they launch their deal?

The Seller-Investor's Listing Agreement

The seller usually proclaims his joint ownership intent when signing the listing agreement with the real estate agent. This document, with its accompanying property profile, prepares the stage to market the property as a joint ownership. It also establishes the agent's commission and the terms under which it will be earned. Some joint ownership sellers feel the agent's commission should be based on the *cash out* price, as opposed to *purchase* price. Agents counter that a joint ownership transaction takes significantly more effort and time than a conventional transaction, entitling them to commission on full value. The seller and his agent should iron out these details at the listing agreement stage.

A larger group of qualified Occupier buyers is attracted by a clear statement – featured prominently in the listing agreement and property profile – that the seller is willing to sell by joint ownership. A seller who decides he wants a joint ownership deal after signing a listing agreement can amend that agreement accordingly.

Of course, it is always the seller's prerogative to market the property on his own without the services of a real estate agent. It would be well worth it in commission savings if a large enough market can be reached on your own. It will all depend on the time of year and the amount of consumers reached through targeted marketing.

The Purchase Documents

The joint ownership process begins with the deposit receipt, also referred to as the *purchase agreement*. The deposit receipt and all addenda and counter offers make up the purchase documents. The deposit receipt is the buyer's offer – usually the first document presented to the seller in the purchase process. The seller either accepts the offer, amends it with an addendum, or counters it with a counter offer. The counter offer process can go back and forth any number of times. Once the parties have reached an agreement on all terms, the purchase agreement is complete and the parties are in contract. These documents dictate the terms of the purchase and launch the joint ownership.

A choice of two scenarios governs the content of the joint ownership purchase documents. Scenario one: an Investor and Occupier buy someone else's property. Scenario two: a seller becomes an Investor in his own property.

When the Parties Buy an Outside Property

When the Occupier teams up with an Investor to buy an outside property, they make a joint offer on the property as co-purchasers. Together they generate a deposit receipt specifying that the offer is made "subject to execution of a Joint Ownership Agreement" between them. The wise Investor and Occupier have already declared their joint ownership terms and splits in a *Joint Ownership Preliminary Commitment.* That preliminary commitment then becomes a formal attachment to the deposit receipt by stating that "this offer is made subject to execution of a Joint Ownership Agreement incorporating the terms of the preliminary commitment, attached." See Chapter Five for a sample of this commitment.

Why is this an important event for the joint ownership? When the joint ownership transaction is referenced in the purchase documents, it becomes a condition of the sale. It sets forth, in black and white, the serious intent of the Investor and Occupier to lending institutions, the title company, and taxing agencies who dictate the deductions and tax breaks.

When the Seller Is the Investor

When a seller decides to sell his property by joint ownership, the documents are the same as those generated in any real estate sale: the listing agreement and deposit receipt. The listing agreement, signed by the Seller-Investor, hires the real estate agent and describes his job. The deposit receipt, executed by the Buyer-Occupier, fixes the terms of the sale.

The Occupier makes an offer to his potential Investor by generating a deposit receipt stating these conditions:

1. Initial deposit and additional cash deposit vary, depending upon the Occupier's cash commitment to the

purchase, which is often 5% of purchase price apportioned toward closing costs.

2. Loan information should indicate the desired financing and should specify in other terms: "Seller to be on first loan with buyer."

3. Title vesting, if contained in the deposit receipt, should state: "Title to be taken in the joint names of seller and buyer as tenants in common."

4. Additional terms and conditions should state: "Seller agrees to sell this property by joint ownership. The basic terms of the joint ownership are that seller defers (dollars or percentage) of the down payment, which amount constitutes his initial contribution to the joint ownership in the form of retained equity. Buyer is to deposit at closing at least 5% of the purchase price, which may be used for payment of loan fees and closing costs, or an amount sufficient to pay the selling and buying agents' commission, loan fees, and closing costs, whichever is greater. Buyer is to be reimbursed at term of the joint ownership for amounts contributed for agent's commission. Buyer shall not be reimbursed for loan fees and closing costs paid. Within 30 days of date hereof, the parties shall enter into a Joint Ownership Agreement to fully memorialize all terms of this joint ownership sale." [Optional: "The attached Joint Ownership Preliminary Commitment sets forth additional basic terms of the joint ownership as agreed upon by buyer and seller."]

His conditions thus stated, the Occupier presents an abundantly clear offer to his potential Investor. If the seller is interested, negotiations will no doubt result in counter offers. Perhaps the offer will be accepted with minor revisions. Thus, deposit receipt and ensuing purchase documents incorporate the joint ownership feature and launch the joint ownership transaction.

Apportioning Initial Cash Outlay

The seller's joint ownership participation creates an additional issue. Who will pay the real estate agent's sales commission? In the typical *third-party* joint ownership, sales commission is not the responsibility of the Occupier-Investor team. But an *Occupier-Seller* team must decide how sales commissions will be paid.

In formulating their joint ownership structure, the team tallies the initial cash necessary to close the transaction. From a new loan, the seller will receive only cash left over after his existing loan is paid. This is sometimes insufficient for the seller to buy a new property *and* pay the sale commission. In these limited situations, the joint ownership transaction can produce enough cash for the seller if the Occupier advances a portion or all of the sales commission and pays the closing costs.

Or the co-owners – the seller and the purchasing Occupier – can offer the buyer's agent an attractive package in return for deferring payment of the commission. What would that be? First, the seller would offer the agent a Joint Ownership Note and Deed of Trust/Mortgage senior to the Joint Ownership Deed of Trust/Mortgage. The agent will ask, "Why do I want to wait for my commission when I'm entitled to it now?" Buyer's answer: "Because if we can't close on this because of your commission, you won't earn a commission. A belated commission is better than none at all." Or try this: "The note will bear interest at 10% per annum, which will earn you a better return than nearly any available investment. On top of that, you'll be secured by the property. The seller will be the one to sign the note to be paid out of the seller's proceeds at termination of the joint ownership."

The reason we choose the buyer's agent to ask for commission deferral is because the buyer's agent is the most motivated. The seller's agent will ultimately close since he has the listing. He'll earn his commission through any transaction that closes during the listing period. Thus, seller's agents are not motivated to compromise. But buyer's agents are motivated because they have less of a chance of finding a suitable seller and property for their joint ownership buyer.

Sale Commission

Thus, when an Occupier teams up with a seller, the Occupier's cash requirements often increase. He usually commits to a cash outlay of 8 to 10 percent of the purchase price — including agent's commission, acquisition costs, and loan origination fees — as opposed to 5% when he teams up with the third-party Investor. Since the seller is responsible for commissions, the Occupier's commission payment is treated as an advance to the joint ownership, which is later reimbursed.

In summary, when the Occupier teams up with a seller, his initial cash outlay is sometimes higher because he may have to advance some or all of the sales commission.

Closing Costs

Loan fees and closing costs are treated as acquisition costs and are not reimbursed. The party paying the closing costs recoups these costs in part by claiming tax deductions to acquire the property, and in part by increasing his tax basis.

Payment of acquisition closing costs is another item subject to negotiation. More often, the acquisition closing costs are fully paid by the Occupier. Sometimes they are shared by the parties in accordance with their ownership splits. Sometimes the Investor pays title insurance, which is deductible to him but not to the principal residence Occupier. It's all up to the parties and what works for them.

Title Vesting As Strategy

Tenants in Common Ownership

The co-owners' best strategy is to take title to the property as tenants in common. Each party's ownership interest should be reflected on title. For example, if Occupier and Investor agree to a 50/50 ownership split, title would be held as follows: "Orville Occupier, an undivided 50% interest, and Ingrid Investor, an undivided 50% interest, as tenants in common."

Why are both parties and their ownership interests on title? Unless the Occupier *and* Investor are both on title in their own names, they do not have a clear, qualifying ownership interest, placing their tax status in jeopardy. Ironically, if both parties indicate their respective percentage interests on title, judgment creditors find it difficult to attach the entire property.

Preserving Tax Status

Both parties are on title with interests clearly shown. This qualifies both Occupier and Investor for their tax deductions and gain deferral. The tax treatment of the joint ownership property differs for Occupier and Investor, depending on how each co-owner uses the property. Under tax law it is the Occupier's principal residence and the Investor's investment property. Each type of use brings its own set of deductions and tax deferral options into the picture. When both parties are on title, they are deemed to have separate *ownership interests* in the joint ownership property. This proves their individual tax status.

The Investor should be on title for practical reasons. First, he will likely defer taxes on his profits by utilizing the exchange provisions of Internal Revenue Code §1031. Since *partnership interests* – without a valid exemption – are specifically excluded from exchange treatment, the Investor's name on title establishes that his interest is an ownership, not a partnership. Second, the Investor claiming investment deductions under Internal Revenue Code §280A is entitled to them only if a qualifying ownership interest is clearly held – proven by title in his name.

The Occupier also takes title for tax reasons. He will most likely defer taxes on his profits by rolling out of the property under Internal Revenue Code §1034. The Occupier qualifies when named directly on title. By being on title, the Occupier qualifies to claim ownership deductions ranging from interest to property taxes. In addition, the Occupier on title is a true owner – not merely a renter occupying the property. Hence the property becomes a recognized personal asset to him.

Protecting the Property from Judgment Creditors

Of course, our *ideal* joint ownership will not be set upon by creditors. But in the first-rate Joint Ownership Agreement we anticipate the unexpected by setting up the right defense. *Tenancy in common* means that the co-owners own undivided interests of the entire property. By defining their interests on title, their holding becomes separate from those of the remaining co-tenants. Certain legal presumptions arise which do not need any discussion here. Its importance to our co-owners is this: if the Occupier has a 40% interest and is beset by creditors, they can only attach his 40% interest. The Investor's 60% interest remains undisturbed. For these reasons, the joint ownership co-tenants hold title as individual tenants in common with their respective interests clearly specified.

Joint Tenancy As an Estate Planning Strategy

What will happen to the Investor or Occupier couple's collective joint ownership interest upon death of a spouse? Joint ownership co-owners who are married couples are surprised to learn they can structure title to automatically establish their survivorship rights. They do this by creating a joint tenancy relationship as part of their tenancy in common.

The majority of joint ownership participants are married couples. A *joint tenancy* designation keeps title intact during the term of the Joint Ownership Agreement. It is relatively simple to create this joint tenancy within the joint ownership. Title would read as follows: "an undivided 45% interest to Mr. and Mrs. Occupier, husband and wife, as joint tenants, and an undivided 55% interest to Mr. and Mrs. Investor, husband and wife, as joint tenants, all as tenants in common."

Under joint tenancy, a deceased party's interest automatically passes to the surviving spouse on death. Thus the parties are assured that despite death of a spouse, the joint ownership title remains intact until term. For survivorship reasons, if you have not otherwise provided for transfer of this property at death, joint tenancy is a practical means to do so. It does not provide optimum tax treatment of the community property designation, (below), but it fills survivorship needs.

Community Property As a Tax-Saving Strategy

The married couple residing in a community property state can hold title as community property. Community property status merely confirms that the married couple is holding their interest as property of the marriage. The joint ownership couple may designate their interest as community property between themselves, within their tenancy in common. Title would read as follows: "an undivided 45% interest to Mr. and Mrs. Occupier, husband and wife, as community property, and an undivided 55% interest to Mr. and Mrs. Investor, husband and wife, as community property, all as tenants in common."

Community property status does *not* confer the survivorship rights of joint tenancy. But it does confer a tax benefit that can mean substantial savings. In concise terms, a property held as community property receives a full step up in value for tax purposes when one of the parties dies. The result is that, for tax purposes, the value of the property is stepped up to fair market value at the time of the spouse's death – which can result in hefty capital gains tax savings to the surviving spouse.

The end result: for tax purposes, community property is the best designation; for purposes of directing title to the joint tenant at death, joint tenancy is best. A will or living trust would alleviate the need for joint tenancy.

The Joint Ownership Agreement

Joint ownership is a highly specialized acquisitional device. The underlying Joint Ownership Agreement must meet the personal needs of Occupier and Investor, insure conformity with the Internal Revenue Code, and adequately protect the

Investor's security. This is accomplished by a customized agreement with all necessary attending documents.

In a standard purchase when title passes, all duties and obligations of ownership are transferred to a single buyer. In the joint ownership purchase, title passes to *two or more* individuals – the Investors and Occupiers. An agreement must be created to allocate ownership duties, responsibilities, and beneficial interests between co-owners. The Joint Ownership Agreement and its accompanying documents are the keys to successfully document and earmark the respective ownership benefits and burdens.

Now that you have lined up your joint ownership team and property, Chapter Five features the basic provisions of your Joint Ownership Agreement. The Joint Ownership Preliminary Commitment gets you started. You'll see the long form agreement later, in the *Appendix*.

Chapter Five

TERMS OF THE JOINT OWNERSHIP AGREEMENT

The Joint Ownership Agreement is the core of a joint ownership. Like the nucleus of a cell, it contains all information necessary for the life and health of its system. The first-rate Joint Ownership Agreement uses the law and tax codes to achieve optimum tax strategies and profits for its co-owners. It defines and apportions their rights and responsibilities. It protects the joint ownership from outside threat and risk. This chapter profiles the basic performance terms while Chapter Seven outlines the default penalties. For those who want to get started, a sample Joint Ownership Preliminary Commitment is provided. Later in the *Appendix*, an actual Joint Ownership Agreement weaves all these provisions together.

*T*he joint ownership is guarded and directed by a carefully structured Joint Ownership Agreement. The better a system prepares for events, the better it is equipped to survive.

A first-rate Joint Ownership Agreement anticipates the foreseeable *and* the unexpected. You will see how the agreement deals with foreseeable events – term of the joint ownership, duties of occupancy, allocation of payments – and how it prepares for the unexpected – bankruptcy, death, and liens by creditors.

When Should the Agreement Be Prepared?

The intent to joint ownership is declared on paper as soon as the parties have agreed to joint ownership – by a Joint Ownership Agreement or a shorter form preliminary commitment. Declaring intent early helps guide the joint ownership through its many formative phases. The Joint Ownership Agreement itself should be prepared and signed as soon as possible. Often the parties wait until the lender has conditionally agreed to fund the loan. The expense of the joint ownership process is justified by knowing that all pre-purchase contingencies, including lender approval, have been satisfied.

The Joint Ownership Preliminary Commitment

If the parties join together *before* a property is found, they should enter into a Joint Ownership Preliminary Commitment shown on the following page, as it creates the basic terms for the formal Joint Ownership Agreement. If the parties come together *after* the property is located, the preliminary commitment is unnecessary. The Joint Ownership Agreement can then be prepared in final form.

Joint Ownership Preliminary Commitment

Investors:

Occupiers:

We, Occupiers and Investors, enter into this Preliminary Commitment prior to preparation of a Joint Ownership Agreement. Occupiers and Investors agree to the following terms which shall be incorporated into the Joint Ownership Agreement. The parties agree to be bound by the following terms until such time as the Joint Ownership Agreement is entered into:

1. The parties shall acquire property to be held by them as tenants in common.

2. Investors shall contribute _____% of the purchase price/ $_____ as their initial capital contribution.

3. Occupiers shall contribute ____% of the purchase price/ $_____ as their initial capital contribution.

4. Acquisitional closing costs are not reimbursable and shall be paid _____% / $_____ by Occupiers and _____% / $_____ by Investors.

5. With Seller as Investor, Occupier shall advance, subject to Seller reimbursement, $_____ of the real estate commission.

6. Ownership split shall be _____% to Investors and _____% to Occupiers.

7. The Agreement term will be:
    ☐ 3 years   ☐ 5 years   ☐ 7 years   ☐10 years

8. Occupier shall be granted exclusive occupancy during term.

9. Purchase price shall be [in the range of] $_____.

10. Additional terms:

Executed this ___ day of _____, (year)

Investors: Occupiers:

_____   _____

Related Documents

Four key documents are prepared with the Joint Ownership Agreement – the Joint Ownership Note confirming Investor contribution and Occupier obligation, the Deed of Trust/Mortgage to the Investor to protect his investment if the unexpected occurs, the Memorandum of Joint Ownership Agreement to legally record the transaction, and the Joint Ownership Lease, which achieves compliance with the rental tax code. These documents may be executed separately before close of escrow or at close of escrow, at the parties' discretion. A sample of each document is included in the *Appendix*.

Since the escrow closing is often complex in its own right, the parties usually choose to complete the joint ownership portion of the transaction separately. A separate *joint ownership closing* often takes place in the attorney's office, before the purchase close of escrow. The joint ownership documents may also be signed at the title company when escrow closes. The sequence should always be, however, that the joint ownership documents are signed *before* the loan documents are signed.

General Provisions of the Agreement

Investor and Occupier create a *joint ownership system* between themselves by negotiation. Except for the distinct set of tax deductions and requirements dictated by the Internal Revenue Code, all benefits and responsibilities of the joint ownership are negotiable. Assuming they have met Internal Revenue Code requirements (see Chapter Eight), the parties negotiate the joint ownership terms to their mutual advantage.

For example, they can share in mortgage payments and take the tax deductions accordingly. The Occupier can agree to a 70% Investor ownership interest if desired. The Investor can make property tax payments and claim that deduction if he wishes. The payment allocations and ownership splits are negotiable between the parties, as long as the tax law is followed and the parties agree the result is fair. We've had Occupiers who can't use the tax deductions, but Investors who can. In those situations many tax-deductible payments have been allocated to the Investor who can claim them. With this variation of the *normal* joint ownership, the Investor's projected return needs to be correspondingly increased. The *typical* joint ownership structure described below is not cast in concrete. It can be modified to serve the unique interests of both parties.

In the most common joint ownership structure the Occupier lives in the property and makes all of the payments. He has exclusive occupancy with the privacy and duties that accompany it. He maintains and repairs the property. With the consent of the Investor, he makes improvements. The Investor, a silent co-owner, is uninvolved with daily responsibilities of the property. Thus the meaning of *Occupier* and *Investor* become clear – the Occupier has a home, and the Investor awaits his profit and tax-deferral at term.

Term of the Joint Ownership As Strategy

The Investor and Occupier decide on the joint ownership's term – how long co-ownership of the property will last. How is the term chosen? Some agreements are written for three, seven, or ten years. A five-year term is the norm with seven years running a close second. It's all up to the parties. Since property is generally expected to appreciate over time, the longer the term the greater the profit.

To make their decision, the Occupier and Investor consider various needs. The Occupier may anticipate a job relocation within two years – or the Investor may have to liquidate his investment in three years to cover a balloon payment. Some lenders require a seven-year agreement for greater property appreciation. Setting the term of a joint ownership becomes a financial and personal strategy.

Again, it is always wise to remember that joint ownership is not considered a profitable short term investment. Our market just doesn't bring rapid considerable appreciation as it once did. The profit comes with long term holding. Because of this, many of our joint ownership participants now begin with a seven year term. Seven years is considered a better curve for realization of appreciation. It is also the average time frame for owning a principal residence. By comparing the two sample transaction in Chapters Nine and Ten, you will see how the seven-year transaction worked out better for the co-owners, especially when it came to buying one another out by refinance.

Payments

The Joint Ownership Agreement directs the *payment system* of the joint ownership. Using tax law and each party's tax strategy, it assigns joint ownership expenses to co-owners. In the typical joint ownership the Occupier pays all expenses and claims mortgage interest and property tax deductions. The Investor is entitled to depreciate his portion of the property if his portfolio otherwise allows it.

Internal Revenue Code §280A dictates a vital aspect of the joint ownership – rental by Occupier of the Investor's interest in the property. Joint ownership co-owners comply with this tax law, particularly if the Investor is claiming any tax benefit from his co-ownership. If they do not, their tax benefits – especially the Investor's – may be in jeopardy.

Under Internal Revenue Code §280A the Investor collects rents from the Occupier, to be offset in large part by investment property expenses paid by the Investor – such as home owner dues, insurance, maintenance, and management fees. If rental income exceeds investment-related expenses, the remaining rent is returned to the property as mortgage interest and property taxes. The Investor makes these payments directly to the creditor. These payments are calculated and specified in the Joint Ownership Agreement. The Occupier is responsible for all property-related expenses above and beyond Investor rental reimbursement. Thus, the Occupier pays the vast majority of joint ownership expenses – and claims nearly all property taxes and mortgage interest as deductions.

In summary, rent and rental reimbursement under Internal Revenue Code §280A do not increase either party's cash commitments. The Occupier's cash commitment remains equal to all property expenses, while the Investor's commitment is up-front money and nothing more. Although the distributions shift around, the totals remain the same. For details see *IRC §280A Rental Requirement* in Chapter Eight.

Loan Principal Reductions

The amount by which the loan principal is reduced is returned to the paying party as part of the equity. This payment is made out of equity immediately after capital contributions are returned to the contributing parties. If both owners have made mortgage payments, the loan principal reduction is proportionately credited. This feature of the joint ownership is important to credit the mortgage payer with the principal reductions that have resulted to the loan. If this feature was not included, both co-owners would benefit from the loan principal reduction – which should not be the case. Since the Occupier is typically the party making the mortgage payments, the Occupier usually receives the loan principal reduction.

Exclusive Occupancy

The Joint Ownership Agreement and the Investor's Deed of Trust/Mortgage set up an important legal condition – *exclusive occupancy*. Under this provision the Occupier is assured his rights of privacy – the Investor must give him written notice of intent to inspect the property.

For the Investor it is a declaration of his faith in the Occupier – and a powerful protective device under law. Exclusive occupancy assures the Investor that the Occupier will not lease out his interest in the property without his written consent. Expressed simply, this assures the Investor that only his carefully chosen Occupier will care for and maintain the joint ownership property and protect its value. The Investor has based his decision to joint ownership on that assurance.

Expressed legally, exclusive occupancy carries a much weightier message. Under the Investor's deed of trust/ mortgage, the exclusive occupancy provision is essential to his decision to jointly own the property. Under law, the Occupier's failure to occupy the property without Investor written consent is cause for default – an event at which the Occupier can lose his entire ownership interest.

The Investor's Deed of Trust/Mortgage clearly states that the Investor's decision for joint ownership was largely based upon exclusive occupancy by the Occupier. Had it not been for the Occupier's unique personal characteristics, the Investor would not have acquired the property nor granted exclusive occupancy to the Occupier. His agreement to exclusively occupy the property was therefore an inducement for the Investor to jointly own the property. As such, if that agreement is violated, the Investor may foreclose under his Deed of Trust/Mortgage.

Unexpected events can happen. The Occupier may need to relocate – for career or other personal reasons. The ideal agreement and Deed of Trust/Mortgage anticipate and prepare for these events at the initial joint ownership conference. Any such needs should be covered in the agreement. Otherwise, the Investor's written consent is required for any change in the exclusive occupancy provision, and his consent should not be unreasonably withheld.

Maintenance

The model Joint Ownership Agreement assigns care of the property to the Occupier. He must do all things required to preserve the joint ownership property, including all necessary repairs. He agrees to maintain and repair the property in the same condition it was in when the joint ownership began, less reasonable wear and tear. Although the Occupier is not repaid for *ordinary* repairs, he is reimbursed for capital improvements he makes which meet certain tests. (See *Improvements* below.) Those reimbursements come from the joint ownership proceeds when the Joint Ownership Agreement expires or upon earlier buyout.

In granting exclusive occupancy to the Occupier, the Investor retains a right of reasonable inspection. It is important for the Investor to inspect the property to ensure that it is being maintained – notifying the Occupier in writing, typically three days in advance.

Improvements

Improvements to the joint ownership property are *necessary* or *voluntary*. The Joint Ownership Agreement sets up definitions and procedures that govern the making of improvements. Necessary capital improvements preserve the value and integrity of the joint ownership property and they are always subject to reimbursement to the co-owner who pays for them. Voluntary improvements are optional, more aesthetic in nature, and may or may not affect the property value.

Necessary Improvements

The Joint Ownership Agreement assigns responsibility and procedures for making necessary capital improvements. The co-owners may share these expenses, using their percentages of ownership, or the Occupier may be solely responsible. These decisions are written into the agreement, providing reimbursement to the contributing party at term. Necessary capital improvements always require written estimates and *written co-owner approval.*

Voluntary Improvements

The Joint Ownership Agreement sets up procedures for voluntary improvements by either co-owner. Each intended voluntary improvement is handled separately. Usually, those which cost more than $750 require approval in writing by both Investor and Occupier. The logic behind the approval process is that one owner may feel that adding a hot tub will increase the value of the property, but the other disagrees. The same with adding skylights, fencing the property and other such voluntary improvements. A co-owner does not want to approve of an improvement unless it will increase the value of the property at least as much as the improvement cost.

We had an Occupier who wanted to landscape the property. When presented with the estimate for approval, the Investor sought an appraiser's opinion as to whether the value of the property would be increased dollar for dollar by the cost of the landscaping. The Investor was advised that although the contemplated landscaping would certainly add to the looks of the property, the value increase would not equal or exceed its cost. In fact, about $3,500 would not be recovered by increase in value. Hence, before making a voluntary improvement the owners should be careful to make sure that the improvement will at the very least increase the value of the property by its cost.

The co-owner proposing the voluntary improvement gets estimates and presents them to his counterpart for written approval. If he seeks reimbursement, he requests written approval regardless of the expenditure amount. Without his co-owner's consent, an improvement above the $750 mark isn't made, nor is reimbursement promised. Approved reimbursements are calculated at cost plus reasonable interest from the date of improvement, and are paid from the joint ownership proceeds or at buyout.

Assignment and Transfer Prohibition

The classic Joint Ownership Agreement and Deed of Trust/Mortgage entitle the Investor to performance of all the Occupier's duties, which are non-transferable. Therefore, the Occupier agrees not to sell, transfer, assign, or encumber his interest in the property without the Investor's written consent, not to be unreasonably withheld. Like the occupancy requirement, the restriction against assignment or transfer protects the Investor's interests and affirms the Occupier's promise to perform his obligations.

The Occupier may not encumber his interest in the joint ownership property without the Investor's written consent. In the Deed of Trust/Mortgage, the Occupier has pledged his joint ownership interest to the Investor in the event that he fails to perform his promises. If the Occupier were to obtain a loan against his joint ownership interest, it would jeopardize his pledge to the Investor. That pledged interest must be preserved.

The Investor, on the other hand, is typically able to freely assign or encumber his interest in the property. As a silent co-owner waiting for his profit, he has no duties to perform under the Joint Ownership Agreement. If the Investor assigns his interest to someone else, the Occupier simply pays off that person at buyout or sale.

The Options at Term

Five options sequentially arise 150 days before the Joint Ownership Agreement expires. Each option lasts for 30 days. First, the co-owners may mutually agree to extend the agreement. Second and third, the co-owners are granted options to buy out one another. If the buyout options are unexercised, the next step is reached. Fourth, if the property appreciation the parties require has not been achieved, the agreement is automatically extended. This option is a guarantee against loss. Finally, if no other step has produced buyout or continuation, the property is sold. The first-rate agreement specifies each step to follow upon buyout or sale and diaries each interval.

Extension by Mutual Agreement

150 days before the agreement terminates, the parties are given a 30-day period to mutually agree to extend the agreement for any period of time they agree upon. If they do

so, a new termination schedule is set. If all co-owners do not agree, extension is not effective.

Terminating Buyout Options

120 days before the agreement terminates, the buyout sequence begins by granting the Occupier, who has occupied the property for the past many years, an exclusive 30-day option to buy out his co-owner. He may elect to buy out the Investor's interest to enjoy uninterrupted occupancy and ownership. If the Occupier does not exercise buyout, 90 days before the agreement terminates the exclusive 30-day option passes automatically to the Investor. If the Investor does not exercise buyout, 60 days before the agreement terminates the agreement is automatically extended if the required appreciation rate set by the parties has not been reached. 30 days before term, if neither party has exercised their buyout option, the property is listed for sale with the agent designated in the Joint Ownership Agreement.

Buyout value is agreed upon by the co-owners or determined by appraisal by an MAI certified appraiser. If the parties cannot agree upon one appraiser, each chooses one and the average of both appraisals establishes value. See Chapter Six for detailed discussion of buyout calculations and procedures.

Automatic Extension to Prevent Loss

In order to prevent a situation whereby at termination of the agreement the market has fallen prey to recession, the parties should agree that if the property has not retained value – or if a certain amount of appreciation has not occurred – the agreement will automatically extend at term. The amount of appreciation is all up to the parties' agreement. This provision is important to prevent a situation where the property has not appreciated, the property must be sold and the Investor ends up losing all or part of his investment.

The automatic extension provision comes into play sixty days before term, if the co-owners have not exercised their buyout options. We recommend the automatic extension provision after the buyout sequence to allow a party, who needs to terminate the transaction during the anticipated term, an opportunity to do so by buying out his co-owner. If the buyout election was not first afforded before the automatic extension, a party may be stuck in his co-ownership for an undeterminable number of years until the required appreciation rate was met. By exercising the buyout option – although the property has not appreciated as expected – a co-owner can terminate his investment by buying out his co-owner and liquidating his investment by selling the property. He won't see a good return, but at least he will be able to close out his investment.

Sale at Term

Thirty days before term, if the co-owners have not exercised their buyout options and if automatic extension does not occur, the property is listed for sale with the agent named in the agreement. If the Joint Ownership Agreement expires before an offer has been made on the property, the agreement is automatically extended until sale occurs.

Closing Costs at Term

We structure the joint ownership transaction so that seller's closing costs, which we generally project as a 6% sales commission, come off the top. In this manner the co-owners bear the closing expenses commensurate with their ownership interest. The Investor must understand, in projecting his return on investment, that if he is not bought out and the joint ownership terminates with sale, his projected annual return will effectively be reduced by about three percentage points.

Since the future can't be predicted, including whether the joint ownership will terminate with buyout or sale, the Investor cannot count on reaching his projected return. Thus, he is wise to also analyze the transaction with termination at sale. Typically, the Investor will find that his projected annual return generally decreases 3% with sale as opposed to buyout. This is due to the closing cost expense. But for the tax-wise Investor, he recoups some of this decrease in profit by a decrease in his property basis due to payment of these closing expenses.

The key to successful projections is to sit down and perform calculations. This is especially important for the sage Investor since his primary motivation is to earn a hearty return. Our software, the *Joint Ownership Calculator*tm, available by the Order Form at the back of the book, does this for you, but you can do it too. Take the time to project the net result after deducting sale expenses to best determine your split and how closing costs at sale will affect your projections. Again, the Investor must analyze the bottom lines of buyout and sale at term, and project returns that are realistic.

Spirit of the Agreement

The Investor and Occupier have declared their faith in each other by entering into a Joint Ownership Agreement. Although the agreement sets up legal remedies for each to pursue, the spirit of their agreement encourages good faith efforts and honest communication. The parties should always attempt to solve problems informally before resorting to those remedies. The sample Joint Ownership Agreement in the *Appendix* includes a useful *mediation – arbitration* provision. By initialing this provision, the co-owners agree to submit any dispute first to mediation for settlement, then to binding arbitration. Foreclosure or unlawful detainer actions may be pursued separately, even if mediation and arbitration are elected.

Default Buyout Provisions

The model Joint Ownership Agreement contains clear buyout remedies for a party which arise if his co-owner defaults. Buyout options often require court approval. Therefore, these options must be fair and expressed in appropriate legal terminology in the Joint Ownership Agreement.

These buyout options entitle the innocent co-owner to buy out the defaulter at a reduced value. Some defaults trigger an 80% buyout payable in a lump sum – others activate a 75% buyout payable in installments. Buyout is based on fair market value at the time of default as agreed upon by the co-owners or by appraisal. The type of default dictates which of the two buyout remedies apply. An owner does not have to exercise his buyout option. Instead, the innocent co-owner can sell the property under the agreement's default sale provision. Chapter Seven titled *Protection Against Co-owner Default,* describes each possibility of co-owner default. These provisions are necessary to protect the Investor's position in the joint ownership.

Mediation and Arbitration As Remedies

The sample Joint Ownership Agreement includes a mediation-arbitration provision. By initialing this provision the co-owners agree to resolve any joint ownership property dispute *outside the court system.* Foreclosure and unlawful detainer proceedings don't apply – these actions are not subject to mediation and arbitration, and may be pursued.

By selecting this provision, the co-owners agree to submit their dispute to mediation first. Mediation is a process which appoints a specially trained mediator to facilitate the parties to their own settlement. Mediation is non-adversarial and has a high success rate.

If the parties are unable to resolve their dispute through mediation, they may then submit the matter to binding arbitration. Arbitration is an adversarial process, similar to a mini-trial. The arbitrator hearing the case renders a binding, enforceable judgment.

Both processes take place outside the court system. They are brief and highly cost-effective. Usually the dispute can be resolved in one day – avoiding a three-year process through the court system. Vast amounts of time and attorneys' fees are saved in this way.

The uniform Joint Ownership Agreement is legitimized through its hand-tailored terms, assuring maximum tax benefits for joint ownerships. With this legitimacy, an important challenge to the residential real estate market is met. Joint ownership is now ready to be a dynamic force in the residential market – bringing it into popularity as the banner acquisitional device to meet the needs of the 21st century's residential real estate market. Now that we've reviewed the primary directives and duties assigned by the first-rate Joint Ownership Agreement, Chapter Six brings you the vital joint ownership numbers – the splits, values, and profits.

Chapter Six

CALCULATING THE JOINT OWNERSHIP NUMBERS

The last chapter created an outline for your joint ownership. This chapter fills in the blanks with real figures. Before this book and its software, calculating an ownership split was a real challenge. Here, various ownership splits are computed and a list of recommended splits are offered. Buyout is calculated for most circumstances, including death, bankruptcy, creditor lien recording, and payment default. Distribution of profit at sale is analyzed – so you can project your profit at the end of the joint ownership. Without further delay, let's move on to *the bottom line*.

*T*he joint ownership venture begins in the minds of Investor and Occupier. That's part of its charm. Each looks at the past – what's the appreciation history of the potential property?

They contemplate the present – financial standing, tax portfolio, cash available, and cost of the property. Then they take an informed look into the future – the best anyone can do, using what's happened before – market trends, supply and demand, and their own requirements. Finally, they decide how much money they want to generate from their joint ownership and make a plan.

At the outset, the Investor provides part or all of the down payment on the property and in return he receives an *equity interest* – a percentage of the property's appreciation when it is sold or bought out. How, then, do the parties determine their ownership split?

Determining the Ownership Split

Before this book, establishing ownership splits confused even the most seasoned mathematician. To simplify this process for everyone, we created a math-based software application known as the Joint Ownership Calculator™ which instantly calculates "what if" for every major variable in the joint ownership decision – in the time it takes to input your entries, press a button, and print.

Here are the numerical entries for any joint ownership:

- Purchase price of the property
- Down payment contribution by each party
- Loan interest rate
- Term of the joint ownership
- Investor's desired rate of return, simple interest
- Projected property appreciation rate

Here are the results:

- Value of the property at term
- Loan pay off at term
- Investor's interest (%)
- Occupier's interest (%)
- Investor's projected cash return
- Occupier's projected cash return
- Occupier's loan principal reduction for return
- Investor's deductions for payments made
- Investor's depreciation deduction
- Occupier's property tax deduction
- Occupier's mortgage interest deduction
- Internal Revenue Code §280A rent
- Refinance at Term: Cash result
- Buyout at Term: Cash result
- Sale at Term: Cash result

If you find the Joint Ownership Calculator™ of interest, see the Order Form following the index. For your guidance without our software, we have created a money map of *norms* to assist you in creating your ownership split. For the simplified Joint Ownership Money Map, read on.

The Joint Ownership Money Map

Most people are surprised to learn that mathematics is not an exact science. All mathematics is based on *assumptions*. Thus we approach ownership splits with assumptions necessary to calculate the joint ownership. But, like mathematicians, we will set up the *best* assumptions possible. The joint ownership projections are only as good as the assumptions upon which they are based.

When you have selected a property and have a good sense of its expected appreciation rate, the term of your Joint Ownership Agreement, and the Investor's desired return, you are ready to calculate your ownership split.

Projected Appreciation Rate

As mentioned before, you can't tell the future – but you can come close. The property's projected appreciation rate is a key factor in calculating the suitable ownership splits. To best estimate your property's appreciation rate, determine the term of your joint ownership. Then do your research – how comparable properties in the vicinity have appreciated in prior years, current real estate market conditions, and real property supply and demand.

Term of the Joint Ownership

Establish the desired term of your joint ownership. Will it be three, five, seven years, or some other period? Apply those years to your research on comparables and market conditions. If the term of your agreement is expected to be five years, find out how much nearby comparable properties have appreciated in the last five years. For a seven-year agreement, look at comparables over the past seven years. Be conservative. If there has been an unusual real estate boom in a prior year, don't consider that year – take an average of the other years for that number.

Projected Investor Return

The Investor indicates the *projected* return on investment he requires to enter the joint ownership transaction. This return is expressed as annual *simple* interest on his dollar investment.

But, always keep in mind – the Investor's return is only projected – there are no guaranteed returns in the joint ownership. In other words, an Investor may join in the transaction if he can reasonably expect a 12% annual return on his investment, simple interest. The Investor determines this percentage by researching comparable investments. How much could he make if he invested in the current market-place? Would the return be simple or compound interest? The Investor increases the comparable marketplace rate of return to compensate for the increased risk he takes in the joint ownership transaction – since his return is not guaranteed.

The Investor also needs to take into consideration that if the joint ownership terminates by sale instead of buyout, some of the return he projects will be eaten up by closing costs. The Investor ends up paying his ownership interest percentage of the closing costs at sale. Closing costs are generally 6% of the sale price. Depending upon the sale price of the property, the difference could be consequential or not.

Since the Investor doesn't know in advance whether he or his Occupier will be exercising their buyout options or selling the property at term of the joint ownership, he cannot precisely predict a single rate of return. We handle this by the Investor projecting a rate of return higher than he requires to compensate for the situation where the property is sold instead of the parties buying out one anther. Generally speaking, the Investor will net about 3% less than his target projected return if sale of the property terminates the joint ownership instead of buyout.

Other Built-in Adjustments

The model joint ownership calculation returns all loan principal reduction to the party making loan payments, typically the Occupier. The important feature credits what could be a significant amount to the paying party. Also, the closing costs at sale come off the top, resulting in each party paying in proportion to their ownership percentage. This results in the Investor receiving about a 3% less annual projected return on his investment. The Investor needs to carefully consider this fact. If he's projecting an 11% return on buyout, he'll get about an 8% return at sale. At the beginning of the co-ownership, no one knows how it will terminate – through buyout or sale. Thus, if the Investor must receive a certain projected return, he should set his projected return to correspond to sale, instead of buyout. These two factors are built into our recommended program.

Suggested Ownership Splits

We now chart several recommended ownership splits based on three essential factors – projected appreciation rate, term, and Investor's desired return at buyout. Since one chart can't possibly illustrate all the possibilities, we've shown some of the most popular transactions with their suggested owner-ship splits.

In all of the examples which follow, the Investor has contributed the full 20% down payment to the joint ownership property, which is worth $225,000. If your Occupier contrib-utes any portion of that 20%, these charts must be adjusted in favor of the Occupier. If the value of your property differs, your splits will differ. In these calculations the purchase loan is fixed rate at 7.5% per annum. The loan interest rate is important since loan pay-off at term will vary with varying loans, and so will the ownership splits. Keep all this in mind when selecting your split. The only way to be truly accurate is to base your split on your own specific calculations – either by using the Joint Ownership Calculator™ or calculating it out yourself.

Suggested Ownership Splits

7-year Agreement / 3% Appreciation		
Investor Return	Ownership Split	
	Investor	Occupier
14%	85	15
13%	79	21
12%	73	27
11%	67	33
10%	62	38
9%	54	46

5-year Agreement / 3% Appreciation

Investor Return	Ownership Split	
	Investor	Occupier
14%	89	11
13%	81	19
12%	75	25
11%	69	31
10%	64	36
9%	56	44

7-year Agreement / 4% Appreciation

Investor Return	Ownership Split	
	Investor	Occupier
14%	62	38
13%	58	42
12%	54	46
11%	49	51
10%	45	55
9%	39	61

5-year Agreement / 4% Appreciation

Investor Return	Ownership Split	
	Investor	Occupier
14%	65	35
13%	59	41
12%	55	45
11%	51	49
10%	47	53
9%	41	59

7-year Agreement / 5% Appreciation

Investor Return	Ownership Split	
	Investor	Occupier
14%	48	52
13%	45	55
12%	41	59
11%	38	62
10%	35	65
9%	30	70

5-year Agreement / 6% Appreciation		
Investor Return	Ownership Split	
	Investor	*Occupier*
14%	42	58
13%	38	62
12%	36	64
11%	33	67
10%	30	70
9%	26	74

Once the ownership split is calculated, it becomes the ownership interest of Investor and Occupier. Cash contributions advanced to buy the property or equity retained by a Seller-Investor, although reimbursed later, no longer represent ownership interests. Ownership is now expressed as an equity percentage. For example, the Investor may have advanced 20% toward the purchase price. However, once the joint ownership relationship is created, the Investor's interest is converted to an ownership split. Based on the previous chart, the 20% Investor receives a 55% ownership split based on a five-year agreement, 4% appreciation, and a 12% annual return projected to the Investor, simple interest.

The primary assumption in these charts is the property's *appreciation rate.* It is the pivotal factor in planning the joint ownership. Investor and Occupier must strive to identify a rate that conforms to the property and the market. Obviously, if their property appreciates at a different rate, their profits will suffer – or soar. Their best strategy is to be informed, reasonable, and conservative.

Your Protection Provision

We've built a protection factor into the Joint Ownership Agreement – to protect against loss if the property has not appreciated. The Joint Ownership Agreement promises that the co-owners will share the value of their property at term, according to their percentage interests. As we know, that future value is unknown. It was an educated guess – if the property depreciates, even their initial cash contributions would not be returned. For this reason, realizing that the real estate market sometimes experiences recession, we have built a protection factor into our model agreement. This provision states that if the property has not appreciated an average of 1.5% per year, the joint ownership will automatically be continued.

We suggest a minimum of 1.5% to protect the Investor's contribution from being eaten up by a sale commission. But, again, the required appreciation percentage is up to the parties' mutual agreement. When defining a required appreciation rate they should consider the benefits and burdens that an extension or many extensions will confer. The Occupier will be living in the property longer than expected. The Investor will not be cashing out as early as expected. But, any detriment these factors may create will likely be offset by the profit they will make when selling in a better market.

On the other hand, a boom may have hit when the agreement terminates. If the property appreciates substantially, the co-owners may become two more real estate tycoons.

Guarantees: The Defeat of a Joint Ownership

The only unconditional guarantee for the joint owner-ship Investor and Occupier is this: their return on investment is not guaranteed. Ironically, this is *good news*. Unconditional guarantees would be the ruin of their joint ownership.

This ruin could come about in several ways, had we not written the Joint Ownership Agreement free of unconditionally guaranteed returns. First, guaranteeing return to an Investor makes him a *lender* under tax law, voiding ownership tax benefits and tax-deferral options. Second, a guaranteed Investor return – if a property doesn't appreciate enough – might result in large sums owing by an Occupier who can't pay them back. Third, if a third-party Investor were deemed a lender, an excessive return on his *loan* would violate usury laws.

Lender Status Nullifies the Joint Ownership

The Investor with a guaranteed return is considered a *lender* by taxing agencies. He loses his ownership deductions and his right to exchange out of the property to defer tax on gain. The Internal Revenue Service has a simple explanation as to why these benefits are forfeited – if the Investor is a lender he is not an owner, nor is he entitled to ownership tax benefits. Our Investor will not experience this kind of disaster. Because he looks only to the property's appreciation for his return, he retains *bona fide* owner status.

The ownership split method of return was created for the joint ownership in order to avoid this lender status issue. A joint ownership transaction does *not* guarantee the Investor's return – thereby establishing ownership status and protecting the Investor and his tax benefits.

Usury Limits

If the third-party Investor is deemed a lender, he is subject to usury laws which limit loan charges to 5% above the federal discount rate. If lender status is found, the Investor's return would be limited to his capital contribution plus the usury limit – the average usury limit has generally been about 8%. If categorized as a lender, the Investor experiences both loss of tax benefits and loss of profits. As a note, *seller status* is an exception to the usury laws. If the Investor is the seller of the joint ownership property, usury limitations don't apply – but he must still avoid dreaded *lender status.*

No Guarantees As Good News

In light of the property's unknown future value, guaranteed return to either party isn't realistic. But our co-owners' shared belief in the appreciation of real estate has brought them together, and they have agreed to do what they can to make it happen.

You can't read the future – but when you come close, it's a truly profitable result. By avoiding unconditional guarantees, the conservative Joint Ownership Agreement protects both Investor and Occupier by establishing tax status – and realistic expectations.

Our co-owners believe in real estate appreciation as a good source of investment return. It is the basis for their Joint Ownership Agreement and their ownership split. Their faith is rewarded. The ownership split, by definition, defines the parties' profit as appreciation in the property. Regardless of the amount of appreciation, both parties preserve ownership status which entitles them to substantial deductions against income. At the same time, the Investor retains the right to exchange out of the property at term and defer tax on any gain. The Occupier also retains his right to roll into another principal residence and defer his tax. Finally, and most importantly, the required appreciation rate the co-owners set protect against loss.

The Bottom Line

If you've done your research and come up with the best possible assumptions, you've determined an ownership split that suits both Investor and Occupier. Now you can use this percentage split to calculate the bottom line profits to each co-owner at sale, buyout, or refinance. Our software (available through the Order Form at the back of the book) performs these calculations with a return of your computer cursor.

On its way to the bottom line, the joint ownership can proceed uneventfully to its conclusion – or the unexpected may happen. In a joint ownership, preparing wisely for the unexpected can transform a bottom line trauma into a triumph. An uneventful joint ownership reaches the bottom line at term upon sale or buyout. Unexpected events – Occupier default, death of a co-owner, or bankruptcy – generate special default buyout options that are anticipated by the first-rate Joint Ownership Agreement. We've created an overview of buyout and sale events in this section. For step-by-step illustrations of sample transactions, see Chapters Nine and Ten.

Buyout at Term

One hundred and fifty days before the Joint Ownership Agreement expires, its termination buyout options take effect. The co-owners decide whether to extend their joint ownership, buy out the other's interest, or sell the property. The buyout sequence is set forth in Chapter Five. The co-owners usually refinance the property to complete buyout. How is buyout calculated and who establishes the values?

Value is set by agreement or appraisal. Appraisal is performed by a single appraiser selected by both parties or by averaging separate appraisals. Buyout calculation follows the steps specified in the Joint Ownership Agreement. First, the loan pay-off amount is deducted. The Occupier is then charged for loan negative amortization, if any. Then the parties' initial capital contributions are reimbursed to them. Next the Occupier is credited for any loan principal reduction he has made. Finally, the parties are credited for reimbursable improvement contributions they have made. *Net equity* remains only after these amounts are credited. Last, net equity is divided between Investor and Occupier using the percentages of their ownership split. For example, if net equity is $100,000 and the Investor is entitled to a 45% ownership split, the Investor receives an additional $45,000 on buyout by the Occupier. The $45,000 is added to his capital contribution for the aggregate buyout amount.

Sale of the Joint Ownership Property at Term

If the co-owners do not extend the agreement or exercise their terminating buyout options, the property is sold unless the required appreciation rate set by the parties is not reached. At sale, value is based on the price the property brings on the open market. The calculations are the same as they are upon buyout, except sale commissions and closing costs are deducted from the net equity before the parties receive any return.

Due to the commission expense, sale produces less equity to the co-owners than they would receive at buyout. For this reason, the Investor projecting return on buyout must also calculate his projected return at sale — which will be less.

Buyout on Mutual Agreement

Suppose one of our co-owners decides early to buy out his counterpart? All it takes is mutual agreement by both Investor and Occupier. Even though the agreement did not contemplate early buyout, the co-owner proposing buyout may find his counterpart willing to liquidate his interest early – there's no penalty. Upon early buyout, the same calculations are performed as when the co-owners buy one another out at term. Value is based on appraised value or as agreed upon.

Buyout on Default

The first-rate Joint Ownership Agreement contains special buyout provisions to handle unexpected events. Two distinct buyout provisions are used – 80% of value payable in one lump sum and 75% of value payable in installments. Buyout is based on appraisal less loan pay-off – unless the parties agree on value.

The type of default dictates which remedy applies. Eighty percent lump-sum buyout arises upon co-owner death, bankruptcy, conservatorship, or creditor lien recording. Seventy-five percent buyout is the general default buyout provision. A 75% buyout arises upon default on any obligation undertaken in the Joint Ownership Agreement. Buyout is payable in installments authorizing payment of half at the time of buyout and the other half over the next six months in equal payments without interest. Chapter Seven details these default buyout provisions.

Default Sale

A co-owner is not required to exercise his default buyout remedy. Instead, he may sell the property under the agreement's default sale provisions with the defaulter paying sale costs and reimbursing him for payments advanced to the extent of the defaulter's sale proceeds. The non-defaulting party must consider that reimbursement for sale costs and payments advanced is limited to defaulter's sale proceeds. Both procedures – default buyout and default sale – should carefully be analyzed before one is selected. See the Joint Ownership Agreement provision in the *Appendix* for the suggested schedule showing how proceeds are divided at default sale.

We've determined ownership splits and value on buyout and sale, and how our co-owners apply these principles. For actual bottom lines, see Chapters Nine and Ten. Cash return is just one profitable result from the joint ownership – there are others. The Internal Revenue Code itself has created many beneficial results for the co-owners in the form of tax deductions and tax deferral, as you will discover in Chapter Eight. But first, let's explore what happens when a co-owner defaults.

Chapter Seven

PROTECTION AGAINST CO-OWNER DEFAULT

This chapter is written by the realist. The realist anticipates the *what ifs* of the joint ownership transaction and provides solutions for them. These solutions are conferred by the documents which accompany the Joint Ownership Agreement – the Memorandum of Joint Ownership Agreement, Joint Ownership Note, Deed of Trust/Mortgage, and Lease Agreement. In the standard joint ownership the Occupier assumes all property obligations. What happens if the Occupier fails to carry out his promises? For the Investor, these concerns are vital. This chapter spells out the co-owners' default remedies – ranging from good faith problem solving to buyout, sale, or foreclosure.

*W*hat if the Occupier moves from the property and leases it out? What if he stops making payments on the loan or the property taxes? What if he refuses to vacate the property after he defaults? These concerns are real to the Investor. This chapter is written for the Investor to answer each and every one of his concerns. The joint ownership protects him all the way around.

In the joint ownership transaction the obligations are distributed between Investor and Occupier. Typically, the Investor funds acquisition costs and the Occupier assumes ownership duties and obligations. Protecting the Investor's security interest – and defining the Occupier's interest – are vital functions of the joint ownership documents. Since the Occupier bears the joint ownership responsibilities, should default occur, he will most likely be the co-owner to default. The Investor must have clear and adequate remedies in the event of Occupier default. The specially designed default provisions of the agreement, the Investor's deed of trust/ mortgage and the lease agreement are his protection.

With the standard structure Investor obligation default is virtually unknown. For events creating court involvement – death, bankruptcy, creditor liening, and conservatorship – the model Joint Ownership Agreement defines these events as *defaults*, confirming the Occupier's ownership rights and granting remedies to him under these circumstances.

What Happens When an Occupier Defaults?

The joint ownership property interest conferred upon the Occupier is actually an *advance* return – it assumes faithful performance of all Occupier joint ownership obligations. When the Occupier defaults, what happens to his interest?

Does it also cease? No. The defaulting Occupier remains on title holding his full property interest. When an Investor assumes a defaulting Occupier's duties – as he undoubtedly will – he deserves to receive the Occupier's property interest as well. But this doesn't happen automatically.

In the real world of the defaulting Occupier, the Investor's property rights and credit become jeopardized. To protect himself, the Investor must step in and remedy the Occupier's defaults. He takes on a whole new set of obligations – without the accompanying property rights. While the defaulting Occupier remains on title holding an unearned property interest, the Investor inherits the Occupier's property obligations. How, then, does the Occupier's property interest shift to the Investor?

The Investor must set mechanisms in place that will shift a defaulting Occupier's property rights to him. The Joint Ownership Agreement and Deed of Trust/Mortgage arm him with a range of remedies. He can buy out the Occupier at a reduced value – otherwise, the property is sold under general default provisions, with sale costs borne by the Occupier to the extent of his sale proceeds. Lastly, if the default involves one of the primary money or performance obligations, the Investor is entitled to foreclose under his Deed of Trust/Mortgage.

What if a defaulting Occupier is truly uncooperative and refuses to vacate the property? In this unlikely event, the Investor must be able to gain possession of the property. The Joint Ownership Agreement and accompanying lease arm the Investor with eviction rights.

The Joint Ownership Agreement provides a range of remedies for various defaults. The type of default dictates its remedy. Those defaults which entitle the Investor to foreclose under his Deed of Trust/Mortgage fall into a category of their own. They include money defaults – on mortgage, property taxes, and insurance – and default on the Occupier's *primary three obligations* – his duty to occupy the property, repair and maintain it, and refrain from assigning or encumbering his interest.

These obligations, entitled primary defaults, are discussed later in this chapter. The less serious defaults entitle the co-owners to buy out one another. When faced with a problem, and before exploring their formal remedies, the co-owners should always attempt to come up with their own solution.

The Important Accompanying Documents

The Joint Ownership Agreement forms the core of the joint ownership transaction – but it is only the starting point. Several additional documents must be prepared to adequately document and secure the transaction – the Joint Ownership Note, the Deed of Trust/Mortgage, the Memorandum of Joint Ownership Agreement, and the lease agreement. These documents add a multitude of checks and balances to the joint ownership transaction. This chapter explains why these documents are needed, and their requirements. Hand-tailored samples in the *Appendix* illustrate how these accompanying documents meet the unique needs of a joint ownership. Forms of these documents are also available by fax-on-demand by the Order Form at the back of the book.

Memorandum of Joint Ownership Agreement

The Joint Ownership Agreement averages 40 pages. Due to its private nature and its length, a shorter *memorandum* is prepared for recording purposes publicly announcing the existence of a longer version of the Joint Ownership Agreement. Since the co-owners' interests and how they hold title are clearly stated in the memorandum, it settles any questions that may arise on those points. The memorandum is also used as a vesting instruction to issue title identical to that recited in the memorandum.

The Joint Ownership Note

The Joint Ownership Note, secured by the Deed of Trust/Mortgage, creates a money obligation running from the Occupier to the Investor. The money obligation is *contingent,* meaning that it is due only if the Occupier defaults on payments or other obligations he has assumed in the Joint Ownership Agreement.

The note amount represents two different sums – the amount of the purchase loan and a valuation of the Occupier's interest in Investor-contributed equity. It includes and repeats the purchase loan obligations, reinforcing the lender's security – while specifying the parties' direct obligations.

The *all-inclusive* feature of the Joint Ownership Note and Deed of Trust/Mortgage is the Investor's best protective measure if the Occupier defaults on mortgage payments. Although the Investor and Occupier are both liable on the loan, the all-inclusive feature confirms that it is the Occupier's duty to pay the mortgage.

The Joint Ownership Note also includes a value of the Occupier's interest in Investor-contributed equity. The Occupier's property interest pledge to the Investor is based upon that value. By a carefully drafted liquidated damages provision in the Joint Ownership Agreement, the parties agree that damages would be difficult to determine upon the

Occupier's default; hence the valuation set forth in the note prevails.

Note Calculation

The sample Joint Ownership Note uses Chapter Nine's sample transaction. Their purchase loan was $108,000 with initial funds contributed by Investor of $27,000. This calculation is only based on Investor's contribution – it does not include Occupier's contribution to initial capital, if any. This is because we only want to reflect the Occupier's equity interest in the Investor's contribution. The aim is to give back what the Occupier has not earned.

In our sample transaction, the Occupier has a 45% ownership interest, yielding an equity interest in the Investor's initial capital of $12,500. For purposes of the note, only initial capital is considered – subsequent capital contributions made by the parties are not. The Joint Ownership Note for the sample transaction is in the face amount of $120,150, representing the $108,000 purchase loan amount plus $12,150 as the Occupier's cash equity interest.

If the Occupier in Chapter Nine fails to make a loan payment, the obligation under the Investor's all-inclusive note becomes due and payable by the Occupier. In the sample transaction the Occupier's promissory obligation in the amount of $120,150 would then become due. If the Occupier fails to pay the note amount, the Investor may foreclose on the Occupier's property interest under his Deed of Trust/Mortgage. Of course, foreclosure would proceed subject to the Occupier's right to reinstate his position under the Joint Ownership Note and Deed of Trust/Mortgage. At sale, the $108,000 first loan is deducted from the Investor's note, leaving the Occupier's interest in the equity as his obligation to the Investor – here in the amount of $12,150.

The Occupier's pledge arises for the following reasons. Under the Joint Ownership Agreement the Occupier has agreed to perform certain property obligations. In return, he has received a co-ownership interest in the property *in advance* and far earlier than he could have on his own. The Occupier's primary obligations include his promises to occupy the property, make payments, refrain from encumbering or transferring his interest, and maintain and repair the property so it will hold its value.

The Occupier received his property interest in return for his promise to perform these obligations, which are essential to the parties' joint ownership of the property. If an Occupier defaults in performing these obligations, the burden falls solely upon the Investor. Along with such a burden, the Investor deserves to receive the Occupier's benefits. Thus, it is fair that the Occupier pledges his property interest to his co-owner if he fails to perform his promises. The Joint Ownership Note and Deed of Trust/Mortgage provide this pledge.

The Joint Ownership Deed of Trust/Mortgage

To protect the Investor, the Deed of Trust/Mortgage grants him a security interest in the Occupier's portion of the property. Both the Joint Ownership Note and Deed of Trust/Mortgage require skillful crafting to create – and protect – the Investor's foreclosure rights. The joint ownership Investor is in a vulnerable position since he is *not* a lender, and there is no current money obligation running to him from the Occupier. The *contingent* money obligation from Occupier to Investor occurs only if the Occupier defaults under the Joint Ownership Agreement. The Investor enforces the note obligation against his defaulting and uncooperative Occupier by foreclosing on his Deed of Trust/Mortgage, clearing the way for him to claim the defaulting Occupier's property interest. Since the Occupier owns a percentage of the property, that specific percentage interest is pledged in the Deed of Trust/Mortgage. If an Occupier holds a 45% equity interest, the trust deed will state:

> Trustor hereby irrevocably grants, transfers, and assigns to Trustee, in trust, with power of sale, Trustor's forty-five percent (45%) tenancy in common interest in the property.

Some states use trust deeds, while others use mortgages. The language in the mortgage is similar to that quoted above. In the long run these security instruments are substantially the same, serving to protect the Investor's investment. Without these security instruments, the Investor cannot properly protect his co-ownership interest.

The joint ownership Deed of Trust/Mortgage must include the purchase loan obligations. In most joint ownership transactions, a new purchase loan is obtained by the co-owners. Although both Investor and Occupier are typically liable on the loan, under the Joint Ownership Agreement the Occupier agrees to make all payments. The all-inclusive feature of the Deed of Trust/Mortgage confirms the Occupier's primary responsibility to pay the mortgage. Thus, the joint ownership Deed of Trust/Mortgage allows the Investor to foreclose if the Occupier fails to make those loan payments. In this manner, an Occupier's default on the purchase loan creates simultaneous default under the Investor's Deed of Trust/Mortgage. The Investor needs this added security.

Subordination Feature

The Deed of Trust/Mortgage is further customized by a subordination clause, giving the lender's loan priority. The purchase lender requires this subordination as a part of the joint ownership transaction. The subordination provision states that the Investor's Deed of Trust/Mortgage is junior to the lender's, which must be honored first.

Power of Sale

The Deed of Trust/Mortgage must contain a *power of sale* provision. Power of sale entitles the Investor to sell the Occupier's interest in the property to satisfy his Occupier's unfulfilled obligations. Without this provision, the Investor cannot sell the Occupier's property interest – nor can he obtain full title to the property by making his own credit bid at the trustee sale. This is why the Investor must ensure that the trust deed contains a power of sale.

Occupancy Requirement

Another hand-tailored feature is the *occupancy requirement*. This provision restates Occupier's duty to occupy the property for the term of the agreement. Both the Deed of Trust/Mortgage and the Joint Ownership Agreement authorize foreclosure by Investor if the Occupier fails to fulfill his occupancy requirement. Of course, the Investor may choose to waive the occupancy requirement, whereupon the Deed of Trust/Mortgage will not be enforced on this issue.

Maintenance and Repair Requirement

The joint ownership Deed of Trust/Mortgage contains specific maintenance and repair requirements. Although the

Joint Ownership Agreement requires the Occupier to maintain and repair the property in the same condition as acquired, less reasonable wear and tear, the Deed of Trust/Mortgage defines the criteria for reasonable maintenance and repair. If the Occupier fails to meet those criteria, the Investor is authorized to foreclose. This provision must be included within the Deed of Trust/Mortgage. Without it, the Investor may not foreclose in the event that the Occupier lets the property fall into disrepair.

The default must be clear and unquestionable to the foreclosure trustee, who will hesitate to undertake foreclosure if the breach is discretionary in any way. Because they must make a judgment to determine whether maintenance and repair provisions have been violated, some foreclosure trustees refuse to service default based on this provision alone. A foreclosure trustee will accept the ruling of an outside authority, such as a city government, which has condemned the property due to inadequate maintenance. A similar finding by a homeowners' association may also be sufficient grounds for breach. Absent such evidence, the professional foreclosure trustee may decline foreclosure based on failure to maintain and repair. The best way to proceed is to check with a foreclosure trustee or your attorney before proceeding to foreclose upon default on these obligations. Nevertheless, the provision should be included in the Deed of Trust/Mortgage in the event that the breach can be clearly established.

Due on Encumbrance Provision

The joint ownership Deed of Trust/Mortgage also includes a *Due on Encumbrance* provision. Under the Joint Ownership Agreement the Occupier is prohibited from transferring or pledging his interest in the property without Investor consent. The Deed of Trust/Mortgage reiterates these requirements and authorizes foreclosure in the event of breach. The provision defines the situations causing breach as transfer, sale, assignment, or further pledge of the Occupier's interest. Further pledge would include obtaining a loan secured by the Occupier's interest in the property.

Request for Notice of Default Under Purchase Loan

The joint ownership Deed of Trust/Mortgage also requests Notice of Default, requesting the lender to give the Investor notice of foreclosure. With Notice of Default the Investor has time to protect both his ownership and lien interests long before the purchase lender concludes foreclosure.

Nevertheless, the Investor must carefully monitor the Occupier's loan payments. The status of the loan is crucial to the Investor since he is named directly on the loan and is responsible to the lender for its repayment. Often the lender refrains from issuing a Notice of Default until the loan is two to three months late. The Investor should not rely solely on this notice as his firsthand source of loan status. He must know early on when any payment is late.

The lender should not object to issuing joint statements to both co-owners as co-borrowers, at their respective addresses. The Investor should set up this dual statement method with the purchase lender to be immediately advised of delinquencies. This is done at the time of the loan application. This way, all notices mailed to the Occupier will also be mailed to the Investor.

There are other reasons for the Investor to monitor loan progress aside from Investor liability on the loan. Occupier non-payment of the purchase loan creates default under the Investor's Deed of Trust/Mortgage. Upon the Occupier's first payment default, Investor and Occupier should communicate honestly in an attempt to solve the problem. If this doesn't work, the Investor should timely pursue his own remedies under the Joint Ownership Agreement and Deed of Trust/Mortgage.

The Joint Ownership Lease

In order to conform to the requirements of Internal Revenue Code §280A, the Investor claiming tax benefits for the property must rent his interest in the property to the Occupier. (See Chapter Eight.) Although Internal Revenue Code §280A does not *require* a separate lease between the parties, we recommend preparation of a separate lease agreement to protect the Investor's legal remedies.

The lease creates separate obligations running from the Occupier to the Investor – and distinct remedies available to the Investor if the Occupier defaults on his rental obligation. The lease agreement defines these landlord-tenant issues and segregates them from those of ownership.

Tenant Status Gives Remedies

Owners are not subject to eviction, while tenants are. To pave the way for eviction, should it ever be necessary, the Joint Ownership Agreement and lease anticipate this unlikely event. The Occupier has agreed to revert to *tenant status* in the event of his default. The evicting Investor may be met with resistance in his unlawful detainer or ejectment action because of policies against owner eviction. Armed with the Occupier's voluntary assumption of tenant status in both the lease and agreement, the Investor has a better chance to prevail.

Thus, the Investor's most important remedy under the lease agreement is his right to evict. The lease agreement authorizes the Investor to commence eviction proceedings against a defaulting Occupier. In the unlikely event of a disruptive and uncooperative Occupier, the eviction remedy is the Investor's key protection.

If the Occupier defaults on his Internal Revenue Code §280A rent obligation, the separate lease agreement also entitles the Investor to exercise his landlord possessory right. The lease agreement confirms that, although the Occupier does own a portion of the property, his ownership does not extend to the portion subject to the lease. Thus, the Investor's eviction remedy for the Occupier's breach of the lease is consistent with their landlord-tenant status.

Remedies at Co-Owner Default

Good Faith Cooperation Above All

Although the ideal Joint Ownership Agreement and Deed of Trust/Mortgage provide a full range of remedies, the co-owners should first try to solve their problems reasonably and amicably between themselves. When something unexpected occurs, the parties should first sit down and discuss all possible solutions. The co-owners should treat one another with utmost good faith, attempting to resolve problems before resorting to more drastic procedures. The remedies provided in the agreement represent the final pit stop available to the co-owners – after pursuing all other solutions.

If the parties are unable to resolve the issue on their own, they should enlist a trained mediator to assist them. Mediation is required by the model Joint Ownership Agreement. It is best to enter mediation early on, long before a minor issue escalates into major battle. If resolution is not possible, then the co-owners should invoke the remedies detailed in the Joint Ownership Agreement as a last resort.

Buyout As a Remedy

Default by an owner creates a buyout option for his co-owner. Buyout provisions are a major deterrent to default, with a fair result to both parties. Buyout should approximate the amount the co-owners would have received had the property been sold, with closing costs assessed to the defaulter. The innocent party should be favored in a reasonable manner, but he should not receive a windfall. These buyout provisions and the security they provide – to the Investor, in particular – have created respect for the first-rate Joint Ownership Agreement, bringing legitimacy and widespread acceptance to the joint ownership transaction in today's residential real estate market.

Two different buyout options are available in the Joint Ownership Agreement. One variety of default entitles the innocent co-owner to an 80% buyout of his co-owner, payable in a lump sum. Remaining defaults entitle the co-owner to a 75% reduced co-owner buyout, payable in installments.

The buyout values recommended here are not engraved in stone. They are merely suggested default values and procedures found to be fair to both co-owners. If the non-defaulting party chooses buyout as settlement during foreclosure, the co-owner in default receives a return not possible in the foreclosure process – and ready cash in a time of financial hardship. Installment buyout allows the non-defaulting co-owner to sell the property before he has to pay full buyout.

80% Buyout: Death, Bankruptcy, Creditor Lien, or Conservatorship

Under the model Joint Ownership Agreement, a lump sum 80% buyout option arises when an event precipitates court involvement – at co-owner death, bankruptcy, creditor lien recording, or conservatorship. The Joint Ownership Agreement defines these four events as defaults, to be remedied by buyout options. The buyout amount, determined by agreement or appraisal, is paid in one lump sum. The innocent party can either exercise his buyout option or sell the property under general default sale provisions, explored later in this chapter.

Each of these four events generates expensive and time-consuming court involvement. The goal of the court system is to pursue justice. Often this pursuit involves a great deal of time and expense – especially the processes of probate, conservatorship, bankruptcy, and execution on creditors' liens. Death brings potential probate court expense and delays. Personal bankruptcy pulls the property into the bankruptcy court system. Creditor lien recording subjects the property to execution. Conservatorship involves court proceedings.

The first-rate Joint Ownership Agreement prepares for these unexpected events, decreasing the likelihood that a joint ownership property will be suspended in the courts. By labeling these events as defaults, the Joint Ownership Agreement creates an immediate buyout option in favor of the unaffected co-owner. Hence, the co-owner has an opportunity to by-pass the court system except for a brief appearance to obtain the court's consent – by exercising buyout for 80% of appraised value.

At Death of a Co-Owner

If a co-owner dies, the Joint Ownership Agreement decides the fate of his joint ownership interest. Several provisions are available. The preferred choice is reduced buyout by the surviving co-owner at 80%, described above, allowing the property to by-pass probate. If the deceased co-owner's interest is held in joint tenancy with a spouse, the buyout option is not triggered unless both joint tenants die.

In selecting a death provision, the co-owners should project what may happen at death and choose an appropriate provision. The co-owners may will away their property interests, rather than grant buyout options. An elderly widowed Investor may want her fortune to pass intact to her beneficiaries. Under this provision, buyout is not triggered upon the party's death. If the Investor is the decedent, her heirs take her place as joint ownership co-owners. If the decedent is the Occupier, the property is sold under default sale provisions and the decedent's proceeds pass on to his estate. This option may cause the property to be held up in the court system.

Of course, the parties can also hold their interests in the name of their living trust (see Chapter 14).

Upon Bankruptcy or Conservatorship of a Co-Owner

Suppose a co-owner files a petition in chapter seven personal bankruptcy or a conservator is appointed to manage his affairs? In the model Joint Ownership Agreement the unaffected co-owner avoids the long, intricate bankruptcy and probate court processes by exercising buyout of the estate. The court is notified and petitioned for confirmation, and the buyout funds are deposited directly to the court upon receipt of the appraiser's report. Thus, the property stays relatively free of court delay and expense.

Upon Filing of a Creditor's Lien

A buyout option is triggered when a creditor lien is recorded on the property for a 90 day period. If the creditor lien goes unsatisfied, the property is in danger of being sold. Under this provision, the innocent co-owner avoids sale by exercising an option to buy out the debtor co-owner's interest. The buyout funds are deposited in escrow and the creditor's lien is paid in the process. The creditor usually reduces his claim in return for voluntary payment. The result – the property, clear of the creditor lien, now belongs to the innocent co-owner.

75% Buyout – General Default

A 75% buyout arises on all defaults not specifically covered by the 80% buyout provision. This provision, referred to as *general default buyout*, is more generous to the innocent party – reducing buyout to 75% and allowing payment to be made in installments. The installment schedule requires half payment at the time of buyout and the other half payable over the next six months in equal payments without interest.

A promissory note for the installment portion of buyout is executed by the Investor, who further secures the obligation with a Deed of Trust/Mortgage to his exiting co-owner. The installment method gives the innocent co-owner an opportunity to sell the property before full buyout is due. Under the installment method he can list the property for sale right after he receives full title in the buyout escrow. The defaulting owner receives the balance of buyout upon sale of the property or as note payments come due, whichever occurs first. By reducing buyout to 75% of value on a payment schedule, this provision relieves part of the innocent co-owner's burden brought about when his co-owner defaults.

General default occurs when co-owners fail to perform specific obligations they have agreed to in the Joint Ownership Agreement. The Occupier's primary duties are to pay the expenses, occupy the property, repair and maintain it, and refrain from encumbering or assigning his property interest. Default on any of these obligations entitles the Investor to two remedies – he may foreclose under his Deed of Trust/Mortgage or buy out the Occupier. Generally, the Investor takes on no duties and is not subject to general default.

Buyout Notice – Appraisal

The buyout option is the innocent party's choice, but mandatory to the defaulting party – if the innocent party chooses to exercise a buyout option, the defaulter must sell. If buyout is not exercised, the non-defaulting party may proceed with default sale of the property instead. (See *Sale of the Property Under the Agreement,* below).

When a party decides to exercise his buyout option, he provides his co-owner with written *Notice of Intent to Buy Out.* This notice specifies the Joint Ownership Agreement's relevant buyout provision and a proposed buyout valuation. Under the Joint Ownership Agreement, value is determined by agreement or by an MAI certified appraiser appointed by the co-owners. If they cannot agree on one appraiser, each selects his own and the average of the two appraisals is adopted as value. If the party being bought out rejects the proposed valuation set forth in the notice, the appraisal process commences.

From the resulting value, loan pay-off is deducted with credit for principal reduction and the co-owners are credited for their capital contributions, leaving net equity. Net equity is divided according to the co-owners' ownership splits. This process establishes market value of the co-owner's interest.

Buyout is then determined by applying the proper buyout percentage. The defaulting co-owner pays any escrow costs generated by the buyout.

The Buyout Escrow

Buyout is accomplished through escrow. Escrow expenses are paid by the defaulter, who receives payment upon transferring his interest by grant deed. A *buyout agreement* is prepared stating that the defaulter conveys his interest freely and voluntarily in exchange for what he considers to be fair and reasonable compensation. Part of that compensation is his innocent co-owner's willingness to release him from liability on the primary loan. (Whether the lender will release him is an entirely different matter.) Since the defaulting party will no longer be on title, it follows that he should not be responsible for the underlying loan.

Suppose an uncooperative defaulter resists buyout? If he refuses to sign over his property interest, escrow is canceled and the buyout deposit is returned to the innocent party. The parties then pursue the Joint Ownership Agreement's remaining remedies – liquidation of the property by sale and possible eviction of the uncooperative party.

Buyout for More Than One Default

If more than one default applies in any given situation, the buyout provision yielding the least proceeds to the defaulting party takes precedence. For example, if the Occupier is in default for assigning his interest without Investor consent, and he subsequently files for bankruptcy, 75% buyout under *assignment* – one of the primary three obligations – prevails over 80% buyout under bankruptcy.

Default Sale

Upon default, a co-owner doesn't have to exercise his buyout remedy. It may be more profitable to do so, but he does not have to exercise the buyout option. Instead, he may elect to sell the property under the agreement's default sale provisions. Default sale proceeds are shared by the parties with the defaulting owner paying all sale costs and reimbursing his co-owner for payments advanced – to the extent of sale proceeds to defaulting party. Always remember that neither party is responsible beyond his interest in the property. See the Joint Ownership Agreement in the *Appendix* for a proceeds distribution schedule.

Sale of the Property Under the Agreement

This section covers sale of the property under the Joint Ownership Agreement, as opposed to under the Deed of Trust/Mortgage (covered below under *Foreclosure by Investor*). The party granted a buyout option is not required to exercise it. Instead, with the cooperation of his co-owner, the property can be sold in accordance with default sale provisions. Similar to sale at term, the proceeds at default sale are shared by the parties – with two major differences. First, the innocent party is reimbursed for all payments advanced on behalf of his defaulting co-owner. Second, the defaulter is assigned responsibility for all seller sale expenses. Of course, just because the defaulter is responsible for these expenses doesn't mean he'll pay them. In the real world of default, payment comes only when the defaulter receives sale proceeds in the escrow process. It never comes out of his pocket; only from his interest in the property.

Foreclosure by Investor

So, how does the Investor foreclose on his co-owner? First, he always attempts good faith cooperation in an effort to obtain cooperative resolution. Suppose his efforts fail? Suppose the Occupier is uncooperative? In this case, the Investor is left holding the bag, and he may foreclose upon his Deed of Trust/Mortgage under certain circumstances. Foreclosure is authorized if the Occupier fails to make payments on the loan, insurance, and property tax or to perform the primary three obligations – to occupy the property, to repair and maintain it, and to refrain from assigning or encumbering his interest.

Payment default and default on the primary three obligations are handled differently – the latter requires a written Notice of Breach before commencing foreclosure with a Notice of Default. Let's look at these two default categories separately, beginning with default on payments.

Foreclosure for Payment Default

Although all property obligations are in both Investor's and Occupier's names, in actual practice in the typical joint ownership they are fully assumed by the Occupier – with the exception of rental reimbursement by the Investor (see Chapter Eight). Of course, we do have variations on the standard joint ownership. The Investor can share in the payments and obligations. But typically, the Investor is just the "money man." For purposes of illustration, we discuss the typical structure.

The Occupier's primary payment obligation is the mortgage. If the Occupier fails to make loan payments, the Investor is particularly vulnerable – since he is liable on the loan, his credit will be jeopardized and his property interest threatened by lender foreclosure. To protect himself, it is in the Investor's interest to remedy any payment delinquency, especially on the loan. Then he should proceed to foreclose under his Deed of Trust/Mortgage.

When the Occupier is 30 days late on the mortgage, property tax or insurance payment, the Investor is entitled to record a *Notice of Default* under his Deed of Trust/Mortgage. He should also pay any missed payments. Missed loan payments affect the Investor's credit standing and threaten foreclosure by the lender. Skipped property tax payments bring penalties and foreclosure in the long run. Uninsured property can bring ruin in the event of fire or other disaster. By covering missed payments, the Investor protects his own interests.

Foreclosure for Primary Three Obligations Default

In addition to payments, the Occupier has agreed to perform a range of obligations essential to retain the value of the joint ownership property. These obligations, referred to as the *primary three obligations,* are to occupy the property, repair and maintain it, and refrain from encumbering or assigning his property interest. If the Occupier fails to perform any one of these primary three obligations, the Investor may enforce his remedy by foreclosing under his Deed of Trust/Mortgage.

Does the Investor's foreclosure procedure differ when the Occupier defaults in performing his primary three obligations? Yes. Before the Investor can record his Notice of Default, he is required to give written *Notice of Breach* to the Occupier, followed by a 30-day correction period. This notice is different from the official Notice of Default recorded under the Deed of Trust/Mortgage. The Notice of Breach specifies the nature of the breach and the manner in which the Occupier may cure that breach within 30 days. It is only after written Notice of Breach is given and the Occupier has failed to correct the condition within 30 days that the Investor may step forward to file a Notice of Default under his Deed of Trust/Mortgage, commencing the foreclosure process.

The Foreclosure Demand

The Investor's all-inclusive Joint Ownership Note and Deed of Trust/Mortgage name two sets of obligations – those under the joint ownership and those stemming from the mortgage loan. When the Investor forecloses under his joint ownership Deed of Trust/Mortgage and the property is sold, these obligations separate and stand alone. The Investor's demand at sale is then limited to amounts due him under the Joint Ownership Note minus the purchase loan amount. Reviewing the sample transaction in the *Appendix,* the Investor's foreclosure demand would be $12,150 – the note amount less the first loan obligation.

Although it appears inconsistent to include the purchase loan in the note and omit it at sale, this process serves a very important purpose. Under the all-inclusive feature, an Occupier's default on the purchase loan triggers the Investor's right to foreclose on his junior trust deed. Upon default the Investor becomes the Occupier's loan guarantor, and foreclosure entitles him to the Occupier's property rights. The all-inclusive feature of his Joint Ownership Note and Deed of Trust/Mortgage achieves his right to foreclose.

By removing the purchase loan amount from the note at foreclosure sale, the Occupier's distinct obligation to the Investor is defined and separated. The all-inclusive feature of the Investor's Deed of Trust/Mortgage and Joint Ownership Note has served its purpose.

The Steps of Foreclosure

Both the mortgage and deed of trust foreclosure processes begin with recordation of the Notice of Default. This provides public notice that the Occupier is in default — thereby protecting a potential lender approached by the defaulting party from advancing a loan when the Occupier is in default. After this initial notice, foreclosure under a deed of trust and a mortgage differs.

Deed of Trust Foreclosure

The deed of trust foreclosure process is entirely a statutory process whereby property rights – in our scenario, the Occupier's rights – are terminated in quick, concise fashion. Thus, foreclosure under the deed of trust prescribes strict guidelines which must be carefully followed.

These strict guidelines begin with recordation and publication of the Notice of Default for a 90 day period followed by recordation and publication of the Notice of Trustee Sale for 21 days. The Occupier has until five business days before the date of the trustee sale to reinstate his money obligations. The Occupier reinstates by curing the default and paying the Investor's foreclosure costs and all amounts the Investor has advanced for payments due on the property. Only after this notice and reinstatement period has expired can the property be sold. The wise Investor will hire a trust deed service to handle the foreclosure process for him, which takes about four months.

Foreclosure on a Mortgage

While foreclosure on a deed of trust is quick and streamlined, foreclosure on a mortgage takes longer and is more complicated. The deed of trust foreclosure occurs entirely outside of the court system employing the gavel of the trained foreclosure trustee, while the mortgage foreclosure requires the court's review and blessing. Because of required court involvement, mortgage foreclosure usually takes a few months longer and costs more. The result is the same – the non-defaulting co-owner receives full title to the property in this important process. With a trust deed, the sale is conducted by the trustee named in the trust deed. With a mortgage, the sale is conducted by the sheriff.

Investor Makes Payments During Foreclosure

The foreclosing Investor should make all payments due to creditors while the foreclosure is pending. He is reimbursed for these amounts by a reinstating Occupier or by a third party who purchases the Occupier's interest at the sale. It is unlikely, however, that a third party will bid at the sale, since only the Occupier's interest is on the block. A co-ownership interest is not typically marketable. If no third-party bid is received, the Investor registers his credit bid and receives the Occupier's interest – joining both interests in the Investor's name. The Investor then becomes the sole owner of the property with the flexibility and equity that accompany title.

Buyout As Settlement During Foreclosure

Foreclosure, whether on a trust deed or mortgage, is a time-consuming, expensive process fraught with confrontation, anxiety, and bad feeling. Although these conditions create an Investor's opportunity to acquire the property for less than fair market value, buyout deftly avoids the foreclosure process while bailing out an Occupier in financial trouble.

While foreclosure is pending, the co-owners should explore settlement in line with the Joint Ownership

Agreement's general default provisions. The first default provision grants reduced buyout of the Occupier's interest at 75% of value. The second default provision requires sale of the property with all sale expenses borne by the Occupier. At this point, buyout becomes a voluntary settlement to foreclosure – buyout values become a guideline instead of a rule.

By choosing buyout, the defaulting Occupier receives a cash return he would be hard pressed to realize in foreclosure. The Investor exercises an opportunity to buy out his co-owner for less than fair market value, saving the time and expense of foreclosure. Hence the parties can turn a serious default situation into a positive result by selecting buyout.

The Investor should proceed prudently and with legal counsel when he begins settlement discussions with the Occupier either before or after filing his Notice of Default. His all-important foreclosure rights may be *waived* in the process – leaving him with no remedy if the Occupier fails to conclude buyout or cooperate at sale.

If voluntary buyout occurs after a Notice of Default has recorded under the Investor's deed of trust or mortgage, recording a *Rescission of Notice of Default* terminates the foreclosure process. Any pending eviction process is also dismissed. All of these steps are accomplished as part of the buyout process.

Eviction of the Uncooperative Occupier

The co-owners should always strive to work out default reasonably and amicably. What if good faith doesn't exist – and the Occupier won't cooperate? The wise Investor should pursue all remedies under the Joint Ownership Agreement and his Deed of Trust/Mortgage – including unlawful detainer or foreclosure. These remedies are distinct and should not be pursued together.

Two distinct features of the joint ownership documents authorize eviction of the occupying co-owner. The agreement itself provides eviction rights if the occupying party breaches his obligations. The separate lease permits eviction if the Occupier fails to pay his IRC §280A rent to the Investor.

In the Joint Ownership Agreement the Occupier clearly declares that if he defaults, he forfeits ownership status and becomes a tenant. The terms of this automatic tenancy require monthly payment to the Investor equal to all monthly expenses due under the agreement. Thus, the defaulting Occupier loses his ownership status and becomes a tenant – subject to eviction, should that become necessary.

Is a Separate Lease Required?

A separate lease agreement is not required by Internal Revenue Code §280, but to address certain legal consequences we usually prepare a separate lease agreement to document the rental relationship. This lease agreement, illustrated in the *Appendix*, segregates the co-owners' landlord-tenant responsibilities from those of ownership. The lease agreement creates a separate, distinct rental obligation running from Occupier to Investor.

The lease agreement serves another purpose. It clearly defines the Investor's remedies if the Occupier defaults on his rental obligation. While the Joint Ownership Agreement and Deed of Trust/Mortgage give the Investor his foreclosure remedies, the lease agreement provides an eviction remedy. Under the lease agreement the Investor is authorized to commence unlawful detainer process to evict the defaulting Occupier from the property.

Since the Occupier is both an owner and tenant, the court may frown on an unlawful detainer action against him. The eviction rights conferred by the separate lease agreement enhance the Investor's chance to prevail in an unlawful detainer action. Prepare a separate lease agreement to arm the Investor with all available legal remedies – in the unfortunate and unlikely event of an uncooperative defaulting Occupier.

The Eviction Process

When a defaulting Occupier refuses to vacate the joint ownership property, the Investor should serve *eviction* process on that Occupier. Eviction, referred to as *unlawful detainer* in some states, may begin when the defaulting Occupier fails to cure his default within the allotted 30-day period. The Investor foreclosing under his deed of trust or mortgage must carefully observe a certain sequence in exercising his remedies. Depending upon the laws of his state, the evicting Investor may want to refrain from exercise of his eviction rights under the lease until the foreclosure process is complete. Check with counsel before beginning the eviction process. There may be no problem at all or there may be a big problem. As always, caution prevails.

The Occupier Is a Co-Owner and a Tenant

Some may question whether the Occupier's waiver of his ownership rights in the Joint Ownership Agreement and accompanying lease is valid and enforceable. Some may argue that the Investor cannot successfully pursue seemingly contradictory remedies against co-owner and tenant at the same time. They claim that contradiction arises when the Occupier is described as an owner in the buyout escrow and as a tenant in the eviction action. There is no contradiction. In the joint ownership transaction, ownership of part of the property and tenancy *do* co-exist.

A separate lease agreement proves rental of the Investor's property interest under Internal Revenue Code §280A, as well as the Occupier's clear promise to waive his ownership rights on default under the Joint Ownership Agreement. These provisions give the Investor valid legal arguments in support of eviction of a defaulting co-owner.

Specific Terms Ensure Remedies

These are the co-owners' many remedies in the unfortunate event of default and inability to resolve it. If default occurs, remedies in existing written agreements between the co-owners must be available. Again, it is highly unlikely that these parties will ever have to resort to the remedies described above, but in isolated instances, they must be available to protect the innocent party.

The foreclosure, buyout, default sale, and eviction provisions of the Joint Ownership Agreement and the Investor's Deed of Trust/Mortgage must be specific, accurate, and detailed. The agreement and its key accompanying documents must pass court inquiry in the event of legal action, pass scrutiny of the sheriff or trustee performing the foreclosure sale and meet title company requirements for insuring title – whether default-related or not. If the provisions are clear and fair, these agencies will not hesitate to render judgment, foreclose, or ensure title.

We've described the co-owners' remedies in the event of default. The chart on the following page specifies the remedies available to the co-owners at default. The *Appendix* contains samples of the documents which enforce them. These documents endow the joint ownership transaction with legal weight that should make any Investor feel secure. Now, let's see how the all-important joint owner-ship tax deductions give co-owners maximum tax efficiency.

CO-OWNERS' DEFAULT REMEDIES

Event	Remedy	Value
Money Default	Foreclosure	The parties' initial capital contributions multiplied by Occupier's ownership interest
	*Buyout	75% of value, installment payment
	*Sale	Sale price; defaulting party pays closing costs
Primary Three Obligations	Foreclosure	The parties' initial capital contributions multiplied by Occupier's ownership interest
	*Buyout	75% of value, installment payment
	*Sale	Sale price; defaulting party pays closing costs
Bankruptcy, Death, Creditor liening, Conservatorship	Buyout	80% of value, lump sum payment
	Sale	Sale price; defaulting party pays closing costs
Other defaults	Buyout	75% of value, installment payment
	Sale	Sale price; defaulting party pays closing costs

* These foreclosure settlement options could result in waiver of foreclosure rights. Consult counsel when exercising these options.

Chapter Eight

TAX DEDUCTIONS OF JOINT OWNERSHIP

A bonus of real property ownership lies in its tax benefits. How are joint ownership tax deductions allocated to the co-owners, and why? Is the entire interest deduction claimed by the Occupier, or is it split between the co-owners? What is the definition of depreciation under a joint ownership? How is it calculated? This chapter addresses joint ownership's short-term tax deductions. It also resolves the rental issue once and for all. Must the Occupier rent the property from the Investor? IRC §280A is explained and applied in a straightforward way. With an understanding of these joint ownership tax deductions, you can plan your transaction for maximum tax benefit and defend against audit.

$\mathcal{T}$here is only one set of deductions available to a joint ownership property. They may be shared by the Occupier and Investor, but not duplicated. The Joint Ownership Agreement carefully blends co-owners' needs, tax law, and property deductions into a formula that distributes those deductions fairly and lawfully. The results: a legally sound basis for joint ownership tax deductions, and a defense against audit.

Under tax law, co-ownership creates a distinct set of tax deductions for the joint ownership property – interest, property taxes, depreciation – and under Internal Revenue Code §280A, a set of rental/reimbursement conditions. The Joint Ownership Agreement assigns these deductions and obligations among the co-owners.

Deduction Entitlement

A taxpayer may claim a deduction upon two conditions – he must be responsible for the obligation and he must have paid the amount claimed. In the typical joint ownership transaction, *joint liability* is created when both co-owners appear on title and on the loan documents. The condition of joint liability makes interest and property tax deductions available to both Investor and Occupier in proportion to the payments each has made. The Joint Ownership Agreement clearly assigns these deductions to Investor and Occupier, assuring clarity and avoiding duplication.

The Occupier usually makes mortgage and property tax payments except, in some situations, for a small contribution by the Investor as reimbursement of rental income under Internal Revenue Code §280A, discussed in detail below. The parties claim these deductions according to their actual payments. In a 50/50 ownership split, the Investor qualifies to claim depreciation for his 50% investment interest in the joint ownership property. On the other hand, under Internal Revenue Code §280A, the 50% Occupier is entitled to claim *all* interest and property tax deductions. First, the Occupier should comply with the rental requirements of §280A. In the rental reimbursement process, the Occupier gives up 10 to 20% of his deductions, netting the remaining principal residence deductions – an enormous tax benefit.

IRC §280A Rental Requirement

Conformity with Internal Revenue Code §280A has brought uniformity and legitimacy to all joint ownership transactions, especially those between family members. In the past, proving joint ownership between family members was a problem. Taxing agencies labeled many such transactions as *between related persons,* disallowing many tax benefits. Today's first-rate Joint Ownership Agreement solves this problem. Clear co-ownership is established, entitling co-owners – even when related – to their respective ownership deductions. Internal Revenue Code §280A's rules are an integral part of the agreement – and a blessing in disguise.

The Rules

All joint ownerships are governed by Internal Revenue Code §280A, which applies to every dwelling acquired by more than one owner and exclusively occupied by less than all co-owners. The Occupier must pay rent to the Investor for the use of the Investor's portion of the property if the Investor is to claim any tax deductions associated with this property. (See *Appendix* for this code section.)

What Does IRC §280A Do?

Internal Revenue Code §280A, properly integrated into the Joint Ownership Agreement, gives co-owners optimum tax deductions. How does it achieve this result?

The Investor and §280A

Section 280A is vital to the Investor who typically enters the joint ownership either exchanging in or intending to exchange out. His interest in the joint ownership property must be defined as an *investment*. To achieve this definition, the joint ownership property cannot be owner-occupied for more than 14 days or 10% of rental days per year. Since the owner-Occupier is exclusively and fully occupying the property, how does the Investor qualify as an owner of investment property?

Internal Revenue Code §280A comes to the Investor's rescue by removing the personal use designation created by his Occupier. The Investor rents his interest to the Occupier, whereupon it qualifies as investment property under Internal Revenue Code §280A and §1031. Thus, the Investor benefits under Internal Revenue Code §280A. He may now claim depreciation on his property interest and is entitled to tax-defer exchange out of the property at term under Internal Revenue Code §1031.

The Occupier and §280A

Generally, deductions by *partners* in real estate are restricted to their percentage interest – own 30%, take only 30% of the property's deductions. This is called *claiming deductions ratably* and is a conservative interpretation of partnership tax treatment. For this reason, the co-owners are careful to define their relationship as co-ownership instead of partnership.

Because of his co-ownership status, the Occupier is not limited by partnership ratable deduction rules. Thus, the Occupier owning 50% who pays all property expenses can claim all expenses without rental payment to the Investor, as long as the Investor does not claim any tax benefits relative to the joint ownership property. However, since use of joint ownership in the residential arena is new, do confirm this with the taxing authority and/or your accountant.

Meeting the Criteria of §280A

First, the joint ownership property should be held in co-ownership as opposed to partnership. The joint ownership property is held by individuals with *ownership* interests – not as partners owning *equity* interests. The parties to the joint ownership hold title individually as tenants in common, thus satisfying this requirement.

Note: Regulations under Internal Revenue Code §1031 now authorize partnership ownership as long as a §761 exemption from partnership treatment is claimed. Partnership definitions contained in these regulations are expected to apply to §280A. Nevertheless, title in tenancy in common is recommended for the joint ownership.

Second, Internal Revenue Code §280A requires the Investor *claiming tax benefits* for this property to rent his property interest to the Occupier. This rental must equal *fair rent* determined when the parties enter into the joint ownership. Rental reflects only the Investor's interest in the property. If the Investor has an ownership interest of 45%, he will rent his 45% of the property based on 45% of rent value.

These are the two primary requirements of Internal Revenue Code §280A. Before we look at how the Joint Ownership Agreement puts Internal Revenue Code §280A into practice, let's explore what happens if the joint ownership does not comply with §280A.

Penalty for Non-Compliance with §280A

Given the lack of relevant cases, each co-owner must determine the result of failure to comply with §280A. This is one more reason why each party should first consult with an accountant. Without compliance, the Occupier should be able to steer clear of *ratable deduction* limits under the concept of *economic risk* – since he is primarily liable for the property's expenses. Thus, the non-complying Occupier should be able to claim deductions for expenses he pays, even if they exceed his ownership interest. But the non-complying Investor's result is far more serious.

Compliance with §280A is imperative for the joint ownership Investor claiming tax benefits for this property. Without §280A the Investor cannot establish his use of the property as an investment. An Investor who does *not* intend to claim depreciation, deduct payments he makes, or defer tax on his profit has little reason to comply with §280A. But the Investor who wishes to claim interest, property taxes, depreciation or exchange tax-deferred at term must comply with its rental requirements. The bottom line: if the Investor intends to benefit from the Internal Revenue Code, he must comply with it – including §280A.

Thus, if the parties do not comply with §280A, the Investor could lose virtually all his joint ownership tax benefits. Before electing to forego the provisions of §280A, each co-owner is strongly urged to consult with his tax advisor.

How Is the Monthly Rent Established?

The Joint Ownership Agreement establishes a formula for determining Occupier rental under §280A, as well as a system for efficiently returning that rental income to the property. The monthly rent is based on a comparative rental market analysis of other properties in the area. An alternate, simpler formula we use is explained below under *Calculating the Rent.*

Is the Rent Actually Paid?

Together, Investor and Occupier develop a payment schedule that conforms clearly to Internal Revenue Code §280A, and assures that significant tax deductions won't be lost. The Occupier should make actual monthly rental payments to the Investor. The Investor claims the rent as income and returns it to the property by paying expenses that are deductible to him but not deductible by the Occupier. Typical expenses are association dues, insurance, maintenance, and management fees. Usually, these Investor-deductible expenses won't be enough to offset the entire rent amount. If this is the case, the remaining rental income should next be paid by the Investor toward mortgage or property tax payments.

Once these allocations are calculated, the Occupier will know exactly how much of the mortgage and property tax he pays and deducts. In the overall strategy for Internal Revenue Code §280A, it is best to assign the Investor as many Investor-only deductible expenses as possible. By so doing, the Investor takes investment-related deductions – while interest and property tax deductions are preserved for the benefit of the Occupier. In this way, the co-owners collectively claim maximum property deductions.

Calculating the Rent

Internal Revenue Code §280A requires the Investor to charge a fair rental. We calculate that rental as follows:

Fair market value	$135,000
Rent apportionment	x .004
Fair market rent	540
Investor's interest	x .55
Rent – Investor interest	297
Less 20% good tenant discount	x .80
Fair rent to Occupier (rounded down)	240

§280A Rental Calculation

Detail: This sample is taken from the transaction in Chapter Nine. That joint ownership property is worth $135,000. A formula of .004 times purchase price yields fair market rental value of $540 per month. Rent is next adjusted to $297 to reflect only the Investor's 55% interest. The Occupier is then given a *good tenant discount* of 20%, reducing the Occupier's monthly rental to $240.

The 20% Discount

The strict language of §280A states *fair rental.* It does not say fair *market* rental, nor does it specify a discount. Our Occupier has been given a 20% good tenant discount, since his ownership interest and long-term tenancy make him more valuable and more dependable than the typical tenant. This discount is not authorized nor prohibited by the language of the statute, and each transaction must be structured according to the interpretations of each party and their advisors.

The Internal Revenue Service may find such a discount to be reasonable, or they may set it aside as being in violation of the intent of §280A. Joint ownership in the residential market does not have enough history to benefit from issue-specific court and tax rulings. As joint ownership evolves, a good occupier discount is one issue that will be resolved. For now, be aware that this is one area where caution and conservatism should prevail.

Calculating Rental Reimbursement

In our sample this Occupier pays rent of $240 a month to the Investor, who is claiming tax benefits. In turn, the Investor reimburses $240 to property expenses for which the Occupier is responsible. Thus, the rent and reimbursement process merely shifts the co-owners' obligations without increasing actual cash outlay. It also offsets the Investor's rental income with equal deductions. Annualized, the $240 rent equals $2,880. The parties must decide the best way to reimburse this sum to the property.

Expenses deductible by the Investor, and not the Occupier, are first selected for rental reimbursement. These expenses are association dues, insurance, maintenance, and management fees. Since only the interest portion of the loan payment is deductible, fully deductible property taxes are next selected. The final item of rental reimbursement is the mortgage payment.

Let's assume the joint ownership property was purchased January 1. The following chart depicts the rental reimbursement method selected.

Annual rental income	$2,880
Annual condominium dues	- 1,260
Remaining income	1,620
Annual insurance	- 350
Remaining income	1,270
Property taxes	- 1,270
Remaining income	-0-

Rental Income and Reimbursement to Expenses

Detail: The sample property has monthly condominium dues of $105, for a yearly total of $1,260. The Investor will pay the condominium dues – leaving $1,620 remaining to reimburse. Yearly insurance is $350, leaving $1,270 remaining to reimburse. Remaining expenses deductible by the Investor only – management fees and recurring maintenance costs – are not associated with this property. Thus, the $1,270 remaining will be reimbursed to general property expenses – in the sample above, to property taxes. Annual property taxes on this $135,000 property are $1,690 of which $1,270 is allocated to this Investor, exhausting his rental reimbursement and offsetting all his rental income.

The bottom line: the Investor has been able to deduct all rental income received, leaving no taxable income. By first claiming expenses deductible by the Investor only, the parties collectively achieve maximum tax benefits. In this transaction the Occupier has lost an annual tax deduction of $1,270, but as you'll see in Chapter Nine, he is able to claim annual deductions of about $9,000. In the rental reimbursement process, this Occupier has lost only 13% of his principal residence deductions. See *Interest and Property Tax Deductions* later in this chapter.

Thus, the benefits of §280A far outweigh its burdens. The Occupier loses between 10 and 20% of the overall interest and property tax deductions, but both Investor and Occupier preserve their rights to hefty tax benefits.

Interest and Property Tax Deductions

One of the Occupier's primary benefits is his ability to deduct interest and property tax payments. In the standard joint ownership transaction the Occupier pays these expenses, beyond the Investor's nominal rental reimbursement. Thus, he claims deductions for all amounts he pays. In the Chapter Nine sample transaction, the five-year Occupier pays all mortgage and some property taxes on a $135,000 property with a $108,000 loan. That Occupier deducts $8,800 annually and $44,000 over term for mortgage interest and property taxes.

These deductions are the Occupier's tax haven. Of course he'd rather not lose any of these valuable deductions. But if the Investor requires tax shelter from this property, it is the only answer. In the rental reimbursement process, the Occupier loses no more than 20% – and sometimes only 10% – of these principal residence interest and property tax deductions. His ownership status is well worth that price.

The Depreciation Deduction

One of the Investor-favored tax aspects of joint ownership is the depreciation deduction. This tax benefit is only second in the joint ownership transaction to the long-term tax benefits he may obtain from exchanging into and/or out of the property. More on his valuable long-term benefits in Chapter Twelve, *The Investor's Method of Sheltering Gain*. Tax savings from depreciation is one of the important benefits of an investment in real estate, recovering a substantial portion of the Investor's acquisition cost. Since the depreciation deduction is limited to property used in business or investment, the joint ownership Investor qualifies to claim it – as long as he complies with §280A.

Since the property is only partially owned by the Investor, the depreciation deduction must be limited to his ownership interest. Thus, if the Investor has a 45% interest in the property, his depreciation deduction is limited to 45% of overall cost. The depreciation deduction is not available to the typical Occupier since he is using the property as his personal residence.

Calculating Depreciation

In calculating depreciation for the Investor, the property's cost establishes its depreciable basis. Calculation of depreciation in the joint ownership transaction is a three-step process.

The first step calculates the value of improvements, since only improvements are depreciated – depreciation cannot be taken for the land. Improvement value is first segregated from land value. Some choose to use the assessor's values. Otherwise, a ratio is used for apportionment. With the current high cost of construction in California, we use a 75% improvement ratio. Before using 75%, however, you should contact your local Internal Revenue Service representative to determine the ratio in your area. Some locales have substantially lower construction costs, and in those areas the improvement ratio would be lower.

The second step is to apply the Investor's ownership percentage to depreciable improvements. Only that portion of the joint ownership property owned by the Investor can be depreciated by him.

Third, the applicable depreciation schedule is applied. Since the Tax Reform Act of 1986, only straight line depreciation is available. Straight line depreciation is applied at the rate of 27.5 years for residential property and 31.5 years for commercial property. Since joint ownership property is typically residential, the applicable depreciation term is 27.5 years.

Let's go through those three steps following the sample transaction in Chapter Nine. First we'll look at the transaction treating the Investor as an "outside Investor" *beginning* a new investment with the joint ownership purchase. The second example will feature the seller-turned-Investor who *continues* his investment.

Outside Investor's Depreciation Deduction

The outside Investor uses the joint ownership purchase price as his depreciable basis, as shown in the chart below.

Depreciable basis		$135,000
Improvements allocation	x	.75
Value of improvements		101,250
Investor interest	x	.55
Investor interest in improvements		55,687
Years for residential depreciation	÷	27.5
Investor annual depreciation		2,025
Five-year term	x	5
Investor depreciation over term		$ 10,125

Outside Investor's Depreciation Deduction

Detail: The outside Investor is able to use the property's present cost of $135,000 as his depreciable basis. Using the 75% improvement ratio, the improvements are valued at $101,250. This Investor owns a 55% interest, reducing his depreciable basis to $55,687. Depreciated over the applicable 27.5 year period, this Investor claims a yearly depreciation deduction of $2,025. By the fifth year this Investor has a cumulative deduction of $10,125.

Seller-Investor's Depreciation Deduction

Let's now take a look at the Seller-Investor's depreciation deduction. The seller-turned-Investor usually captures a much lower depreciation deduction than the outside Investor because *his cost* is used in calculating depreciation. The Seller-Investor's cost of the property is traced back to what he paid when he originally bought it – usually far less than the joint ownership purchase price.

This Seller-Investor, from the sample in Chapter Nine, bought the joint ownership property ten years ago for $75,000. He is cashing out of 80% of the property and entering the joint ownership with 20% of retained equity. Thus, his depreciable basis is 20% of $75,000, or $15,000.

Depreciable basis	$15,000
Improvements allocation	x .75
Value of improvements	11,280
Years for residential depreciation	÷ 27.5
Investor annual depreciation	409
Five-year term	x 5
Investor depreciation over term	$ 2,045

Seller-Investor's Depreciation Deduction

Detail: 20% of the property's cost reflects the Seller-Investor's depreciable basis – $15,000. The 75% improvements allocation is applied to his depreciable cost, valuing improvements at $11,280. (Investor's interest is already allocated in the $15,000; thus step two is unnecessary.) The final step applies the 27.5 year depreciation schedule. If this seller had held this property for investment purposes before the joint ownership, he would have taken this deduction in prior years.

Depreciation Varies with Investor Status

The two charts show the Seller-Investor's depreciation deduction can be significantly less than the outside Investor's. The vast difference lies in continuation of depreciable basis for the Seller-Investor and beginning of depreciable basis for the outside Investor. The Seller-Investor is continuing his ownership, unable to step up his basis to current market value.

Depreciation for the Seller-Investor varies with his cost basis, depending upon the original property price. Here, the Seller-Investor who bought the property ten years ago claims a depreciation deduction about $1,750 less per year and $7,000 less over a five-year term. This depreciation deduction is often substantially less when a seller becomes the Investor.

Deduction Limitations

The depreciation deduction is limited. First, it cannot exceed the amount of income produced by the investment property. Here, rental income on this $135,000 property with a 55/45 ownership split is $240 a month and $2,880 a year. The annual depreciation deduction for the outside Investor is $2,025 and $409 for the Seller-Investor. The depreciation deduction does not exceed the amount of rental income either Investor claims for that year, entitling each Investor to deduct full depreciation on his portion of the property.

In the typical joint ownership transaction, rental income completely offsets the depreciation deduction, and passive loss rules will usually not apply. But, if rental income does not fully offset the depreciation deduction, passive loss rules come into play. The Investor qualifies to claim up to $25,000 of loss per year, including depreciation, when he *actively participates* in managing the joint ownership property. The Investor actively participates by making major ownership decisions regarding leasing, assignment, and improvements and is the major decision-maker for long-term management of the joint ownership property.

With active management participation in the property, he may deduct depreciation up to $25,000 a year – beyond rental income – with certain limitations. If the Investor's adjusted gross income exceeds $100,000 the $25,000 is reduced by $1 for each $2 of income above $100,000. If gross income exceeds $150,000, he loses all passive loss advantages. However, a heavy income investor can carry excess depreciation forward as a loss and offset it against gain on sale.

Now that we have reviewed some of the short-term tax aspects of the joint ownership, we'll look at two sample joint ownership transactions in Chapters Nine and Ten. Chapter Nine's Investor is the seller. In Chapter Ten, he's a third party. IRC §280A rent is calculated and reimbursed to the property. You will see how the co-owners claim deductions and depreciation and compare their bottom lines.

Chapter Nine

SELLER AS INVESTOR
SAMPLE TRANSACTION

Joint ownership comes to life in this and the next chapter. Actual transactions are demonstrated from start-up to term. In this chapter the sellers become the Investors. In Chapter Ten, a very different scenario takes place – the seller is uninvolved in the joint ownership and the Investors are *third parties*. Here, we begin with purchase, calculate the ownership splits, rental amount and reimbursement, and assign tax deductions. The joint ownership proceeds to term, when the co-owners choose their terminating options – buyout by Occupiers, buyout by Investors, or sale. Each option is calculated and illustrated. The transaction concludes with tax deferral by both parties – and the joint ownership's bottom line.

$\mathcal{T}$his chapter and the next present sample joint ownership transactions. These samples allow you to preview two transactions from beginning to end. You'll see the results based on the beginning choices these parties made. These chapters will help you understand how the joint ownership concept works in real life – to help you plan your own joint ownership.

This transaction, where the sellers become the Investors, differs greatly from the one illustrated in Chapter Ten, in which the Investors are third parties. The primary differences can easily be detected by comparing the *Summary of Basic Terms* in each chapter.

Summary of Basic Terms

The Investors in this sample transaction are the sellers of the property; term is five years. The annual assumed appreciation rate is 4%. Projected annual return required by the Investors is 12% at buyout. Sellers have deferred the 20% down payment, which has been credited as Investor-retained equity.

At purchase, non-reimbursable closing costs were paid by the Occupiers. Using the guidelines from Chapter Six, the ownership splits were set at 45% to Occupiers and 55% to Investors. Investors are paying association dues, insurance, and some property taxes as reimbursement of rental income. Occupiers make the remaining payments.

Scenario

In this transaction the sellers participate in the joint ownership as Investors. The property is worth $135,000.

Occupiers confirmed sellers' valuation from the lender's appraisal. The wise Occupiers made their joint ownership offer contingent upon the bank's appraisal coming in at or above the sellers' valuation. The Seller-Investors retained 20% of value in the property, which is described as $27,000 seller-retained equity. Internal Revenue Code §280A rent is calculated at $240 per month.

Fortunately, these sellers funded the real estate agent's commission from sale proceeds. Their loan pay-off was substantially less than the new loan, leaving them with about $45,000 to cover the sale commission and a down payment on a new home. Purchase closing costs were paid by Occupiers.

Although some Seller-Investors receive surplus cash from sale, sometimes sellers' cash out is insufficient to pay the selling agent's commission. In that case, the Occupiers advance the agent's commission to begin the joint ownership transaction. The Occupiers receive credit for the advanced commission in the same way as the seller receives credit for his retained equity. The chart below depicts the basic terms of this joint ownership. See the end of this chapter for a comprehensive chart containing these figures and calculations.

Purchase price	$135,000
Seller-retained equity	27,000
80% loan at 8% fixed	108,000
Term	5 Years
Ownership split	Occupiers 45% / Investors 55%
§280A rental	$240/mo. / $2,880/yr.
Projected annual appreciation rate	4%
Projected annual return to Investor	12%

Joint Ownership Terms – Seller As Investor

The Basic Terms

The appraisal prepared in the lending process satisfied Occupiers that the property was worth its $135,000 selling price. The 80% loan is $108,000; term is five years. The parties agreed to an ownership split of 55% to Investors and 45% to Occupiers. How did the parties achieve their ownership split?

Ownership Split

Appreciation Rate

Investors and Occupiers agreed upon an assumed annual appreciation of 4% per year over the five-year term of their joint ownership. Since the seller bought this property ten years ago, the parties compared the original purchase price with current value to compute *actual* appreciation. In five years the property appreciated 8%, but now the market had slowed down considerably. The Investors selected an assumed appreciation rate of 2% to include a risk factor; Occupiers selected 5%. The parties agreed upon 4% as a reasonable midway point.

Projected Investor Rate of Return

The Investors wanted to achieve a 14% annual projected return on their $27,000 retained equity. Occupiers and their accountant thought that was too high. The Occupiers were willing to agree to a projected Investor return on buyout of 8% maximum. At this point they were too far apart for agreement.

Occupiers then reviewed the market again, looking at several other properties. Investors reviewed comparable returns they would make on a $27,000 investment in the open market. Occupiers confirmed their strong desire to purchase the sellers' property. The property suited their needs and would make the ideal first home for their family. Moreover, their joint ownership offers on other properties were not accepted.

In re-evaluating their position, Seller-Investors confirmed their decision to enter into joint ownership for several key reasons. They felt it would be a better investment than those available in the general marketplace – particularly attractive due to tax-deferred exchange benefits under Internal Revenue Code §1031. The property had been on the market for eleven months without selling and if they lost this transaction, it might be on the market for another year. They were rolling over into a less expensive principal residence, creating a tax burden. Through this joint ownership they could reduce their principal residence tax basis by 20%, more closely matching the value of the new property and eliminating any tax in the rollover process. For the Seller-Investors, this transaction ideally suited their tax needs. Given these motivating factors, Occupiers and Investors were willing to adjust their positions. The parties agreed to a projected Investor annual rate of return of 12% on buyout and 8% on sale.

Calculation

Based on the selected 4% assumed appreciation, it took an ownership split of 55% to the Investors to achieve a projected 12% annual return at buyout on the $27,000 down payment they waived.

Each transaction consists of a unique property and two individuals with unique characteristics and requirements. The ingredients necessary to create the ownership split differ for every transaction. The final decision is reached by combining the parties' needs, motivations, assumptions, research, and negotiation. Other needs and assumptions alter the parties' result. (See Chapter Ten for contrast.)

Title

Occupiers and Investors are married couples. The Occupiers want their spouse to immediately inherit their interest if one of them dies. Thus they take title in joint tenancy. The Investors are more interested in maximum tax benefit, taking title as community property. Collectively, they hold title as tenants in common: "a 45% undivided interest to Orville Occupier and Margie Occupier, husband and wife, as joint tenants, and a 55% undivided interest to Harold Investor and Ingrid Investor, husband and wife, as community property, all as tenants in common."

The Loan

Occupiers and Sellers-Investors obtained an 80% loan together. They all signed on the loan. When sellers remain on title, they should explore refinance with their existing lender, who may offer special packages to refinance an existing loan. This lender did, resulting in reduced loan origination fees to the Occupiers. Often refinance is limited to 75% of value, but this lender agreed to 80%.

Customarily the Occupier is subject to strict lender scrutiny. When an existing loan is refinanced, the lender relies more heavily on the seller's loan history. The seller must then scrutinize the Occupier's credit profile and financial history, satisfying himself that his co-owner will conscientiously meet the property ownership expenses for the term of the joint ownership. Otherwise, the Investor will be obligated to take back the property and return to square one, listing it for sale.

Investor Approval of Occupier

When the seller receives the buyer's joint ownership offer, he conditions acceptance upon approval of the Occupier's financial profile, specifying a 15- to 20-day approval period. Our potential Investors established the following criteria to approve their Occupiers – a clear credit report and solid job and rental history for the past five years, prior housing expenses approximating 65% of joint ownership expenses including insurance, mortgage and property taxes, and gross income about three times the joint ownership expenses. These Occupiers then satisfied the Investors' criteria.

These criteria are particularly strict. Investors may choose to be more flexible when considering all circumstances. For example, the Occupiers may have recently relocated from an area with a different economy, or a spouse may be returning to the work place. The Occupier may be a college graduate entering his first full-time job.

Rent

Internal Revenue Code §280A rent was calculated with the following formula: ".004 times purchase price times Investor equity interest less a 20% *good tenant discount.*" Based upon this formula rent was computed at $240 per month.

Fair market value	$135,000
Rent apportionment	x .004
Fair market rent	540
Investors' interest	x .55
Rent - Investor interest	297
Less 20% good tenant discount	x .80
Fair rent to Occupiers (rounded)	$240

§280A Rental Calculation

To assure the seller his valuable long-term capital gain tax benefits, rent under IRC §280A must be charged to the Occupiers. Occupiers paid rent to the Investors at $240 a month, totalling $2,880 a year. Occupiers made all payments on the property during term, except for the Investors' property payments of $2,880 yearly, reimbursing rent.

Payments and Rent Reimbursement

Investors have $2,880 in rental income to return to the property each year in the form of deductible expenses. In this way rental income is fully returned to the Occupiers. Fully deductible expenses are selected so Investors' deductions equal rental income. Rental reimbursement is determined by reviewing expenses *deductible* by Investors and *non-deductible* by Occupiers. These parties agreed upon the following payment and rental reimbursement allocations.

	Yearly	Term
Rental Income:	$2,880	$14,400
Deductions:		
Association Dues	1,260	6,300
Insurance	350	1,750
Property Taxes	1,270	6,350
	$2,880	$14,400

Rent Received and Reimbursed As Expenses

Detail: The Investors have $2,880 to reimburse to the property annually. This property carried homeowner association dues of $105 a month, at $1,260 a year. Association dues were assigned to the Investor since they are deductible as an investment property expense and non-deductible by the Occupiers. Insurance at $350 per year, also deductible by Investors and non-deductible by Occupiers, was assigned to Investors. After these expenses Investors still tally $1,270 per year of the $2,880 rental income remaining to reimburse to property expenses. However, the Investors have exhausted expenses deductible to them and non-deductible to the Occupiers.

Fully deductible property taxes are selected as the next expense assigned to the Investors. Property taxes in the sample are $1,480 a year. Investors will pay the remaining rental reimbursement due of $1,270 per year towards property taxes. The result – Investor rental income of $2,880, offset by exactly $2,880 in property-related expenses.

Investors completely offset rental income with investment property deductions, about half of which were deductions that could not be claimed by the principal residence Occupiers. The ideal rental reimbursement process preserves as many Occupier deductions as possible. In this sample Occupiers lost only about 13% of the principal residence deductions in the rental reimbursement process.

The lender required advance payment of insurance and a property tax impound. Since Investors became responsible for these payments as rental reimbursement, they made this escrow deposit. This payment represents advance rental reimbursement, subject to receipt of monthly rent from the Occupiers.

Tax Deduction Allocations

The Joint Ownership Agreement assigns all property deductions to the parties. Each claims deductions associated with actual payments made. Here, Occupiers made all loan payments and a portion of property taxes, claiming those deductions. Investors paid and claimed association dues and insurance, as well as a major portion of the property taxes. Investors declared their intent to hold their portion of the property as an investment, to be exchanged pursuant to Internal Revenue Code §1031 and depreciated until term. Occupiers declared their tax-deferral intention under Internal Revenue Code §1034.

Occupier Tax Deductions

The joint ownership continues uneventfully for its five-year term. As shown by the figures in the following chart, Occupiers claimed deductions totaling $44,050 for $43,000 of mortgage interest and $1,050 of property taxes. In addition, Occupiers can elect to shelter their profit by rolling over into a new home.

	Yearly	Term
Interest	$8,600	$43,000
Property taxes	210	1,050
TOTAL	$8,810	$44,050

Occupiers lose approximately 13% of deductions in rent reimbursement.

Occupiers' Tax Deductions - Five-Year Term

Investor Tax Deductions

Over their five-year ownership Investors report rental income of $14,400, fully offset by equal deductions. Additionally, they claim $2,045 in depreciation.

	Yearly	Term
Investor depreciation	$409	$2,045

Investor's Depreciation - Five-Year Term

As featured in Chapter Eight, the Seller-Investor's depreciation deduction is far less than that claimed by the outside Investor. Our Seller-Investors continue their 20% ownership – using 20% of their *original* cost as their depreciable basis. Ten years ago they bought the property for $75,000. Without adjustment, their depreciable basis in the joint ownership property is $15,000.

75% of basis is allocated to improvements, leaving a depreciable basis of $11,250. Divided by the applicable 27.5 year schedule, his depreciation is $409 per year.

Depreciable basis	$15,000
Improvements allocation	x ____.75
Improvements cost	11,250
Years for residential depreciation	÷ ___27.5
Investor annual depreciation	$ 409

Calculating Investor's Depreciation

Investors will be entitled to claim the full amount of depreciation on their interest since rental income is greater than depreciation. Depreciation for the sample Investor is minimal. However, the joint ownership Investor's depreciation deduction pales before his profit potential and his right to exchange out of the property, deferring taxes on that profit.

The Options at Term

The following buyout and sale calculations are based on projections made by the co-owners at commencement of the joint ownership. Potential joint ownership participants envision their future positions in terms of these projections. In this sample, each option and its tax consequence are analyzed.

Buyout of Investor

The buyout process begins with the Occupiers, who are first able to exercise their option to buy out the Investor. Buyout value is determined by appraisal, unless the parties agree on value. In the sample depicted in the following chart, a 4% annual assumed appreciation rate establishes value. Since these parties are *projecting* what they will net at term, they base their calculations on these initial projections instead of actual value.

Appraisal - 4% annual appreciation	$164,000
Loan pay-off	103,000
Equity	61,000
Return of investment to Investor	- 27,000
Loan principal reduction to Occupier	- 5,000
Net equity	29,000
Investor interest	x .55
Investor share of equity (rounded)	16,000
Return of Investor down payment	27,000
Buyout of Investors	$43,000

Buyout of Investor at Five-Year Term

Detail: Based on the assumed appreciation rate this property is valued at $164,000 at five years. In determining buyout, the loan is first paid off. Most loan payments were credited to interest, leaving a principal balance of $103,000 after five years. Deducting the $103,000 loan pay off leaves gross equity of $61,000. Next Investors receive their $27,000 in retained equity and the Occupiers are credited with $5,000 principal reduction to the loan, leaving $29,000 net equity for the co-owners to split. At this point Investors cash in their 55% equity interest for $16,000. In total, Investors receive their

$27,000 original retained equity plus $16,000 as an appreciation re-turn, for a total of $43,000. At term, based upon their projections, it will take $43,000 for the Occupiers to buy out the Investors.

Occupier Refinance

Occupiers will usually refinance the property to buy out the Investor. The following chart depicts refinance by the Occupiers to buy out their co-owner.

Appraised value - 4% appreciation	$164,000
80% refinance	x _____.80
Loan proceeds [$33,000 equity] (rounded)	131,000
Loan pay-off	- 103,000
Net proceeds	28,000
Investor buyout	- 43,000
Deficit to Occupiers	- $ 15,000

Occupiers Buy Out Investors by Refinance at Five-Year Term

Detail: The property will be appraised in the refinance process. For purposes of this sample the 4% assumed appreciation rate establish-es value at $164,000. 80% of value is refinanced for a new loan of $131,000. From loan proceeds the $103,000 first loan is paid off, leaving net loan proceeds of $28,000. It will take $15,000 more to buy out the Investors for $43,000. Investors may be willing to take a note for the remaining $15,000; otherwise, Occupiers will cash out Investors through other sources. Here, the Occupiers have saved $2,000 per year for a total of $10,000 they will add to the pot. The Occupiers' parents, impressed that their children have been able to save $10,000 over the past five years, have agreed to loan the Occupiers the remaining $5,000 they need to cash out the Investors.

With the refinance and Occupiers' payment combination the Occupiers boost themselves to a position of sole ownership – with $33,000 of equity in the property. Although they now face a higher monthly loan payment, through earlier projections they are prepared to make these payments. Many lenders limit a refinance to 75% of value. This Occupiers' refinance at 80% is an exception.

Tax Consequence of Investor Buyout

When the Occupiers buy out the Investors, Occupiers incur no tax liability. The Investors are being cashed out of the property and experience a taxable event. The cashed out Investors should consider deferring their tax obligation by exchanging under Internal Revenue Code §1031.

These Investors will exchange their interest for another property with an equal or greater value. The exchanging Investor will set the necessary exchange mechanisms in motion that reserve and convert their funds upon buyout or sale.

By exchanging into another property our sample Investors will defer taxes on their $16,000 buyout profit. At a 35% combined federal and state capital gains tax rate, the exchanging Investors defer $5,600 in taxes. Chapters Eleven and Twelve present more detailed gain analysis of the co-owners' positions.

Buyout of Occupier

If Occupiers do not exercise buyout, the option passes to Investors. The chart on the next page shows the buyout of Occupiers.

Appraisal - 4% annual appreciation	$164,000
Loan pay-off	- 103,000
Equity	61,000
Less Investor equity	- 27,000
Loan principal reduction to Occupier	- 5,000
Net equity	29,000
Occupiers' interest	x .45
Net Proceeds	13,000
Plus loan principal reduction	5,000
Occupier buyout	$ 18,000

Investors Buy Out Occupiers at Five-Year Term

Detail: Based on a $164,000 value, gross equity of $61,000 remains after the loan is paid off. Investors' original $27,000 retained equity is next deducted, as is Occupier's $5,000 loan principal reduction, leaving net equity of $29,000. Occupiers step forward to cash in their 45% equity chip – for a $13,000 share in appreciation. The loan principal reduction is added to the occupier pot for a buyout of $18,000. At term, Investors cash out their Occupiers for $18,000.

Investor Refinance

The Investor will usually refinance the property to cash out his co-owner. The following chart illustrates Investor refinance upon buying out the Occupiers.

Appraised value- 4% appreciation	$164,000
75% refinance	x .75
Loan proceeds [$41,000 equity]	123,000
Loan pay-off	- 103,000
Net proceeds	20,000
Occupiers' buyout	- 18,000
Residual to Investor	$ 2,000

Investor Buys Out Occupiers by Refinance at Five-Year Term

Detail: Buyout of Occupiers is $18,000. A 75% refinance produces loan proceeds of $123,000. Loan pay off leaves Investors with $20,000. After cashing out the Occupiers, Investors are left with $2,000. Thus, a 75% refinance buys out Occupiers and leaves a little extra cash for Investors – along with equity of $41,000.

Tax Consequence of Occupier Buyout

On Occupier buyout, the Investor incurs no tax liability. The bought-out Occupiers may then roll into another principal residence to defer their tax obligation – the tax on profit of $13,000 – which does not include his $5,000 loan principal reduction return. At a 35% federal and state combined tax rate, the Occupiers can defer $4,550 in taxes in a roll over (see Chapter Eleven).

Sale at Term

If buyout does not occur, the property is sold. The following chart calculates sale proceeds and their distribution.

Sale price - 4% annual appreciation	$164,000
Loan	- 103,000
Seller closing costs (6%)	- 10,000
Gross proceeds	51,000
Investor return of retained equity	- 27,000
Loan principal reduction to Occupier	- 5,000
Net equity	19,000
Investor ownership split	x .55
Investor share of net equity (rounded)	10,000
Investor return of investment	+ 27,000
Investor proceeds on sale	37,000
Gross proceeds (from above)	51,000
Less Investor proceeds	- 37,000
Occupiers' proceeds on sale	$ 14,000

Sale of Joint Ownership Property - Five-Year Term

Detail: Selling price (based on projected appreciation) is $164,000. Loan pay off is $103,000, leaving gross equity of $61,000. The 6% sales commission comes off the top, reducing gross equity by $10,000, leaving $51,000. Investors' $27,000 retained equity is deducted along with the occupier's $5,000 loan principal deduction, leaving $19,000 as net equity. Net equity is shared by the parties per their ownership splits. Occupiers receive $14,000 as their share of sale proceeds. ($9,000 of appreciation and $5,000 of loan principal reduction reimbursement.) Investors receive $10,000 of appreciation – in addition to the $27,000 return of equity – for sale proceeds of $37,000.

Tax Consequence of Sale

How do these co-owners treat their profit at sale? Both Occupiers and Investors experience a taxable event since they are each cashed out of the property. Will they each have to pay taxes now on their profit? No. Each party's profile must be separately considered since Occupiers and Investors defer taxes by different means.

Occupiers will defer taxes by rolling into another principal residence pursuant to Internal Revenue Code §1034. By replacing their principal residence with another of equal or greater value Occupiers defer all tax. At a 35% federal and state combined capital gains tax rate, these Occupiers defer thousands in taxes by rolling over. (See Chapter Eleven.) In the sale process they cash out with $14,000 – probably enough to buy another home with a 10% down payment. If they have to put down the full 20% down, they can pull in another Investor team member, but this time for only half of the down payment. They've got a very impressive record from this transaction. So Investors and traditional lenders will be far easier to impress this time around.

Investors will defer their taxes by exchanging into another property pursuant to Internal Revenue Code §1031. By replacing their joint ownership investment with another investment of equal or greater value, Investors defer all taxes. At a 35% combined federal and state tax rate, these Investors with a $10,000 sale profit defer $3,500 in taxes in an exchange. (See Chapter Twelve.)

The Bottom Line Results

The joint ownership is truly a win-win venture for both co-owners. Occupiers have claimed $44,050 in tax deductions. On buyout they earn $18,000, $13,000 of which is profit. On sale they earn $14,000, $9,000 of which is profit. The Occupiers, armed with sufficient funds for a down payment or an impressive track record to get a loan closer to value or to pull in a "junior" investor, can defer taxes on their profit by rolling into another principal residence pursuant to Internal Revenue Code §1034. By rolling over, these Occupiers defer several thousands in taxes based on a 35% combined capital gains rate. Chapter Eleven begins where this chapter leaves off – calculating these Occupiers' gain and rolling it over.

Investors' benefits parallel their co-owners' benefits. Investors have claimed nominal depreciation, but their profit is great. On buyout they receive $43,000, $16,000 of which is profit. On sale they receive $37,000, $10,000 of which is profit. Investors can defer taxes on their profit by exchanging into another property under Internal Revenue Code §1031. As calculated in Chapter Twelve, Investors also defer several thousands in taxes, based on a 35% combined state and federal capital gains rate. (Tax applications performed in this chapter have been general. Chapters Eleven and Twelve present more specific applications of tax criteria for Investors and Occupiers. For example, the Seller-turned-Investor determines his basis from his purchase price long ago – when he first purchased this property. Chapter Twelve calculates this Investor's adjusted basis and computes *actual gain,* which turns out to be much higher than generally projected in this chapter.)

The Joint Ownership Agreement on which the foregoing sample transaction was based may be found in the *Appendix.* It shows how the co-owners' intentions were incorporated into their formal contract. Turn to the charts at the end of this chapter for full charts of this transaction.

Next, in Chapter Ten, another sample transaction is reviewed – where the seller is uninvolved in the joint ownership purchase of his property. Instead, the Investors are third parties. The Investors and Occupiers in Chapter Ten select options very different from those in this chapter. Chapter Ten's *Summary of Basic Terms* describes the joint ownership structure selected by those parties. The results, summarized at the end of Chapter Ten under *Bottom Line Results,* differ too.   At the end of Chapter Ten the two sample transactions are compared. We recommend reading Chapter Ten in its entirety – but if you are prone to skimming, review the summaries and comparison we've referenced here for the full bottom line impact.

Chapter Nine Sample - Seller As Investor

Initial Purchase

Purchase price	$135,000
Seller-retained equity	$27,000
80% loan at 8% fixed	$108,000
Term	5 Years
Ownership split	Occupiers 45% / Investors 55%
§280A rental	$240/mo. / $2,880/yr.
Projected annual appreciation rate	4%
Projected annual return to Investors	12%

Payments/Rent Reimbursement

Occupiers	Yearly	Term
Mortgage interest	$ 8,600	$43,000
Property taxes	210	1,050
Total	$ 8,810	$44,050

Occupiers lose approximately 13% of deductions in rent reimbursement.

Investors	Yearly	Term
Rental income:	$ 2,880	$14,400
Deductions:		
Association dues	1,260	6,300
Insurance	350	1,750
Property taxes	1,270	6,350
TOTAL	$ 2,880	$14,400
Depreciation deduction	$ 409	$ 2,045

Five-Year Buyout of Investors

Appraisal - 4% annual appreciation	$164,000
Loan pay-off	-103,000
Equity	61,000
Return of investment to Investor	-27,000
Loan principal reduction to Occupier	- 5,000
Net equity	29,000
Investor interest	x .55
Investor share of equity	16,000
Return of Investor down payment	27,000
Buyout of Investors	**$ 43,000**

Five-Year Buyout of Occupiers

Appraisal - 4% annual appreciation	$164,000
Loan pay-off	- 103,000
Equity	61,000
Return of investment to Investor	- 27,000
Loan principal reduction to Occupier	- 5,000
Net equity	29,000
Occupiers' interest	x .45
Occupier share of equity (rounded)	13,000
Loan principal reduction to Occupier	5,000
Buyout of Occupiers	**$ 18,000**

Five-Year Refinance by Occupiers

Appraised value - 4% appreciation	$164,000
80% refinance	x .80
Loan proceeds [$33,000 equity] (rounded)	131,000
Loan pay-off	- 103,000
Net proceeds	28,000
Investor buyout	- 43,000
Deficit to Occupiers	- $ 15,000

Five-Year Refinance by Investor

Appraised value - 4% appreciation	$164,000
75% refinance	x .75
Loan proceeds [$41,000 equity]	123,000
Loan pay-off	- 103,000
Net proceeds	20,000
Occupiers' buyout	- 18,000
Residual to Investor	$ 2,000

Five-Year Sale

Sale price - 4% annual appreciation	$164,000
Loan	- 103,000
Seller-paid closing costs (6%)	- 10,000
Gross proceeds	51,000
Investor return of retained equity	- 27,000
Loan principal reduction to Occupier	- 5,000
Net equity	19,000
Investor ownership interest	x .55
Investor share of net equity (rounded)	10,000
Investor return of investment	+ 27,000
Investor proceeds on sale	37,000
Gross proceeds (from above)	51,000
Less Investor proceeds	- 37,000
Occupier proceeds on sale	$ 14,000

Chapter Ten

THIRD-PARTY INVESTOR
SAMPLE TRANSACTION

How is this chapter different from Chapter Nine? Chapter Nine's Investor was the seller of the joint ownership property. Here, Investor and Occupier purchase *someone else's property*. Thus, they must fully research the property's appreciation rate and provide a cash down payment. Like Chapter Nine, this chapter guides you through each phase of an authentic joint ownership transaction – but the assumptions and projections made by these parties are very different, and so are their results. Let's take a look at the unique strategy these co-owners devised when they bought their joint ownership property from someone else.

$\mathcal{T}$he Investor in this joint ownership is a third party – someone otherwise uninvolved with the transaction.

Summary of Basic Terms

The term is seven years. The loan is fixed rate at 7.5%. Occupier and Investor researched the property and arrived at an assumed annual appreciation rate of 4.5%. Investor's projected return on buyout is 11%; on sale is 8.5%. A cash down payment was required. Both Occupier and Investor contributed to the down payment – $36,000 by Investor, $12,000 by Occupier. Investor also paid title insurance and escrow fees, deductible by him as investment expenses. Remaining non-reimbursable closing costs at purchase were fully paid by Occupier. Ownership splits are 67% to Occupier and 33% to Investor. Investor makes insurance and partial property tax payments as reimbursement of rental income. Occupier makes the remaining payments.

Scenario

Here, the Occupier offered the seller a joint ownership deal. He refused, desiring to cash out entirely to roll into a more expensive property. The Occupier then brought in an outside Investor – his employer, for whom he had recently relocated to the area. Often, relocation is a condition of employment in technologically advanced areas like computer mecca Silicon Valley, near San Jose, California. We find an increasing number of employers willing to assist newly relocated employees in joint ownership transactions. (See Chapter Thirteen.) The employer wants to make a profitable investment and to assist his employee. Our Occupier had 25% of the down payment, and his Investor-employer provided the rest. The purchase price is $240,000. IRC rent is $250 per month.

This transaction is quite different from the one depicted in Chapter Nine. Here the Investor is a third party, and both parties contribute to the down payment. These parties have made projections and assumptions that differ greatly from those in Chapter Nine. For example, the ownership split is 33/67 here, while the split in Chapter Nine was 55/45. The results will also be different. At the end of this chapter the joint ownership structure and results of Chapters Nine and Ten are compared.

Let's take a closer look at this joint ownership to see how it achieved its profile. The chart below depicts the basic terms of this transaction. Its terms and values are illustrated at the end of this chapter. A comprehensive quick reference chart, including all terms and calculations in this chapter, appears at the end.

Purchase price	$240,000
Down payment - Investor paid	$ 36,000
Down payment - Occupier paid	$ 12,000
80% loan	$192,000
Term	7 Years
Ownership split	Occupier 67% / Investor 33%
§280A rental	$250/mo. / $3,000/yr.
Projected annual appreciation rate	4.5%
Projected annual return to Investor	11%

Joint Ownership Terms - Third-Party Investor

The Basic Terms

The purchase price of this property is $240,000. The 80% loan is in the amount of $192,000 at 7.5% fixed interest. A seven-year term has been chosen instead of five years, because Occupier and Investor believed the longer they held this investment the more money they would make. Since the Occupier had just relocated to the area he did not expect to move within the next seven years. The parties agreed upon an ownership split of 33% to Investor and 67% to Occupier. How did they achieve their ownership split?

Ownership Split

Appreciation Rate

Investor and Occupier agreed upon an assumed annual appreciation rate of 4.5% over the seven-year term of their joint ownership. This assumption was based on a seven-year history of comparable properties in the vicinity. An appraiser was hired to compile this data and prepare these statistics. Although comparable properties averaged 5.9% appreciation during that period, Occupier and Investor agreed it was better to *underestimate*. Thus, they chose 4.5% as a conservative estimate of the property's annual appreciation rate for the next seven years. The Occupier had relocated from an area in the Midwest where properties appreciate about 2% a year. Projecting 4.5% appreciation was a real adjustment for him – but so was paying $240,000 for a house.

Note: Be realistic and conservative with your assumed appreciation rate. Select an assumed appreciation rate that conforms to your particular property and location. That might lead you to select a rate as low as 3 - 4% in some areas or as high as 8 - 10% in others. But do be conservative in your projection.

Projected Investor Rate of Return

The parties selected 11% as their annual rate of projected Investor return at buyout. The Investor was in this transaction primarily to allow his valued new employee to relocate, and thus desired to project an average return. The Investor employer felt that an 8.5% projected return at sale was fair – if the employee did not buy out and sale occurred. The main concern of the parties was that the transaction be mutually fair.

Calculation

Based on the selected assumed appreciation rate, it took an ownership split of 33% to the Investor to yield his 8.5% annual return at sale – an 11% return at buyout – on his $36,000 down payment contribution. Rate of return is not projected for the Occupier, who contributes little to the down payment. One of the Occupier's greatest joint ownership returns is in the form of mortgage interest and property tax deductions. Thus, the Occupier's return analysis would necessarily encompass payments he makes and tax deductions he receives, in addition to the initial cash he contributes. (Scanning forward to this Occupier's bottom line return of $74,290 on buyout, his return will be substantial when compared with his $12,000 initial contribution.)

Title

Investor and Occupier were both married persons. Neither couple desired the joint tenancy right of survivorship to pass between spouses. These couples, living in a community property state, decided to hold title in community property with their spouses. They took title as community property as to one another and as tenants in common collectively, as follows: "a 67% undivided interest to Orville Occupier and Margie Occupier, husband and wife, as community property, and a 33% undivided interest to Harold Investor and Ingrid Investor, husband and wife, as community property, all as tenants in common."

The Loan

Occupier and Investor shared the down payment and acquired a $192,000 loan. Since the Occupier makes all loan payments, he must meet the lender's financing criteria, and he chooses the loan package. This Occupier shopped for a loan package and decided upon a fixed rate at 7.5%. Once the Occupier qualified for the loan, the lender required only a quick qualifier application from the Investor. If an Occupier cannot qualify on his own, the Investor must provide complete financial history and be subject to strict lender scrutiny. Due to several factors, including the high purchase price of this property, this employer-employee team did not qualify for the *Magnet Loan* program described in Chapter Thirteen.

Rent

Internal Revenue Code §280A rent was calculated with the following formula – ".004 times purchase price times Investor ownership interest less a 20% *good tenant discount.*" (See Chapter Eight.) Thus, rent was computed at $250 per month.

Fair market value	$240,000
Rent apportionment	x .004
Fair market rent	$ 960
Investor's interest	x .33
Rent - Investor interest	$ 317
Less 20% good tenant discount	x .80
Fair rent to Occupier (rounded)	$ 250

§280A Rental Calculation

The Occupier paid rent of $250 a month to the Investor, totalling $3000 a year. The Occupier made all payments on the property except the Investor's yearly payments of $3000 to offset rent.

Payments and Rent Reimbursement

The Investor has $3000 in rental income to return to the property each year in the form of deductible expenses. Expenses deductible to the Investor and non-deductible to the Occupier were first selected as the means of rental reimbursement. Let's take a look at how this Investor returned that rental income to the property.

	Yearly	Term
Rental income:	$3,000	$21,000
Deductions:		
Insurance	1,200	8,400
Property taxes	1,800	12,600
TOTAL	$3,000	$21,000

Rent Received and Reimbursed As Expenses

Detail: Investor has $3,000 to reimburse to the property annually. With no association dues or maintenance fees, the only item deductible by Investor and non-deductible by Occupier was insurance. Thus, the annual insurance payment of $1,200 was assigned to Investor, leaving another $1,800 of rental income to reimburse to the property each year. No other expenses were deductible by the Investor and non-deductible by the Occupier. Property taxes were the next choice. For this property, those taxes were $3,000 per year. Investor was assigned payment of $1,800 toward property taxes, fulfilling his rental reimbursement obligation.

The result – Investor rental income of $3,000, offset by exactly $3,000 in property-related expenses – $1,200 for insurance costs and $1,800 for property taxes. The Occupier paid the remaining property taxes and made all mortgage payments. Rental reimbursement shifted about 10% of the Occupier's primary residence deductions to the Investor – but the Occupier retained a hefty 90% of all property deductions available to him. Bottom line: although the Occupier did lose some tax deductions by compliance with Internal Revenue Code §280A, he still retained the vast majority. This joint ownership still remained a tax haven for the Occupier.

Tax Deduction Allocations

Under this Joint Ownership Agreement the Occupier makes all loan payments and claims the entire interest deduction. The Investor pays and claims insurance and a portion of property taxes. The Investor depreciates his portion of the property and claims that deduction. The Investor has declared his intent to hold the property as his investment to be exchanged at the end of the agreement, pursuant to Internal Revenue Code §1031. The Occupier has declared his tax-deferral intention under Internal Revenue Code §1034.

Clearly, the majority of tax benefits go to this Occupier. For that reason, we try to achieve a greater profit allocation to the Investor. The Occupier's greatest benefit is his tax deductions while the Investor's greatest benefit is profit. But in this transaction, the Investor is motivated more by employee relations than by profit.

Occupier Tax Deductions

The joint ownership continues uneventfully for its seven-year term. As shown by the following figures, the

Occupier claims interest deductions of $97,000 and property tax deductions of $8,400. In addition, the Occupier can shelter his profit by rolling over into a new residence.

	Yearly	Term
Interest	$13,850	$ 97,000
Property taxes	1,200	8,400
TOTAL	$15,050	$105,400

Occupier loses approximately 10% of deductions in rent reimbursement.

Occupier's Tax Deductions - Seven-Year Term

Investor Tax Deductions

Over the seven-year ownership this Investor reports rental income of $21,000, fully offset by the same amount of deduction. He also claims a depreciation deduction in the amount of $15,120, calculated below.

	Yearly	Term
Investor depreciation	$2,160	$15,120

Investor's Depreciation - Seven-Year Term

Investor's Depreciation Deduction

This Investor, as an outside Investor, is able to benefit from a far greater depreciation deduction that the Seller-Investor. This Investor uses the current cost of the property as his depreciable basis, entitling him to deduct $2,160 yearly and $15,120 over the term.

Depreciable basis		$240,000
Improvements allocation	x	.75
Improvements cost value		180,000
Investor interest	x	.33
Investor interest – improvements		59,400
Years for residential depreciation	÷	27.5
Investor annual depreciation (rounded)		2,160
Seven-year term	x	7
Investor depreciation over term		$ 15,120

Investor's Depreciation Deduction

Detail: In reviewing this Investor's portfolio he qualifies to claim all depreciation on his 33% interest for a deduction of $15,120 in depreciation over the seven-year term.

The Options at Term

The following buyout and sale calculations are based on the projections these parties made at commencement of the joint ownership.

Buyout of Investor

At term, the first buyout option passes to the Occupier, who can buy out the Investor based on the calculations on the following page.

Appraisal - 4.5% annual appreciation	$327,000
Loan pay-off	- 176,000
Equity	151,000
Return of investment to Investor	- 36,000
Return of investment to Occupier	- 12,000
Loan principal reduction to Occupier	- 16,000
Net equity	87,000
Investor interest	x .33
Investor share of equity	28,710
Return of Investor down payment	36,000
Buyout of Investor	$ 64,710

Occupier Buys Out Investor at Seven-Year Term

Detail: **4.5% annual assumed appreciation establishes value of $327,000. Deducting the $176,000 loan pay-off leaves gross equity of $151,000. Next the Investor receives his initial $36,000 contribution. The Occupier's initial $12,000 contribution is then returned to him. Next, the Occupier's loan principal reduction of $16,000 is returned to him. Net equity for the co-owners to split is $87,000. At this point the Investor receives credit for his 33% equity interest, giving him $28,710 of the accumulated appreciation. In total, the Investor receives his $36,000 original contribution plus $28,710 as his appreciation return, for a total of $64,710. Based upon these projections, it will take $64,710 for the Occupier to buy out the Investor at term.**

Occupier Refinance

The chart on the following page illustrates Occupier refinance to cash out the Investor at term.

Appraisal - 4.5% annual appreciation	$327,000
75% refinance	x .75
Loan proceeds [$82,000 equity]	245,000
Loan pay-off	- 176,000
Net proceeds	69,000
Investor buyout	- 64,700
Cash proceeds to Occupier	$ 4,300

Occupier Buys Out Investor by Refinance at Seven-Year Term

Detail: Value determined by assumed appreciation is $327,000. It will take a 75% refinance to cash out the Investor. The 75% loan is in the amount of $245,000. From loan proceeds the $176,000 first loan is paid off, leaving $69,000 cash to the Occupier. Buyout of the Investor is calculated at $64,700. Occupier can cash out the Investor with $4,300 left over, most of which will go to refinancing fees.

Through refinance this Occupier is able to cash out his co-owner, move into a position of sole ownership and assume $82,000 in equity. His monthly payment is higher than it was, but after seven years of working for his Employer-Investor, he's able to afford it. Co-owners often find a seven-year term better than five years for buyout and refinance.

Tax Consequence of Investor Buyout

Let's review the co-owners' tax consequences when the Occupier buys out the Investor. The Occupier incurs no tax liability in continuing his ownership. The Investor, cashed out of the property, experiences a taxable event. The cashed out Investor will want to exercise his tax deferral option pursuant to Internal Revenue Code §1031 by exchanging his joint ownership property interest for another similar property of equal or greater value. (See Chapter Twelve.)

Here, the exchanging Investor defers taxes on his $28,700 buyout profit. Before adjusting basis, at a 35% combined federal and state tax rate, the exchanging Investor defers $10,000 in taxes.

Buyout of Occupier

If the Occupier does not exercise his buyout option at term, it passes to the Investor. See calculations below:

Appraisal - 4.5% annual appreciation	$327,000
Loan pay-off	- 176,000
Equity	151,000
Return of investment to Investor	- 36,000
Return of investment to Occupier	- 12,000
Loan principal reduction to Occupier	- 16,000
Net equity	87,000
Occupier interest	x .67
Occupier share of equity	58,290
Occupier down/loan reduction	28,000
Buyout of Occupier	$ 86,290

Investor Buys Out Occupier at Seven-Year Term

Detail: Value based on assumed appreciation is $327,000. The $176,000 loan is paid off, leaving $151,000 gross equity. Investor's original $36,000 equity interest is deducted next. The Occupier's original $12,000 equity is then returned to him. Occupier is then credited for the $16,000 loan principal reduction he made. Remaining is net equity of $87,000. The Occupier steps forward to cash in his 67% equity interest – $58,290 for his share of appreciation. At term the Occupier receives $86,290 – $58,290 for his 67% share of the appreciation and $28,000 as return of his original cash contribution and loan principal reduction.

Investor Refinance

This chart illustrates this Investor's refinance to cash out his co-owner at $86,290.

Appraised value - 4.5% assumed apprec.	$327,000
80% refinance	x .80
Loan proceeds [$65,400 equity]	261,600
Loan pay-off	- 176,000
Net proceeds	85,600
Occupier buyout	- 86,290
Deficit to Investor	- $ 690

Investor Buys Out Occupier by Refinance at Seven-Year Term

Detail: Value based on projections is $327,000. It will take an 80% refinance to buy out the Occupier, providing loan proceeds of $261,600. The $176,000 first loan is paid off, leaving $85,600 cash to the Investor. After cashing out the Occupier for $86,290, the Investor needs to add only $690 to the Occupier buyout pot.

Tax Consequence of Occupier Buyout

What is the Occupier's tax consequence when he is bought out by the Investor? The Investor continuing his investment incurs no tax liability, while the cashed out Occupier does confront a taxable event. To defer his tax this Occupier may roll over into another principal residence under Internal Revenue Code §1034. By replacing his residence under those guidelines, this Occupier will defer taxes on $58,290 of profit which amount does not include his $12,000 down payment or his $16,000 return of loan principal reduction. Before computing basis or deduction adjustment, at a

35% combined federal and state capital gains rate, the rolling over Occupier defers $20,401 in taxes. Chapter Eleven more precisely calculates the Occupier's gain and explores his Internal Revenue Code §1034 option in depth.

Sale at Term

If neither Occupier nor Investor exercise buyout at term, the property is sold. Proceeds distribution at sale is calculated on the following chart for these parties.

Tax Consequence of Sale

At sale, Investor and Occupier each experience a taxable event since they are both cashed out of the property. Each party's tax profile must be considered separately, since they will defer taxes under different provisions.

The Occupier defers his taxes by rolling into another principal residence pursuant to Internal Revenue Code §1034. By replacing his residence with another of equal or greater value the Occupier defers all taxes. Before basis or deduction adjustment, at a 35% rate, this Occupier defers taxes of $15,712 on his $44,890 profit ($72,890 less $28,000 down payment/loan principal reduction) as shown in the following chart.

Sale price - 4.5% annual appreciation	$327,000
Loan	- 176,000
Seller closing costs (6%)	- 20,000
Gross proceeds	131,000
Investor return of investment	- 36,000
Occupier return of investment	- 12,000
Loan principal reduction to Occupier	- 16,000
Net equity	67,000
Investor ownership interest	x .33
Investor share of net equity	22,110
Investor return of investment	+ 36,000
Investor proceeds on sale	58,110
Gross proceeds (from above)	131,000
Less Investor proceeds	- 58,110
Occupier's proceeds on sale	$ 72,890

Sale at Seven-Year Term

Detail: Sale price projected at $327,000 leaves gross equity of $131,000 after $176,000 loan pay-off and $20,000 in 6% seller closing costs. From the $131,000 proceeds, Investor's $36,000 investment is returned, as is Occupier's $12,000 investment. Occupier's $16,000 loan principal reduction is then returned to him, leaving net equity of $67,000 to be split between the co-owners. Of that Investor receives $22,110 as his 33% interest; Occupier receives the remaining proceeds of $72,890, $60,890 of which is profit to him. At sale, then, the Investor receives $58,110 of which $22,110 is profit while Occupier receives $72,890 of which $44,890 is profit. As you can see, at sale the co-owners share the 6% closing costs, thereby reducing their profit in proportion to their ownership interests.

In the sale process the Occupier cashes out with enough money to buy a new residence – this time, without a co-owner. (See Chapter Eleven.)

The Investor defers his taxes by exchanging into another property pursuant to Internal Revenue Code §1031. By replacing his joint ownership investment with another investment of equal or greater value, the Investor defers all taxes. By exchanging, before basis and deduction adjustment, and using a 35% rate, this Investor defers $7,739 in taxes on his $22,110 profit. (See Chapter Twelve.)

The Bottom Line Results

This seven-year joint ownership transaction proves to be a profitable and tax-wise venture for both co-owners. The Occupier has claimed $105,400 in tax deductions. On buyout he receives $86,290, of which $58,290 is profit. On sale he receives $72,890 of which $44,890 is profit. The Occupier leaves the joint ownership armed with sufficient funds for a down payment. Not only can he now afford to buy a new property without co-ownership – he can defer taxes on his profit by rolling into another principal residence pursuant to Internal Revenue Code §1034.

The Investor's benefits parallel his co-owner's. The Investor has claimed depreciation of $15,120. On buyout he receives $64,710, $28,710 of which is profit. On sale his profit is $22,110. The Investor leaves the joint ownership with enough money to move up into a considerably higher-priced property. He can also defer taxes on his profit by exchanging into another property under Internal Revenue Code §1031. Chapter Twelve takes up where this chapter leaves off – it calculates the Investors' gain and exchanges it into another property.

Comparison of Samples: Chapters Nine and Ten

Let's take a look at the differences between the two sample transactions in Chapters Nine and Ten. The basic terms of the transactions are compared on the following pages.

Beginning Data

Chapter Nine: The co-owners chose 4% as their appreciation rate and 12% as projected Investor rate of return on buyout. Their term was five years with an ownership split of 45% to Occupier and 55% to Investor. The Seller-turned-Investor posted $27,000 retained equity as the down payment, and no down payment contribution was made by Occupier.

Chapter Ten: The co-owners, who bought a property from someone else, made choices very different from those in Chapter Nine. Based on a 4.5% assumed appreciation rate and an 11% projected Investor rate of return on buyout, these parties split the ownership at 67% to Occupier and 33% to Investor. They also split the down payment – the Investor contributing $36,000 and Occupier $12,000. Their term was seven years.

Factor	Chapter Nine	Chapter Ten
Appreciation rate	4%	4.5%
Projected Investor return	12%	11%
Term	5 years	7 years
Ownership split	45/55 Investor	67/33 Investor
Down payment	$0 Occupier	$12,000 Occupier
	$27,000 Investor	$36,000 Investor

Diverse ownership splits arise from different contributions, assumptions, and projections. Let's see how the two sets of ownership splits affect their co-owners' results.

The Results

In Chapter Nine, over a five-year term the Occupiers claimed $44,050 in deductions, and made $18,000 of which $13,000 was profit on buyout and $14,000 of which $9,000 was profit at sale. Investors' profit was $16,000 on buyout and $10,000 at sale. These co-owners' profits were comparable – a far more even distribution of profits than in this chapter. When choosing their ownership splits, the parties should always project their transactions to term to confirm that they will achieve their desired result with the assumptions they have used.

In this chapter the joint ownership term was seven years – two years longer. Keep this factor in mind to account for increase in value and deductions between the two transactions. Occupier claimed over $105,400 in tax deductions, and made $58,290 profit on buyout and $44,890 profit at sale; the Investor's profit was $28,710 on buyout and $22,110 at sale. Note that the Occupier's profit was double the Investor's.

Factor	Chapter Nine	Chapter Ten
Term	5 years	7 years
Occupier deductions	$44,050	$105,400
Occupier Profit – Buyout	$13,000	$ 58,290
Sale	$ 9,000	$ 44,890
Investor Profit – Buyout	$16,000	$ 28,710
Sale	$10,000	$ 22,110

The end result for each of these transactions has been optimum profit and tax benefits through joint mixed use of a single property. The tax calculations performed in this chapter have been general. Chapters Eleven and Twelve apply more specific tax criteria and begin where these samples left off – illustrating the co-owners' rollover and exchange options. See the last pages of this chapter for all charts from this transaction.

We've now seen joint ownership in action. Next up – the actual long-term tax deferrals available to the parties: Chapter Eleven for the Occupier, and Chapter Twelve for the Investor.

Chapter Ten Sample - Third-Party Investor

Initial Purchase

Purchase price:	$240,000
Down payment – Investor paid:	$36,000
Down payment – Occupier paid	$12,000
80% loan	$192,000
Term	7 Years
Ownership split	Occupier 67% / Investor 33%
§280A rental	$250/mo. / $3,000/yr.
Projected annual appreciation rate	4.5%
Projected annual return to Investor	11%

Payments/Rent Reimbursement

Occupier	Yearly	Term
Interest	$13,850	$97,000
Property taxes	1,200	8,400
TOTAL	$15,050	$105,400

Occupier loses approximately 10% of deductions in rent reimbursement.

Investor	Yearly	Term
Rental income:	$3,000	$21,000
Deductions:		
Insurance	1,200	8,400
Property taxes	1,800	12,600
Total	3,000	21,000
Depreciation deduction	$2,160	$15,120

Seven-Year Buyout of Investor

Appraisal - 4.5% annual appreciation	$327,000
Loan pay-off	- 176,000
Equity	151,000
Return of investment to Investor	- 36,000
Return of investment to Occupier	- 12,000
Loan principal reduction to Occupier	- 16,000
Net equity	87,000
Investor interest	x .33
Investor share of equity (rounded)	28,710
Return of Investor down payment	36,000
Buyout of Investor	**$ 64,710**

Seven-Year Buyout of Occupier

Appraisal - 4.5% annual appreciation	$327,000
Loan pay-off	- 176,000
Equity	151,000
Return of investment to Investor	- 36,000
Return of investment to Occupier	- 12,000
Loan principal reduction to Occupier	- 16,000
Net equity	87,000
Occupier interest	x .67
Occupier share of equity	58,290
Return of Occupier down/loan reduction	28,000
Buyout of Occupier	**$ 86,290**

Seven-Year Refinance by Occupier

Appraisal - 4.5% annual appreciation	$327,000
75% refinance	x ___.75
Loan proceeds [$193,000 equity]	245,000
Loan pay-off	- 176,000
Net proceeds	69,000
Investor buyout	- 64,700
Cash to Occupier	$ 4,300

Seven-Year Refinance by Investor

Appraised value - 4.5% assumed appreciation	$327,000
75% refinance	x ___.80
Loan proceeds [$65,400 equity]	261,600
Loan pay-off	- 176,000
Net proceeds (rounded)	85,600
Occupier buyout	- 86,290
Deficit to Investor	- $ 690

Seven-Year Sale

Sale price - 4.5% annual appreciation	$327,000
Loan	- 176,000
Seller closing costs (6%)	- 20,000
Gross proceeds	131,000
Investor return of investment	- 36,000
Occupier return of investment	- 12,000
Loan principal reduction to Occupier	- 16,000
Net equity	67,000
Investor ownership interest	x .33
Investor share of net equity	22,110
Investor return of investment	+ 36,000
Investor proceeds on sale	58,110
Gross proceeds (from above)	131,000
Less Investor proceeds	- 58,110
Occupier proceeds on sale	$ 72,890

Chapter Eleven

THE OCCUPIER'S
TAX HAVEN

A myriad of long-term tax aspects arise in a joint ownership. The parties intend to co-own the property for term, make as much money as they can through tax deductions and appreciation, and defer paying taxes on their profit. The Occupier's tax deferral method is Internal Revenue Code §1034. The Investor's deferral mechanism lies in Internal Revenue Code §1031. These procedures, called *bridges over the taxable event*, are exceptions to the general rule requiring recognition of gain upon sale. The Investor's position is analyzed in Chapter Twelve. Here we see how the Occupier shelters his gain by *rolling over* under Internal Revenue Code §1034, exempting gain under §121, and retaining basis under Proposition 60.

*T*ypically, the Occupier lives in the property as his principal residence for the term of the joint ownership. At term, three terminating options are available. He may buy out the Investor, the Investor may buy him out, or the property is sold.

Buying out the Investor will increase the Occupier's property basis. This will not result in a taxable event to the Occupier since he is not cashing out of the property. Taxable profit will flow to the Occupier only if he is bought out by the Investor or if the property is sold. To defer being taxed on this profit, the Occupier may utilize the provisions of Internal Revenue Code §1034.

Deferral Options

Real estate investment is one of the most economically wise investments that can be made. The Internal Revenue Code sanctions tax-deferred profit as long as the investment continues on in another similar property. The Internal Revenue Code also authorizes deductions for the cost of financing real estate investments. These tax benefits stimulate the economy, promoting property ownership and affordable housing.

The principal residence owner is able to defer tax on his profit by rolling into another principal residence. The investment property owner tax-defers his investment by exchanging into another investment property. The vast majority of property transfers fall into these two categories. Thus, tax deferral options are available in most transactions. Although many people find little personal economic support in the taxing structure of the Internal Revenue Code, savvy real estate investors know otherwise. They realize that as long as they continue their investments, our taxing system sanctions and encourages deferral of tax.

What is *deferral?* Deferral means temporary postponement. Tax is deferred until such time as the investment is discontinued. At that time, the original property basis before exchange or rollover is adjusted by improvements and depreciation to determine gain. That gain is taxed. To postpone that taxable event, the investment perpetually continues into a property of equal or greater value.

Under Internal Revenue Code §1034 the Occupier defers tax on his gain by *rolling his gain over* into another principal residence of equal or greater value than the adjusted sales price. This is referred to as a residential *rollover.* Thus the Occupier defers all profit he has earned from his joint ownership. If the replacement residence is of less value than the adjusted sales price of his joint ownership interest, the Occupier will be partially taxed on what is called a *trade down.*

Exemption Options

Exemption options, as well as *deferral* options, are available to the taxpayer age 55 and over. Later in this chapter we will discuss Internal Revenue Code §121, under which the age-qualified Occupier may claim a once-in-a-lifetime *exemption* to exclude his gain from taxation forever. Under Proposition 60 in California he can exempt his property from local property tax reassessment. Most other states have similar exemptions for the 55 and over owner.

Determining Occupier Gain Without Rollover

Before evaluating tax deferral or exemption options, the Occupier should calculate the amount of gain he will realize on sale. These calculations should be performed well in advance of the joint ownership termination date to assist in deciding whether to buy out the Investor or sell the property. The gain computation will determine whether the Occupier should roll over into another primary residence, or just cash out of the property.

The Occupier computes gain on the sale and tax on that gain. Typically, the Occupier has held the property for the one-year capital gains holding period. Thus, the Occupier qualifies for capital gains tax rates. Capital gains tax rates change frequently, so you would be wise to consult your tax advisor for the current rate.

A Few Definitions

Specific terms are used to describe the property sold and the property purchased. In this chapter, *relinquished* property describes the property the Occupier rolled out of or sold. *Replacement* property describes the new principal residence rolled into by the Occupier.

Calculation

The chart on the following page provides a concise calculation of gain. A blank worksheet is included in the *Appendix* for your use in making your own calculations. The Chapter Nine Occupier, owning a 45% interest, is featured in this illustration.

BASIS AND GAIN CALCULATIONS – OCCUPIER
To Compute Gain Recognized Without Rollover

1. Relinquished property acquisition cost $60,750
2. Capital expenditures   – 0 –
3. Adjusted basis on relinquished property $60,750
        (Line 1 plus Line 2)
4. Relinquished property sales price $73,800
5. Selling fix-up expenses   – 0 –
6. Selling closing expenses   ($ 4,428)
7. Adjusted sales price on $69,372
        relinquished property
        (Line 4 minus Line 5 minus Line 6)
8. Gain recognized without rollover   **$ 8,622**
        (Line 7 minus Line 3)

Adjusted Basis

Generally, the adjusted basis of a principal residence is its original cost adjusted by capital improvements and casualty losses. Item One shows the Occupier's acquisition cost of the relinquished property. The relinquished property cost $135,000, 45% of which is owned by the Occupier. Thus, his portion of the acquisition cost of the relinquished property is $60,750. Added to cost are capital improvements and expenditures. For purposes of this chart only, the Occupier has made no capital improvements; Item Two is therefore zero. Item Three is cost plus improvements, for a total adjusted basis of $60,750 on the Occupier's interest of the joint ownership property.

Adjusted Sales Price

Adjusted sales price is generally the sales price adjusted by selling and fix-up expenses. Item Four asks for the sales price of the relinquished property – which here would pertain only to the Occupier's interest in the sales price. The property sold for $164,000. Applying our Occupier's 45% interest gives him a relinquished property sales price of $73,800 for Item Four. Item Five, selling fix-up expenses, shows a contribution by the Occupier of zero. Item Six is selling closing expenses. Closing costs were $9,840 and the Occupier paid $4,428 as his 45% interest; therefore Item Six is $4,428. All of these sales expenses are deducted from the sale price, resulting in Item Seven – an adjusted sales price of $69,372.

Gain

Gain realized is the difference between the adjusted basis and the adjusted sales price. The adjusted basis is $60,750 and the adjusted sales price is $69,372. The difference, as Item Eight, leaves realized gain of $8,622.

According to these calculations, the Occupier in Chapter Nine will pay taxes on $8,622 of gain. (The calculations in this chapter prevail over the *estimates* in Chapter Nine.) Before deductions, at a 35% capital gains rate, this Occupier will pay nearly $3,018 in federal and state taxes. It would behoove this Occupier to consider his tax deferral and exemption options. The Occupier intending to buy another principal residence will first look to Internal Revenue Code §1034. He wants to exhaust his tax deferral options before he uses his once-in-a-lifetime exemption.

What Does IRC §1034 Require?

Principal Residence

Our Occupier has occupied the joint ownership property as his principal residence for a number of years. Therefore he can use Internal Revenue Code §1034 – providing he leaves one principal residence and replaces it with another he either buys or builds. A copy of this code section is included in the *Appendix*.

Two-Year Limitations

Internal Revenue Code §1034 requires purchase and occupancy of the new principal residence within *two* years before or after disposition of the joint ownership property. This is the rolling over process. The Occupier has a two-year period within which to roll over the sale proceeds. §1034 cannot be used more frequently than once every two years, with a few exceptions. Since the joint ownership transaction is usually five years long, the two-year limitation is typically not a problem.

The typical joint ownership Occupier easily meets the requirements of Internal Revenue Code §1034. At the end of the joint ownership, the Occupier who purchases another principal residence of equal or greater value will shelter all his profit by rolling over under Internal Revenue Code §1034.

§1034 in Operation

The Occupier is able to shelter *all* profit when he buys or builds a new residence at least equal in value to his joint ownership interest. If the new residence is of lesser value, he must pay some tax on his recognized gain. The process of rolling into another residence of less value is called a *roll down* or *trade down*. In a roll down, the Occupier is taxed on the difference between the value of the new residence and his interest in the old residence.

If the Occupier does not roll over into another residence under Internal Revenue Code §1034 he will be fully taxed on his gain. In the sample transaction above, the Occupier's gain is $8,622 and his tax is a few dollars short of $3,018. The Occupier who replaces his joint ownership property interest with a principal residence benefits by using his tax deferral option. Even if he rolls down, he partially shelters his gain.

Age 55 Exemptions

Advantages for the senior taxpayer are conferred by our taxing system. The gauge is set at the 55-year mark. Internal Revenue Code §121 and Proposition 60 in California are two of the provisions which confer tax breaks on property owners age 55 or over.

Internal Revenue Code §121 Exemption

If the Occupier is 55 years of age or older, Internal Revenue Code §121 should be considered. Generally speaking, Internal Revenue Code §121 entitles the 55 plus principal residence seller to a $125,000 gain exemption. A copy of this code section is included in the *Appendix*. The election is granted *once in a lifetime* and the gain exempted is *forever* tax-free. If this exemption has already been taken with a spouse, an accountant should be consulted to see if any part of the exemption remains.

To qualify for Internal Revenue Code §121 the Occupier or spouse must be 55 years of age *before* sale of the joint ownership residence. The Occupier is also required to have used the joint ownership property as his principal residence for three out of the preceding five years. The typical joint ownership Occupier satisfies this requirement by having lived in the property as his principal residence for at least the prior three years.

§121 in Operation

By qualifying under Internal Revenue Code §121, the Occupier age 55 or over may make the following elections in selling the joint ownership property. He can exempt taxes on up to $125,000 of gain he has realized from sale of the joint ownership property. This is accomplished by trading down or electing not to purchase another residence, and designating $125,000 of gain to come within the §121 exemption.

This Occupier can also utilize Internal Revenue Code §1034 in conjunction with Internal Revenue Code §121. With these combined benefits, he'll be rolling *down* into a residence of lesser value and exempting the gain he has not rolled over. Here is how the combined option works. For purposes of this roll down only, let's assume our 55-plus Occupier sells his joint ownership interest for $275,000 and receives $260,000 after closing and fix up costs. He wants to buy a new principal residence worth $150,000. He will be rolling down, as opposed to rolling over, since the replacement property is of less value than his interest in the joint ownership property. The following chart illustrates this transaction.

Sections 1034 and 121 Combined

1. Relinquished property sales price $275,000
2. Selling fix-up expenses   – 0 –
3. Selling closing expenses $ 15,000
4. Adjusted sales price, $260,000
   relinquished property
      (Line 1 minus Line 2 minus Line 3)
5. Fair market value, replacement prop. $150,000
6. Gain realized (Line 4 minus Line 5) $110,000
7. Less up to $125,000, IRC §121 exempt $110,000
8. Gain recognized   – 0 –

Detail: **Assume this Occupier's interest in the joint ownership sales proceeds is $275,000. Item One – relinquished property sales price – is $275,000. He had no fix-up expenses and closing expenses were $15,000. Thus, Item Two is zero and Item Three is $15,000. Deducting these sale costs, he is left with an adjusted sales price of $260,000 for his relinquished joint ownership interest as Item Four. Item Five is $150,000 as the value of his replacement principal residence. The $150,000 fair market value of the replacement property is deducted from the adjusted sales price of $260,000, leaving $110,000 for Item Six as his gain realized in this roll down. As Item Seven he implements his IRC §121 $125,000 exemption and effectively exempts his $110,000 gain from taxation for Item Eight – recognized gain of zero.**

By applying Internal Revenue Code §1034 this Occupier subtracts the value of the replacement property from his adjusted joint ownership sales price, realizing a gain of $110,000. If 55 or over, he uses Internal Revenue Code §121 to exempt the remaining $110,000 from tax. The exemption provisions of Internal Revenue Code §121 can result in substantial savings to the seller aged 55. Considering this is a once-in-a-lifetime exemption, the Occupier should project future investments to insure that he is claiming the exemption as fully and as appropriately as possible.

Reassessment Exemption

Let's explore another option available to the age 55 and over principal residence seller in California and many other states. California's Proposition 60 provides an exemption from property tax reassessment. Many other states have adopted the exemption as well. In states other than California, your local Assessor's Office should be contacted to determine if similar legislation has been enacted.

Proposition 60, and its counterparts in other states, allow homeowners age 55 and over to transfer the current assessed value of their home to a replacement principal residence also located in that county. Proposition 60 requires replacement within the same time frame as Internal Revenue Code §1034 – within two years before or after sale of the principal residence.

The properties on both ends must be the taxpayer's principal residence. The replacement residence must be either equal or *lesser* in value than the relinquished residence. Thus, when applying Proposition 60 the replacement residence *cannot* be of greater value than the relinquished property. There is no exception to this requirement. It is intended to benefit the seller who trades equal or down, but not up. Proposition 60's replacement value requirements should not be confused with Internal Revenue Code §1031 and §1034 – which require the replacement residence to be of equal or *greater* value than the relinquished property.

The states that allow this exemption usually transfer the exemption between counties. Your local Assessor's Office should be contacted in each instance. The reciprocity provisions, if in effect, allow a qualifying taxpayer to retain his basis in, for example, a San Diego County property when relocating to a qualifying Marin County property.

The property tax reassessment exemption can only be used once in a taxpayer's lifetime. In this way, it is similar to the exemption granted by Internal Revenue Code §121. This exemption can allow significant relief to the age 55 taxpayer – many of whom have lived in properties with low assessed value for many years. Under Proposition 60 a qualified taxpayer is able to continue making low property tax payments by retaining his tax basis.

Conversion to Investment Property

There is one more option for the Occupier who does not intend to replace his residence when leaving the joint ownership. That Occupier can *convert* his interest in the joint ownership property to income or investment property. By so doing, the Occupier defers tax on his profit by exchanging out of the joint ownership property and into another income or investment property. He accomplishes this tax-deferred exchange pursuant to Internal Revenue Code §1031. In order to qualify for §1031 exchange treatment, he should convert the property at least one year *before* exchanging out of it at term.

The most obvious method of conversion is for the Occupier to lease out the property for the last year of the joint ownership term, or longer. If this is the Occupier's intention he should revise the occupancy requirement with the Investor's consent. The Joint Ownership Agreement requires the Occupier to occupy the property for term. If the Occupier intends to convert the property, he must revise the occupancy requirement to allow him to lease it out.

Now that we have explored the tax sheltering options available to the Occupier, let's move on to Chapter Twelve. The Investor, too, can shelter the profit he has made in his joint ownership. His option is available under Internal Revenue Code §1031.

Chapter Twelve

THE INVESTOR'S METHOD
OF SHELTERING GAIN

How does the Investor defer paying taxes on his joint ownership profits? This chapter reveals his strategy. The Investor prepares for tax deferral on two occasions – at the beginning and at the end of the joint ownership transaction. Since the Investor usually comes to the joint ownership with a real estate history, his *incoming tax position* receives careful analysis – especially when he is the seller of the joint ownership property. At term, the Investor's *exiting tax status* is scrutinized. At this point the Investor realizes gain and can defer paying taxes on his profit. This chapter presents the Investor's tax-deferral timetable and options.

*A*n Investor comes to a joint ownership transaction in a number of ways – as a relative of the Occupier, an exchanging Investor, or a seller of the property. As the Occupier's relative, he wants to assist in the purchase. If he is the exchanging Investor, he exercises his exchange options under Internal Revenue Code §1031, exchanging out of one property and into the joint ownership property. As seller of the joint ownership property, he continues part of his investment as a joint ownership co-owner. The exchanging Investor and the Seller-Investor begin joint ownership with careful tax strategy.

The Outside Investor

The *exchanging* Investor acquires the joint ownership property as *replacement* property in an Internal Revenue Code §1031 exchange. This Investor exchanges out of his former investment property and defers tax on gain by exchanging into the joint ownership property. At the end of the joint ownership he intends to defer tax on gain once more by exchanging out of the joint ownership property and into yet another. This Investor carefully positions himself into and out of each transaction in order to meet all exchange requirements.

The Seller As Investor

The Seller-Investor must carefully evaluate his tax position upon entering the joint ownership transaction. He simultaneously sells part of his property while continuing part as his investment. Hence the joint ownership transaction triggers differing tax results for his sale and his entry into the joint ownership.

The Seller-Investor who retains 20% of value in a joint ownership sells and realizes gain on 80% of his property. He sets up the appropriate mechanism to defer tax on gain for the 80% portion of the property he sells. He also sets the stage so he can exit the joint ownership with another tax-deferral at term. This taxpayer must carefully monitor his position since he is conducting *two* separate transactions – selling part of his property and entering into a joint ownership on the rest.

The seller's sale status is first assessed. His method of sheltering gain depends on how he has held his property – as an investment or as his principal residence. Let's take a look at each of these seller profiles.

The Investment Property Seller

First we'll explore the tax status of the Seller-Investor who has held his property as an investment. Assume that he goes into the joint ownership by initially retaining 20% of value in the property. For tax purposes, then, he sells and realizes gain on 80% of his investment property. Since *investment property* – not a principal residence – is being sold, this Seller-Investor can utilize the exchange provisions of Internal Revenue Code §1031 to defer tax.

This Seller-Investor *exchanges* out of the 80% portion of his investment property into another in order to defer his tax. In exchanging out, he will acquire a replacement property with equal or greater value than the 80% interest he's selling. For example, if his property has a fair market value of $225,000 he must replace the 80% interest he sells – here $180,000 – with a property worth $180,000. Full value replacement will enable the seller to defer all tax. If the seller does not exchange into another property, he will be fully taxed on all gain he has made. His tax will then be calculated on only 80% of his property basis.

As for the 20% interest he retains for his joint owner-ship, this Seller-Investor continues his investment, planning to exchange out of this portion of his investment at term. It may seem odd that the seller retains 20% equity in the property, while as joint ownership Investor he owns a 50% interest, but these two percentages are correct. They are assigned to the Seller-Investor at two different stages in the joint ownership process. See *The Investor's Two Percentages*, below, for more discussion of this issue.

The Principal Residence Seller

If the seller's residence becomes the joint ownership property, he will defer gain on the portion he sells under Internal Revenue Code §1034 – the residential counterpart to Internal Revenue Code §1031. Under Internal Revenue Code §1034, the Seller-Investor rolls into another principal resi-dence with a value roughly equal to the 80% interest he sold. The seller with a principal residence valued at $225,000 can replace his 80% interest with a residence worth $180,000. By fully replacing the 80% interest he sold, this seller defers tax on all gain. If the seller does not roll over, he will be taxed on all gain. His tax will be based on only 80% of his property's basis, since he is selling 80% of the property.

This Seller-Investor's 20% retained interest in the joint ownership property becomes investment property. He no longer uses the property as his principal residence; instead, he holds it as an investment. Under Internal Revenue Code §1031 only investment or property used in trade or business qualifies for tax deferral. Through joint ownership he converts his retained interest to investment property, qualifying under Internal Revenue Code §1031 to defer tax on his profit when the joint ownership expires. This Investor thus begins the joint ownership holding investment property with the intent of exchanging into another property at term.

The Investor's Two Percentages

You are probably asking yourself about the percentages associated with this Investor. Apparently, he retains a 20% interest in the joint ownership property, yet he owns 50% of it. There is an explanation – the 20% retained interest is used to calculate his ownership interest, which then takes its place.

Two percentages are *always* associated with the Investor. The first percentage – here, 20% – is the percentage of his contribution to the purchase price of the property. Most often the Investor's contribution to purchase price is in the range of 15% to 20%. The next percentage associated with the Investor is the ownership interest he receives in the joint ownership. When the Joint Ownership Agreement is signed the Investor's contribution percentage is converted to an equity interest. Generally, the 20% Investor contributor receives about 50%-60% of equity. When the Investor's equity interest is assigned, his contribution percentage no longer exists – except for purposes of calculating tax basis and gain. When it comes to basis calculation this Investor has a 20% interest; for all other purposes his interest in the joint ownership property, as stated on title and in the Joint Ownership Agreement, rules.

Investor Leaving the Joint Ownership Transaction

In the beginning of this chapter we reviewed how the Investor enters the joint ownership and establishes his interest. Now let's examine the Investor's position as he leaves the joint ownership – and how he defers tax on the profit he made.

The joint ownership Investor's intent is to make a profit. If he achieves his purpose, he will earn profits on his investment. This profit is characterized as gain. The Investor should pre-plan to shelter his projected gain by exchanging out of the property at the end of the joint ownership.

The Investor sets up his shelter plan in the Joint Ownership Agreement. He declares his use of the property as an investment and his intent to exchange out of the property at term. In this way the Investor defers tax on projected gain – much the same as the Occupier has done, but under a different rule. The Occupier deferred his tax under Internal Revenue Code §1034. The Investor accomplishes tax deferral under Internal Revenue Code §1031.

Investor's Terminating Options

At term of the joint ownership, the Investor's interest is calculated under the option elected by the parties. The Occupier is first entitled to buy out the Investor. The buyout option then passes to the Investor if unexercised by the Occupier. If neither co-owner buys out the other, the property is sold. In two of the three terminating options, the Investor terminates his ownership in the joint ownership property, realizing gain. If he is bought out by the Occupier, the Investor leaves the property, realizing gain. If neither party buys out the other, the property is sold and the Investor realizes gain. Therefore, it is most probable that he will realize gain at term of the joint ownership. The Investor shelters his gain from taxation under the exchange provisions of Internal Revenue Code §1031.

In the sample transactions in Chapters Nine and Ten, before basis and deduction adjustment the Investors made profits of $16,000 and $28,710, respectively, on their buyout.

If these Investors were taxed on their profits at a 35% combined federal and state capital gains rate, they would owe $5,600 to $10,049 in taxes. Thus, the Investors want to do whatever they can to defer tax on their profit.

Investor and IRC §1031

Under Internal Revenue Code §1031 the Investor may exchange tax-free out of the joint ownership property and into a new investment property. In the exchange process the Investor formally continues his investment and tax on his gain is therefore deferred.

An exception to deferral occurs if the Investor receives property other than *like-kind* real property in the exchange. Non-like-kind property received in an exchange is taxed on its own value. In a joint ownership, non-like-kind property is anything of value that is not real property held for investment or for use in trade or business. For example, if the Investor receives cash or furniture in the exchange, he is taxed on the value of those items. He is also taxed for *mortgage relief* – if he assumes a mortgage less than his existing mortgage, he is taxed on the difference.

Is exchanging worth the Investor's time and expense? Let's analyze the Investor's tax situation as he exits the joint ownership to determine whether he should exchange or sell his property interest. The best way to decide whether to exchange or sell is to compare the Investor's tax liability in each instance. The worksheets entitled *Basis and Gain Calculations*, found below in this chapter, yield the Investor's taxable gain in a straight sale of the joint ownership property.

A Few Definitions

Specific terms are used to describe the two properties involved in the exchange. *Relinquished* property describes the property the Investor is exchanging *out of* – here, his joint ownership interest. *Replacement* property describes the new property the Investor is exchanging *into*. *Gain realized* is the fair market value of the replacement property minus the adjusted basis of the relinquished property. *Boot* is anything that does not qualify as like-kind real property. *Gain recognized* is the lesser of gain realized and net boot received.

Determining Investor Gain Without Exchange

The Investor is taxed on gain he has made in the joint ownership transaction. This gain must be identified. Gain is the difference between the adjusted sales price and the adjusted basis of his ownership interest. These variables are calculated to determine Investor gain. The gain calculation is performed differently for each type of Investor – the Seller-Investor and the outside Investor. Their tax bases are not the same.

The property basis of the *Seller-turned-Investor* is determined by the property value when he first purchased it – likely long before the joint ownership transaction. On the other hand, the *outside Investor's* basis – assuming no prior exchange and no improvements made to the joint ownership property – is his ownership percentage of the joint ownership purchase price. Adjusted basis is calculated differently for these two Investors. The two differing Investor profiles in Chapters Nine and Ten are separately analyzed in the charts on the following page. The first chart calculates gain for Chapter Nine's Investor, the seller of the property, and the second chart calculates gain for Chapter Ten's Investor, an outside party.

Seller-Investor

– BASIS AND GAIN CALCULATIONS –
INVESTOR AS SELLER
To Compute Gain Realized Without Exchange

1. Relinquished property acquisition cost $ 15,000
2. Capital expenditures $ 3,000
3. Balance (Line 1 + Line 2) $ 18,000
4. Depreciation adjustment   ($ 2,045)
5. Adjusted basis on relinquished property $ 15,955
      (Line 3 minus Line 4)
6. Relinquished property sales price $90,200
7. Selling fix-up expenses   – 0 –
8. Selling closing expenses   ($ 5,412)
9. Adjusted sales price $84,788
      on relinquished property
      (Line 6 minus Line 7 minus Line 8)
10. Gain realized without exchange $68,833
      (Line 9 minus Line 5)

Adjusted Basis

The Investor depicted in the chart above was the Seller-turned-Investor in Chapter Nine. He has allocated his property basis as 80% to the portion of the property he sold and 20% to the portion he retained in the joint ownership. Thus, the acquisition cost for his joint ownership interest is 20% of his cost when he first acquired the property. He bought the property 10 years ago for $75,000.

His unadjusted basis for the entire property is $75,000. $15,000 is the 20% allocated to his joint ownership interest.

Item One, his relinquished joint ownership property acquisition cost, is $15,000. Added to cost are capital improvements and expenditures. (For purposes of this chart only, this Investor made $3,000 in improvements to the joint ownership property.) Item Two is $3,000. Item Three, cost plus improvements, totals $18,000. Item Four, depreciation adjustment, reduces the basis by total depreciation the Investor has taken over the joint ownership term. The Chapter Nine Investor took $2,045 in depreciation deductions over the term of the joint ownership. Item Five, gross cost minus depreciation, yields an adjusted basis of $15,955.

Adjusted Sales Price

Adjusted sales price of the Investor's interest in his relinquished joint ownership property is determined. Item Six asks for the sales price, which is the $164,000 sales price times the Investor's 55% ownership interest – for a sales price of $90,200. Item Seven, selling fix-up expenses, are zero. (In calculating adjusted sales price, fix-up expenses reduce the sales price.) Item Eight, selling closing expenses, is $9,840. This Investor split selling expenses with the Occupier, paying $5,412 as his 55% share. These sale expenses also offset sale price. Item Nine is sales price less sale expenses, for an adjusted sales price of $84,788.

Gain

Our Chapter Nine Investor has an adjusted sale price of $84,788 and an adjusted basis of $15,955. Gain realized upon sale of his interest in the joint ownership property is the difference between these two figures. This Investor will have realized gain of $68,833 (item 10). On a straight sale of this Investor's joint ownership property interest he faces a gain of $68,833. Absent deductions, at a 35% combined federal and state capital gains rate he'll pay about $24,092 in taxes.

The calculations performed in this chapter prevail over the estimates based on profit – as opposed to gain – presented in Chapters Nine and Ten. The Seller-Investor actually faces a much higher tax liability than estimated in Chapter Nine. It is certainly in the best interest of this Chapter Nine Investor to exchange out of the joint ownership property.

The Outside Investor

Let's now take a look at the gain realized by the Chapter Ten Investor. This Investor is an outside party who came into the joint ownership transaction purely for investment purposes. In the following chart, this outside Investor uses the joint ownership purchase price in calculating basis.

– BASIS AND GAIN CALCULATIONS –
OUTSIDE INVESTOR
To Compute Gain Realized Without Exchange

1. Relinquished property acquisition cost $ 79,200
2. Capital expenditures   0
3. Balance (Line 1 + Line 2) $ 79,200
4. Depreciation adjustment   ($ 15,120)
5. Adjusted basis on relinquished property $ 64,080
       (Line 3 minus Line 4)
6. Relinquished property sales price $107,910
7. Selling fix-up expenses   0
8. Selling closing expenses   ($ 6,475)
9. Adjusted sales price, $101,435
       relinquished property
       (Line 6 minus Line 7 minus Line 8)
10. Gain realized without exchange   **$ 37,355**
       (Line 9 minus Line 5)

Adjusted Basis

This third-party Investor did not *exchange* into the joint ownership property. Instead, he entered the joint ownership as a new investment. He claims 33% (his joint ownership interest) of the $240,000 joint ownership purchase price as his acquisition cost of $79,200 – Item One. This Investor made no improvements; Item Two is zero. Item Three – the total of Items One and Two – is $79,200. For Item Four, this Investor claimed depreciation over the joint ownership term in the amount of $15,120. Item Five is cost minus depreciation for an adjusted basis of $64,080.

Adjusted Sales Price

Adjusted sales price of the joint ownership property must next be determined. Item Six asks for sales price. For this Investor that is his 33% ownership interest of the $327,000 sales price – $107,910. Item Seven is selling fix-up expenses, which are zero. Item Eight is selling closing expenses. This Investor paid $6,475 as his 33% of the $19,620 sales commission. Item Nine is sales price less sale expenses, for an adjusted sales price of $101,435.

Gain

The Investor's gain is the difference between his adjusted basis ($64,080) and adjusted sales price ($101,435) – here, $37,355 as Item Ten. On a straight sale of this Investor's joint ownership property interest he will pay taxes on $37,355. Before deductions, at a 35% combined federal and state capital gains rate he'll pay about $13,000 in taxes.

Comparison

These two Investors agree on one thing – they will defer substantial taxes by exchanging out of their joint ownership properties. Collectively, these two Investors will save over $37,000 in taxes by using their tax deferral options.

Internal Revenue Code §1031 Requirements

Since exchanging out of the joint ownership transaction will result in substantial savings to the Investor, let's take a closer look at Internal Revenue Code §1031 as it applies to the joint ownership Investor. A copy of this code section is included in the *Appendix*. Under Internal Revenue Code §1031 no gain or loss is recognized if property held for use in trade or business or for investment is exchanged solely for property of a *like-kind* to be held for use in trade or business or for investment.

Investment Character of Property

To qualify for exchange treatment, the Investor must have held the joint ownership property as his investment or for use in his trade or business. He must also hold the replacement property for the same purpose. The joint ownership Investor satisfies the first requirement by holding the joint ownership property as his investment. The second requirement is also met when the Investor exchanges into *like-kind* property.

Like-Kind Status

Internal Revenue Code §1031 requires the replacement property to be *like-kind*. Like-kind distinguishes between real and personal property. Real property is like-kind to real property and personal property is like-kind to personal property. The Investor satisfies this requirement by exchanging his joint ownership real property for other real property.

Holding Period

The joint ownership property and the replacement property exchanged into should be held for at least one year each. If the exchange is between related persons, the holding period is two years. The joint ownership property easily qualifies since it is typically held for five or seven years. The Investor should hold the new property he exchanges into for at least a year – or two if exchanging with a related person – before he cashes out.

Partnerships Excluded

Partnership holdings have always been excluded from exchange treatment. However, under recently adopted regulations to Internal Revenue Code §1031, partnerships qualify for exchange treatment if a valid exemption from partnership tax treatment is made under Internal Revenue Code §761(a). The joint ownership Investor qualifies for exchange treatment by individually holding his interest as a tenant in common with the Occupier, not in partnership. Then the §761 exemption does not apply.

Simultaneous and Delayed Exchanges

The joint ownership Investor easily qualifies for exchange treatment under Internal Revenue Code §1031. He knows this and he has determined how much he'll pay if he cashes out in a straight sale. The Investor's next step is to analyze potential exchange properties. The Investor analyzes each exchange property under consideration to compare gain deferred on each.

Generally, there are two types of exchanges the Investor can make – simultaneous and delayed. A simultaneous exchange is done by swapping a deed for a deed at the same time. A delayed exchange occurs when there is a delay between giving up the deed on property relinquished and receiving a deed on replacement property. In a simultaneous exchange the exchange expenses are reasonable. A delayed exchange can be expensive, involving fees of an escrow agent, facilitator, or attorney. Thus, the exchange should be evaluated to determine whether the expense of exchanging is justified by its tax deferral.

Calculating §1031 Exchange Treatment

In calculating §1031 exchange treatment, remember one simple rule: tax is calculated on the lesser of gain realized or net boot received. To analyze the exchange, *gain realized* and *boot received* must be calculated.

Calculation

The exchange tax calculation which follows is based on the Investor profile in Chapter Ten. The worksheet computes *gain realized* in the first section and *boot received* in the second section. In the *straight sale* gain calculation earlier in this chapter, our Investor realized gain of $37,355 – if he opts to sell. Faced with a $13,000 tax bill, this Investor has decided to exchange out of the joint ownership. The Investor then evaluates exchange of his joint ownership interest for the following replacement property – rental property valued at $118,000 with a $71,200 existing loan.

First, this Investor prepares his exchange profile, then he calculates the gain he will recognize.

INVESTOR'S EXCHANGE PROFILE

	Relinquished Property	Replacement Property
1. Market value	$107,910	$118,000
2. Existing loans	$58,080	$ 71,200
3. New loans	– 0 –	– 0 –
4. Equity (#1 less #2 & #3)	$49,830	$ 46,800
5. Cash boot	– 0 –	$ 3,030
6. Other (boot) property	– 0 –	– 0 –
7. Loan proceeds	– 0 –	– 0 –
8. **Balance**	**$49,830**	**$49,830**

In calculating his exchange profile, the Investor determines the value of the relinquished property based on sale price and loan pay off prorated to his 33% ownership interest. $107,910 is 33% of the $327,000 sale price (less commission, which is not included in this rough comparison). $58,080 is 33% of the $176,000 loan pay off (a more finite calculation here would also reflect his percentage of the loan principal reduction reimbursed to the Occupier). Thus, this chart represents a rough general comparison for determining the exchange tax calculation with respect to boot received. Here, the Investor receives $3,030 cash boot.

EXCHANGE TAX CALCULATION
To Compute Gain Recognized in Exchange

REALIZED GAIN

1. Fair market value of replacement property	$118,000
2. Fair market value of boot replacement property	– 0 –
3. Liabilities on relinquished property	58,080
4. Cash received	3,030
5. Total	179,110
6. Adjusted basis of relinquished property	64,080
7. Adjusted basis of boot relinquished property	– 0 –
8. Liabilities on replacement property	71,200
9. Cash paid out	– 0 –
10. Total (Lines 6 + 7 + 8 + 9)	135,280
11. Gain/loss realized (Line 5 minus Line 10)	43,830

BOOT RECEIVED

12. Liabilities on relinquished property	$ 58,080
13. Liabilities on replacement property	71,200
14. Line 12 minus Line 13	– 0 –
15. Fair market value of boot relinquished property	– 0 –
16. Difference (Line 14 minus Line 15)	– 0 –
17. Cash received (offset by exchange expense)	1,030
18. Total (Line 16 + Line 17)	1,030
19. Cash paid out	– 0 –
20. Line 18 minus Line 19	1,030
21. Market value of boot replacement property	– 0 –
22. Total boot received (Line 20 + Line 21)	1,030

RECOGNIZED GAIN   **$ 1,030**
(the smaller of Line 11 and Line 22)

A note about forms – For use in analyzing your own exchange, we have included blank forms in the *Appendix*.

Gain Realized

Remember the simple rule for tax treatment in an exchange – tax is calculated on the lesser of gain realized or net boot received. This calculation's bottom line indicates a gain realized of $43,830 and boot received of $1030. The lesser of the two is $1030. This lucky Investor will be taxed on only $1030 if he exchanges with the replacement property described. Let's go through the chart on the preceding page step by step and see exactly how this Investor recognizes only $1030 of his $43,830 gain.

Item One requests the fair market value of the replacement property. In this transaction the Investor is receiving replacement property worth $118,000 – Item One. Item Two is fair market value of boot property received with the replacement property. The Investor is not receiving any personal property, such as furniture and furnishings worth – Item Two, therefore, is zero. Item Three calls for liabilities on the relinquished property. The joint ownership mortgage pay-off was $176,000; the Investor's portion of that pay-off was his 33%, for his mortgage liability of $58,080 – Item Three. Item Four calls for cash received by the Investor. The Investor nets a $3,030 cash residual as joint ownership proceeds not exchanged into the replacement property (see Exchange Profile, featured earlier in this chapter). Therefore Item Four is $3,030. Item Five adds Items One through Four, for a total of $179,110.

Item Six is the adjusted basis of the relinquished property. In performing basis and gain calculations earlier in this chapter we determined that this Investor's adjusted basis is $64,080. (See chart, page 237 – Basis and Gain Calculations.)

Item Seven is the adjusted basis of boot property transferred with the relinquished property – zero here, since this Investor is only transferring like-kind property in the exchange. Item Eight calls for liabilities on the replacement property. The replacement property is encumbered by a $71,200 loan, so Item Eight is $71,200. Item Nine is cash paid out by the Investor. In this transaction the Investor has paid no cash – so Item Nine is zero. Item Ten totals Items Six through Nine – here $135,280. Item 11 is Line Five ($179,110) minus Line 10 ($135,280) for a total gain realized in the exchange of $43,830. Thus Item 11 is $43,830 – the amount of gain the Investor realizes in this exchange. How much of this gain realized does the Investor actually recognize for tax purposes?

Generally *gain realized* is the same as *gain recognized* – and therefore taxed. In an exchange, however, this is often not the case. Here's that simple rule again – tax is calculated on the lesser of gain realized or net boot received. In order to determine how much of the $43,830 gain realized is recognized, the amount of boot received by the Investor must be calculated. Before calculating boot, let's take a look at the nature of boot and how much boot, if any, causes recognition of gain realized in this transaction.

Boot Received

In an exchange assets that do not qualify as tax-free are referred to as *boot*. Boot is any asset received that is not real property held for use in trade or business or for investment. Boot may be in the form of cash, notes, debt relief, or personal property. All boot received by the Investor must be analyzed to determine how much of the $43,830 realized gain will be recognized – and therefore taxed.

The exchange tax calculation performs that function, separately analyzing each item received and given in the exchange. Let's get back to the chart and see how it determines the amount of boot. Item 12 calls for liabilities on the relinquished property. We previously calculated the Investor's portion of the mortgage at $58,080. Item 13 calls for liabilities on the replacement property – here in the amount of $71,200. Item 14, Line 12 minus Line 13, is zero (negative numbers are not used). This process is called *netting mortgage boot.* Item 15 calls for fair market value of boot property associated with the relinquished property – here zero, since the relinquished joint ownership property did not involve any boot property. Item 16 offsets mortgage boot by personal property boot, for a difference of zero.

Item 17 is cash received by the Investor, less deductible exchange expenses. The Investor anticipates $2,000 in deductible exchange expenses. Offsetting the Investor's $3,030 cash received by $2,000 projected exchange expenses nets $1,030 for Item 17. Item 18 nets boot by adding the mortgage boot (here zero) and the $1,030 cash residual boot, for a total of $1,030. Item 19 is the amount of cash boot the Investor has paid out – zero. Item 20 nets boot at $1,030. Item 21 is market value of boot property received by the Investor, which is zero. And finally, Item 22 is total boot received – Line 20 plus Line 21 – which add up to $1,030.

Gain Recognized

Boot received is $1,030. Gain realized is $43,830. Once more, that simple rule: tax is calculated on the lesser of gain realized or net boot received. The lesser of these two amounts is $1,030. Therefore this Investor will recognize a taxable gain of only $1,030 if he exchanges into the rental property under consideration.

Before deductions, the Investor's tax, based on a 35% combined federal and state capital gains rate, is $360. This Investor could reduce his tax bill to zero if he exchanges into another property with net equity equal to his relinquished property. Here he has *exchanged down* in equity, and received $3,030 as cash left over from the joint ownership sale. Therefore he is taxed on these amounts ($3,030) less exchange expenses ($2,000) for a total of $1,030 – as items which do not qualify as continuation of his investment in the eyes of the Internal Revenue Service.

Comparison of Gain Recognition on Sale and Exchange

Now that he has performed his exchange analysis, the Investor can compare his tax profile on sale and on exchange to determine if exchanging is truly worthwhile.

This Investor has recognized an enormous tax break by exchanging. At sale he will pay $13,000 in taxes. If he exchanges, he will pay only $360. By exchanging he shelters over $12,640 in tax dollars. This method of sheltering profit is *deferral* of taxes, a tax bill the Investor must face if he ever terminates his investment. Of course, the Investor's best bet is to continue his investment indefinitely, exchanging into new properties as needed. If he needs cash, refinance would be his best move. In this manner, the savvy Investor is assured of the ultimate tax shelter – when he dies, his heirs will receive his investment portfolio and his deferred income tax liability will pass on with him.

Our taxing bureau has given us two valuable ways to shelter income through real estate ownership. As homeowners, we may continue our principal residence investment under Internal Revenue Code §1034. As investors, we may continue our real estate investments under Internal Revenue Code §1031. We are wise to take advantage of these tax deferral options.

Now that we have fully analyzed the tax benefits available to the Occupier and Investor, we will proceed to Chapter Thirteen – to explore some special circumstances in which joint ownership becomes a *strategy* during times of stress and change.

Chapter Thirteen

SOLUTIONS AT DIVORCE, FORECLOSURE, AND RELOCATION

You've learned how the joint ownership transaction works – from plan design to actual results. This chapter reveals the joint ownership itself as *strategy* – not only for our traditional Investor and Occupier, but in times of change and stress – at divorce, foreclosure, and relocation. Joint ownership can be the perfect solution – providing continuity for a family going through divorce, cash when an owner's property interest is threatened, and the way to buy when you're suddenly relocated. We'll see how joint ownership assists in stressful transitions like these.

*J*oint ownership is a valuable ticket to *acquire, sell, and retain* real estate. Throughout this book we've featured joint ownership as the ideal tool to buy or sell residential property – a buyer in need of a down payment teams up with an Investor. By joining in as Investor, a seller attracts buyers.

This chapter features joint ownership as a way to *retain* or *replace* property. So far, the joint ownerships in this book begin with a real estate purchase – but the joint ownership transaction can also be used as strategy. In times of stress and change, joint ownership can be used to *retain* property that might be lost. Two distress scenarios are especially suited to the joint ownership solution – impending foreclosure and possible loss of property by sale at divorce. Let's see how the properties in these scenarios are *salvaged* by joint ownerships.

But before that, another time of stress comes about with employee relocation. The solution to the relocated employee dilemma is to replace the property that's left behind.

The Relocated Employee

Joint ownership responds particularly well to employee relocation. In fact, the relocated employee finds joint owner- ship with his employer to be the ideal solution in his time of change. This time can be particularly stressful since the employee is relocated, but his house stays behind. How does he go about replacing his property if he moves to a location with much higher prices?

Employer-Assisted Joint Ownerships

Specialized federal loan packages are now available for the employer and employee who team up in a joint ownership. These programs, referred to as *Magnet Loans*, are described later in this chapter. First we'll explore an employer-employee joint ownership without the Magnet Loan program.

With the availability of joint ownership and special loan programs, employers are becoming Investors by offering the joint ownership incentive to long-term and relocating employees. Sometimes the employer's contract terminates the joint ownership if the employee leaves the job. In that event, one co-owner buys out the other or the property is sold. This provision limits the joint ownership incentive to the period of employment.

More employees are relocating to high priced areas for job reasons, assisted by their employer's agreement to jointly own property. Typically, this agreement begins with a preliminary commitment between employer and employee, listing the basic terms to be incorporated into their joint ownership. A sample preliminary commitment is included in Chapter Five, and a blank commitment is found in the *Appendix*.

A Sample Preliminary Commitment

Even if a property has yet to be found, the parties can define the parameters of their joint ownership in a preliminary commitment. In our sample, the purchase price is set at a maximum – let's say $225,000. The employer will be contributing $30,000 and receiving a 24% ownership interest. The employee pays $15,000 of the down payment and pays all closing costs. The agreement is for seven years. The employer and employee calculate the Investor's 24% interest by estimating annual appreciation at 5% and projecting Investor's annual return at 10.5%. The employee will occupy the property and pay all expenses. Internal Revenue Code §280A will be complied with, since the Employer-Investor will tax-defer his investment and claim his portion of depreciation.

In reliance on the preliminary commitment the employee sells his home, assured he will replace it with a comparable residence at his new destination. Confident that all gain will be rolled over into the new residence under Internal Revenue Code §1034, the employee does not have to budget for a tax bill.

Special Loan Packages

Loan packages identified as Magnet Loans are offered by "Fannie Mae" (Federal National Mortgage Association) specially designed for employers to assist employees with housing costs. Although our scenario features the relocated employee, Magnet Loan programs do not require relocation — only an employer-employee team.

Some of the plans offered require only a 5% down payment – 3% paid by the Employee-Occupier and the remaining 2% paid by the Employer-Investor. Compared with the standard 20% down payment, these low-capital packages are invaluable in getting the employee into a property. If the employee earns more than a certain income (presently 115% of the median income in the area), he must contribute the full 5% himself – a far cry from the 20% down payment required by conventional lenders.

Let's take a look at a sample joint ownership under one of the Magnet Loans. The property to be acquired is worth $200,000. The employee pays $6,000 as 3% of purchase price and the employer contributes $4,000 as his 2%. Based on a 5% annual appreciation rate and a 13% annual projected return to the employer, the ownership split would be 8% to the Employer-Investor and 92% to the employee. Given these employer-assisted loan plans and the joint ownership option, there is no reason why the long-term employee should have to resort to property rental. To obtain more information about these loan packages and lenders who offer them, contact your local office of the Federal National Mortgage Association.

Now that we have explored the use of joint ownership in times of employment relocation, let's move on to its uses in other stressful times of divorce and foreclosure. The joint ownership seems to fill the bill at these difficult times as well.

The Answer at Divorce

The couple at divorce often sell the family home and split the equity as part of settlement. Divorce transition, difficult enough, magnifies with sale of the home and relocation. This is especially true when children are involved.

Joint ownership at divorce can bridge the gap by preserving ownership of the family home. The wife and children move through the initial divorce phase in a far more comfortable way. The family unit stays intact in familiar surroundings amid supportive friends and family, decreasing adjustments accompanying divorce. Since it is often the wife who seeks to remain in the family home, our illustration designates the wife as joint ownership Occupier and the husband as the exiting spouse.

There are several ways to structure the joint ownership at divorce. The ex-spouse may be the Investor, or relatives and friends can take that role. The joint ownership structure provides immediate and long-term solutions that benefit both Occupiers and Investors. What's so right about it? The remaining spouse isn't asking a favor – she grants a valuable property interest to the potential co-owner with the prospect of substantial projected return.

Ex-Spouse As Investor

If the exiting spouse – in this example, the husband – becomes the Investor, his family home cashout is deferred for a number of years. This deferral works to his advantage. His potential return is much greater than if he cashed out and invested in the general marketplace. He preserves the equity in his hard-earned community property. Since cash in hand is often cash spent, especially in this early divorce period, deferring cashout becomes a wise choice. Moreover, the exiting spouse avoids regret over his family having to vacate the home. His decision to jointly own the property for the initial divorce phase solves these problems, and many others.

The form of ownership created by the joint ownership structure appeals to a divorced couple. The parties usually want to terminate all joint holdings. The joint ownership clearly divides and defines their interests, allowing them to hold title individually in differing percentages as tenants in common.

Outside Investors

If the exiting spouse rejects joint ownership, the occupying spouse should offer the joint ownership Investor role to relatives and friends. This role can be assumed by a single Investor or many. Most friends and family are more than willing to assist at divorce, and the promise of a valuable investment will pique their interest. Get a proposal together in line with the illustration below, study the information you've read in previous chapters, and make your pitch. You'll be surprised to find potential Investors delighted by the idea and impressed by your knowledge.

Whichever way has produced your Investor, here's how the joint ownership can be structured. In the sample below, the Investor is the ex-spouse and limited refinance provides him with all cash he needs right now. He looks to the joint ownership for the rest. If your joint ownership does not require immediate cash to the ex-spouse, delete the refinance feature. If your joint ownership brings in outside Investors and cashes out the ex-spouse, replace Investor funds with the amount required to cash out the spouse.

An Appraisal

First, have the property appraised or have your friendly real estate agent perform a competitive market analysis. The property must be valued before the joint ownership structure can be designed. If an appraisal has already been performed in the divorce settlement process, this step can be omitted.

Should the Property Be Refinanced?

This question is often asked. Typically, the occupying spouse does not want to make higher payments — especially when just returning to the job market. But the exiting spouse may need ready cash that can only be generated by refinance. The parties will have to work out these needs, usually with the assistance of the attorney preparing the Joint Ownership Agreement. One solution is to have the exiting spouse make the increased portion of the loan payment. He claims a tax deduction for the portion he makes and gets credit for a portion at the end of the joint ownership.

A Sample Situation

Our couple owns a family home with a value of $250,000. The existing loan is $150,000, leaving $100,000 in equity. Equity at divorce has been determined – $40,000 to husband and $60,000 to wife. The parties have joint custody of their two children, who will live with their mother full time with visitation by their father. The wife has been working part-time for the past few years and is now returning full time to the work place. The parties could refinance the property to cash out the husband for his $40,000. Often, the wife lacks credit history to qualify for a loan and needs her ex-husband to remain on the loan. In addition, the wife now faces a mortgage payment alone. A refinance would not only assign her the entire mortgage payment, but increase it as well. Thus, a refinance which completely cashes out the husband does not work. On carefully assessing their positions and requirements, this husband tallied his immediate cash requirements over the next five years and found that he needs only $15,000 of his ownership interest now, deferring the remainder for five years. Joint ownership and a partial refinance became their answer. The following chart shows how their transaction is structured.

Their Structure

Joint ownership value	$250,000
Investor retained equity	$22,500
Occupier retained equity	$57,500
Refinance	$170,000
Term	5 years
Assumed appreciation rate	4%
Projected annual Investor return	11%
Ownership split	77% Occupier / 23% Investor
Loan payments on existing 10.5% $150,000 loan	$1,372
Loan payments on new 8.5% $170,000 loan	$1,307

At Divorce: Joint Ownership Structure

Transaction Summary: In order to meet the husband's need for $15,000 cash the co-owners obtained a refinance at $170,000, paying off their $150,000 loan and providing $15,000 cash and $5,000 for loan origination fees. The co-owners share the $5,000 loan origination fees, reflected by a $2,500 reduction in their retained equity. The Husband-Investor began with $40,000 equity, reduced by $15,000 loan proceeds and $2,500 as his half of the loan origination fees, leaving him with $22,500 in retained equity. The Wife-Occupier began the joint ownership with $60,000 of equity, reduced by $2500 as her half of the loan origination fees, leaving her with $57,500 in retained equity. Their decision to share equally in the loan origination fees was fair, in view of the mutual benefits they will enjoy from continued ownership.

The New Loan Payment

The old loan carried a 10.5% interest rate. The new loan bears an 8.5% rate. Because of the reduced interest rate, refinance actually decreases the loan payment while increasing the loan amount. These parties have agreed that the Occupier will continue to make loan payments without any contribution by the Investor. If interest rates are lower for your refinance, your joint ownership result will be similar.

If payment increases, the parties should consider payment of the increase by the Investor, who will then claim the interest deduction associated with that payment – along with a joint ownership credit for about 15% of total payments made. His credit will be added to his joint ownership retained equity, to be paid before appreciation is shared.

Assumptions and Projections

These parties decided on 4% as an assumed annual appreciation rate over their 5-year holding period. The Investor was assigned an 11% annual projected rate of return on his retained equity. In this situation, since it is so important to the Occupier to retain the property, 11% is projected as an inducement to the Investor. The Investor at divorce, experiencing its consequences emotionally and financially, receives some relief from the security of his joint ownership projections. Based on these assumptions and projections, an ownership split of 77% to Occupier and 23% to Investor is created.

What Happens at Term?

When the joint ownership expires at five years, the standard options apply – the Occupier is given the first buyout option, followed by the Investor, and then sale of the property. Refinance is typically their method of buying out one another. The major difference between the standard joint ownership and the divorce-related agreement is payment of sale costs. In the divorce agreement, the Occupier usually agrees to bear all sale expenses. The reason – it's purely an inducement to the Investor. In this manner, the Investor gets the same return whether the Occupier keeps the property or sells it. The following charts depict their buyout and sale options at term.

Investor's Benefits

The joint ownership has successfully served immediate and long-term needs of the Occupier. It has also provided the following wide range of benefits to the Investor:

· Based on a 4% assumed appreciation rate, he cashes out with $35,000.
· He receives an 11% annual return – the joint ownership yields the same return as if he had received payment on his retained equity at 11% each year.
· He has been able to assist his family in a very important way, while making a hearty profit.
· Since he has continued his interest in the property as an investment, he can defer tax on his profit if he exchanges out.

Buyout at Term

Appraisal - 4% appreciation	$304,000
Loan pay-off	- 162,000
Occupier retained equity	- 57,500
Investor retained equity	- 22,500
Less loan principal reduction	- 8,000
Net equity	54,000
Occupier interest	x .77
Occupier share of equity	41,580
Plus Occ. retained equity/loan reduction	65,500
Occupier buyout	**$107,080**
Net equity (repeated from above)	54,000
Investor interest	x .23
Investor share of equity	12,420
Plus Investor retained equity	22,500
Investor buyout	**$ 34,920**

Buyout at Term

Sale at Term

Investor proceeds	$34,920
Occupier proceeds	$88,840

Sale at Term (Abbreviated)

Detail: The Occupier buys out the Investor for $34,920, whereas the Investor buys her out at $107,080. The Occupier will require a 65% refinance to buy out the Investor. ($197,600 in loan proceeds minus

$162,000 loan pay-off leaves $35,600 proceeds.) If they sell at term, the $20,600 commission is solely paid by the Occupier, leaving the Investor with the same return he received at buyout and Occupier with about $18,000 less than at buyout. In each situation the goal has been reached: one spouse can continue to occupy the house without penalizing the other.

A Happy Solution at Divorce

Despite the lack of positive results flowing from divorce, the joint ownership uniquely meets the following important emotional and financial needs of the divorced couple:

· The spouse occupying the home pools Investor funds from willing family and friends, projecting a hardy return.
· The ex-husband makes a contribution to his family by deferring full pay-off – projecting an excellent profit in the bargain.
· The wife maintains family stability and establishes her own credit standing by paying on the loan over the next five years.
· The children have not been uprooted from their important friendships and school.
· The parties achieve the separation they require by holding title as tenants in common with their own individual percentage interests.
· Exclusive occupancy and all obligations by the Occupier reinforce their separate status.
· At term the property's appreciation allows the Occupying spouse to cash out the Investor through refinance.
· They are able to separately defer tax on their profits.

Now that joint ownership has been able to salvage the divorced couple's home, let's see how the joint ownership structure can rescue the owner faced with foreclosure.

The Owner Facing Foreclosure

Foreclosure visits itself upon the weary owner unable to make his payments. The defaulting owner, amidst financial straits, is often unable to see solutions to his predicament. Joint ownership could be his answer.

The owner faced with foreclosure frequently resorts to marketing his property for sale with little time to pull in a qualified buyer. By offering a joint ownership sale – as an Investor *or* an Occupier – he creates a panorama of buyers. He should also market a joint ownership sale of his property to peers and friends. He has a valuable interest to sell – even more valuable because of the joint ownership feature. Potential Occupiers/Investors will line up asking, "Is it really true that I don't need the down payment?"

Most property owners aren't aware they can sell interests in their property – much the same as corporations sell shares of stock. To by-pass securities regulations, however, the number of Investors should not exceed four. In return for monetary contributions, corporations give shares with stock certificates evidencing ownership. Property owners have a far more valuable commodity to sell – made more valuable by the non-movable permanent nature of real estate. The joint ownership purchaser, whether Investor or Occupier, receives far more than a mere certificate for his investment – he receives an ownership interest evidenced directly on title. As Investor he also receives a Deed of Trust/Mortgage which further secures his investment. As Occupier he receives the right to exclusively occupy the property.

Bringing in an Investor

The owner in foreclosure can structure his joint ownership in several ways. He can obtain just enough money from his new co-owner to cure his default and reinstate the mortgage. The new co-owner would be positioned on title and on the loan as Investor, receiving his return when the joint ownership expires. Because he has fallen behind in payments, it may be difficult for the owner in foreclosure to find a joint ownership Investor – but if the events leading up to foreclosure were the result of an isolated incident, it will encourage Investor participation.

Vacating the Property for an Occupier

The owner in foreclosure often vacates his property to solve the problem. He assumes the role of Seller-turned-Investor. He waives the down payment beyond the amount he needs to reinstate the mortgage. For example, if he is $5,000 in default, he will require a co-owner's cash contribution in that amount. If a sale commission is involved, he will require that amount to be advanced by the entering co-owner. His immediate cash needs will be converted into down payment funds, to be reimbursed to the new co-owner at term of the joint ownership. The smaller his cash requirements, the larger his co-owner market becomes.

Assumption or Refinance?

Either the Seller-turned-Investor and his new Occupier will refinance the property, or the Occupier will assume the existing loan. The lender does not want to take the property back, and will usually consent to the new co-owner's assumption of the loan with the existing borrower.

In the refinance process these co-owners will encounter difficulty due to default status on the existing loan, but a credit-worthy Occupier can surmount the lender's objections. Adding a co-owner with good credit to a dismal loan package sometimes works wonders.

The owner in foreclosure can even cash out with enough money to buy another property. If his mortgage pay-off is less than 80% of value and he structures the joint ownership right, he can cash out for the difference between refinance proceeds and pay off of his existing loan.

A Sample Situation

For example, the property is worth $300,000, loan pay-off is $225,000 and he's in default for $5,000. He offers a joint ownership for $20,000 cash down and retains $55,000 as his joint ownership contribution. Let's take a look at how this savvy owner in foreclosure structures his deal. See the following charts.

Joint Ownership Price	$300,000
Investor retained equity	$55,000
Occupier contribution	$20,000
Existing loan	$225,000
Term	5 years
Assumed appreciation rate	4%
Projected Investor return	11%
Ownership split	53% Occupier / 47% Investor

At Foreclosure: Joint Ownership Structure

Detail: The ownership split he offers is 53% to the Occupier, reserving 47% for himself. This split was calculated assuming 4% annual appreciation and an 11% projected rate of return to himself on the $55,000 retained equity.

Five-Year Buyout

Appraisal - 4% appreciation	$365,000
Loan pay-off	- 214,000
Investor retained equity	- 55,000
Occupier initial contribution	- 20,000
Less loan principal reduction	- 11,000
Net equity	65,000
Occupier interest	x .53
Occupier share of equity	34,450
Plus Occupier initial contribution	20,000
Plus Occupier loan reduction	11,000
Occupier buyout	**$ 65,450**
Net equity (recap)	$ 65,000
Investor interest	x .47
Investor share of equity	30,550
Plus Investor retained equity	55,000
Investor buyout	**$ 85,550**

At Foreclosure: Five-Year Buyout

Detail: This Owner-turned-Investor has retained a 47% interest in the property and retained equity of $55,000. On buyout he gets another $30,550, cashing him out of his property for $85,550. Although not shown on this chart, if the Occupier gets an 80% refinance he receives $78,000 in proceeds. By adding $7,500 or asking the Investor to take a note, he'll completely cash out his co-owner.

The Key at Foreclosure

This Investor facing foreclosure has literally turned a distressed situation into a profitable investment. He has received $85,550 in equity and preserved his credit status – an excellent solution under any circumstance. When compared with the consequences at foreclosure – little or no cash, loss of the property and a severely damaged credit rating – joint ownership has positioned the owner-in-foreclosure with an excellent investment. As long as he acts quickly and structures his deal right, the average owner in foreclosure can turn dire straits into profit that few reap, even under the best of circumstances.

The Occupier hasn't done so badly himself. He's realized a profit of $45,450 – and don't forget the substantial tax deductions of about $80,000 he's taken over the past five years. Now, at refinance he's cashing out the Investor and becoming a sole owner.

In sum, joint ownership can be the key to prosperity for the owner in foreclosure. He should package his joint ownership as soon as possible, long before the foreclosure process begins. He should utilize every possible marketing device, from classified advertising to hiring a real estate agent. He should establish the parameters of his joint ownership early on. As with anything else, a well-packaged plan has a marketability of its own.

In most states, special laws protect the seller in foreclosure from unfair advantage. These laws call for specific agreement provisions and cancellation periods, among other things. Because of these laws, it is best to check with your local real estate attorney before entering into a transaction with an owner in foreclosure.

Now that we've reviewed joint ownership as strategy for distress situations, let's look at an exciting new technique that co-owners have been blending with their joint ownerships – the living trust. Joint ownership purchasers have become quite sophisticated, and now they're taking title in the name of their living trust. Chapter Fourteen explores this popular alternative to a will and how it blends successfully into the joint ownership transaction.

YOUR LIVING TRUST AS A TOOL

You can't take it with you – but you can minimize the stress and cost of passing on your legacy. How? By creating a *living trust*. What is a living trust? How does it take part in a joint ownership? What are its advantages – disadvantages? How will it ease the burdens of your heirs? Is it true that you can gift $10,000 a year tax free? Can your living trust gift for you? By popular demand, we show you how to jointly own property with your own living trust.

$\mathscr{A}$s society becomes increasingly more sophisticated and technologically advances, individual asset portfolios
do the same. Joint ownership co-owners in increasing numbers
have living trusts – and hold title to property in their names.
We devote this chapter to the living trust – an estate planning
option available to you that works especially well with a joint
ownership.

This chapter answers these and other questions: What
is a living trust? Can you hold title to your joint ownership
interest with your living trust? How is this done? Does your
living trust receive tax benefits of the joint ownership Investor
or Occupier?

What Is a Living Trust?

The living trust – recognized in all 50 states – is
basically a will that does not require probate through the court
system. The living trust makes the same provisions as a will,
but takes the process a step further. Its trustees actually transfer their assets, along with instructions for distribution, into
the living trust during their lifetime. Hence, its name.

How Is It Different from Probating a Will?

Probate is the costly, time-consuming court process that
legally transfers an inheritance to heirs. It bridges the gap
between death and distribution. The court gathers the decedent's assets, puts them in a pot called "the estate" and values
and distributes them to the heirs according to the decedent's
will. The probate court acts as temporary public guardian – a
chaperone for the estate's executors, attorneys and referees.

The living trust, on the other hand, is perpetual. It has a life of its own which continues after the death of its owners. The living trust does not require probate court orders to transfer and distribute its assets. Instead, the trustee named in the trust carries out all transfers and distributions. Thus, the living trust continues on with its own appointed trustee in charge.

Emotional Advantages of the Living Trust

Time frames and structures of probate courts are rigidly cast, and sometimes run counter to the heirs' emotional needs. For example, estate assets cannot be transferred by the court for an initial six month period. Then transfer occurs rapidly and completely, regardless of the wishes of the heirs. At a time when gentle, hand-tailored transition is most needed, the impersonal probate process marches on.

The living trust provides far more flexibility to its beneficiaries. Heirs to a living trust have more freedom to carry out the trust provisions at their own pace – whether it be sooner or later. With the assistance of the trustee, heirs can control timing of asset transition. Immediate transfer to a beneficiary, as well as delayed transfer, occur as necessary. Hence, the living trust brings a human element to the delivery of an inheritance to its heirs.

Economic Advantages of the Living Trust

Fees of attorneys, probate appraisers and personal representatives can be quite high – and can take an unnecessary bite out of your legacy. These fees are a necessary part and expense of administering an estate through the probate process.

The well-detailed living trust administers your legacy-to-be, carrying out these important functions without exorbitant administration fees. However, reasonable compensation for your chosen trustee is very important. Your trustee provides a central role as messenger of your legacy, and should be compensated fairly for this service. As long as the living trust is well-detailed, the trustee's steps are far less complicated and time-consuming than those involved in probate.

Whether your wishes are carried out by a living trust or a will by probate, inheritance taxes are always payable. With a will, the probate estate pays taxes before the assets pass to the heirs. With a living trust, the heirs claim inheritance and pay tax on their own tax returns. The tax is the same with both methods of gifting.

Disadvantages of a Living Trust

The only disadvantage of a living trust arises from the appointment of a less than honest trustee. This possibility – a dishonest trustee – is the one scenario which makes court probate, with its scrutiny and expense, worthwhile. Your trustee is the steward of your fortune. As long as the trust clearly specifies gifts and your trustee's instructions, assets cannot be manipulated to anyone's benefit.

Appointment of an honest and able trustee is vital in selecting a living trust over a will. Your choice of trustee is as important as your choice of attorney to draft the living trust. These two ingredients – a good living trust and an able trustee – create a successful living trust estate plan.

Joint Ownership with a Living Trust

Now that living trusts have come into their own, many people acquire assets in trust. Can you joint ownership with your living trust? Yes, you can. Always think of your living trust as *you*. If you can do it, your living trust can do it. The trust can acquire your personal residence – and it can roll out of it. The trust can acquire investment property and it can exchange out of it. Similarly, your trust can acquire a joint ownership interest in property.

Joint Ownership Title with a Living Trust

Your joint ownership title is taken in the name of your living trust. For example, the Investors to the Joint Ownership Agreement in the *Appendix* hold title as "Harold Investor and Ingrid Investor, husband and wife, as community property, as to an undivided 55% interest." If Harold and Ingrid Investor have a living trust, title should read as follows: "Harold Investor and Ingrid Investor, Trustees of The Investor Family Trust dated _____, as to an undivided 55% interest."

When to Take Title in the Name of the Living Trust

If your trust is established when purchasing the property, title should be taken in the name of the trust. You are the trust for all purposes – including tax, liability and ownership. If you establish your trust after taking title, follow the simple instructions under *Transfers to Your Living Trust*.

A Perfect Program for Relatives

Many caring parents and relatives find joint ownership with their living trust the perfect way to help their children acquire a first property – and will their joint ownership interest to the youngsters at the same time. It's the perfect blend of tax benefits to the living Investor relatives, and a gift to their Occupier children if the Investors pass on before the joint ownership term is over.

How do they create this perfect blend? The relatives take title as the joint ownership Investor – in the name of their living trust. The living trust leaves the Investors' interest in the joint ownership to the Occupiers. During the joint ownership the Investor relatives earn depreciation deductions and the opportunity to exchange tax-free out of the property. If the Investors pass away during the joint ownership term, their interest in the property automatically goes to the Occupiers under the living trust as long as the living trust so designates.

Gifting $10,000 of Equity Per Year

Each taxpayer is entitled to gift $10,000 per year to as many different people as desired without any tax consequence. Each gift not exceeding $10,000 annually is entirely tax free to both parties. There is no reporting requirement and the gift does not come off your $600,000 after death exemption. Thus, annual gifting to relatives can be the ideal way to reduce the size of your estate for tax purposes and assist loved ones during your lifetime. Gifting is discussed more in Chapter 15.

Within the joint ownership structure, the relative desiring to gift to the Occupier relative during the joint ownership term will include a yearly gifting provision in the agreement. The provision will provide that the Investor gifts $10,000 of equity to the occupier each year. Married relatives can each gift $10,000; and if the Occupiers are more than one, each Investor relative can gift $10,000 to each per year, achieving a $40,000 gift annually from the married Investors to the married Occupiers. They can also structure their gift for less than $10,000, to skip a year, or any other variation. To be tax-free, the only requirement that must be met is that each individual cannot give more than $10,000 in value to any other individual in a year.

This method of gifting is ideal for the person whose estate exceeds the lifetime exemption amount. He gifts to his loved ones tax-free and reduces the size of his estate – which would have been subject to hefty estate taxes when he died. Of course, the Investor relative does not have to gift; it is merely an option to consider in the event that gifting suits your profile. The joint ownership form with Gifting by Investor to Occupier may be ordered through the Order Form at the end of the book.

With this combination of joint ownership and living trust – whether or not during lifetime gifting is involved – the Investors achieve an excellent result. They have enabled their young relatives to buy a home. They have secured their own contribution with an interest in the home. They have created valuable tax deductions. And, finally, they have willed away their interest to their Occupier heirs in the event that the unforeseen occurs during the joint ownership.

The end result: the Investors have acquired a property and willed it away all in one step – weaving in some valuable tax benefits for themselves in the bargain. It's the perfect program.

Dealing with Lenders

Some lenders who have not updated their lending practices are unwilling to lend to living trusts. If you come up against this practice, reasoning with the lender may go a long way – or it may not. But it can't hurt.

Lending practices are fairly rigid. Traditional lending organizations have delayed entry of the living trust into their practice manuals. It will be accepted, but it takes a long time to change lending practices.

Thus, some lenders object to a living trust as borrower because of insufficient guidelines. Beyond that, a skittish lender may cite its policy against lending to "fictitious entities." These lenders have had bad experiences lending to entities that are actually fronts for fraud. The lender may view the trust as a separate entity similar to a corporation. But this assumption is wrong.

In truth, the trust is *not* a separate entity. You and your living trust are synonymous for all purposes – especially liability. The Internal Revenue Service views you and your living trust as one and the same – just as they do a sole proprietorship and its proprietor. Your living trust's assets and liabilities are included on your own income tax return. In spite of this recognition by the IRS, the living trust remains outside the guidelines of many lenders – and they may view this unknown entity with suspicion – akin to a corporation.

The lender solves its problem with the corporation by obtaining personal guarantees from the principals. You can help the lender solve its problem by offering a personal guarantee. It's really an inconsequential step, since you are already liable for any debt incurred by your trust. But it may be the lender's solution. Tell them you understand their hesitation and you would be happy to personally sign on their loan in your individual capacity, or give them a separate personal guarantee. This should be all they need.

If your lender stands firm in its objection, you will have to take title in your name individually. But after escrow closes, you will deed your interest over to your living trust. This is an extra step, but may be necessary for your trust to take title in its name.

You may wonder, won't the lender call my loan under the due-on-sale provision if I do this? No, they won't. Transferring the property into your living trust will not trigger the lender's right to call your loan under its due-on-sale clause. Although most mortgages allow the lender to demand loan pay-off if you transfer your interest in the property, transferring title into your living trust is a specific exception.

Transfers to Your Living Trust

If you create your living trust *after* you acquire a property, merely transfer the property – or the interest you hold – from yourself to the living trust. How is this done? You sign a Trust Transfer Deed (a Grant Deed will do if you can't locate this form) from you individually to your living trust, and have it notarized.

Since this procedure is technically a *change of ownership*, most county recorders require that a Change of Ownership report be filled out at the time of transfer. This report is for use by the local tax assessor to assess transfer and property taxes. However, transfer of real property to your living trust is an exempt transfer. You only need state on the Change of Ownership form that the transfer is solely for purposes of transferring the property into your trust.

The Memorandum of Joint Ownership Agreement should also be revised to reflect this title change. The deed and new memorandum are recorded to give notice on the public record that title is held in the name of your trust. A one-page addendum to the Joint Ownership Agreement should also be prepared naming the trust instead of the individuals. This simple step requires no notarization or recording. It's just a formality. These are the basic transfers that should flow through to your living trust. Depending on your status as Investor or Occupier, a few more steps may be taken for completeness.

Investor Transfer Documents

If you are the Investor and your package included a Joint Ownership Note and Deed of Trust/Mortgage from the Occupier, those documents should also be transferred to the living trust. The individual Investor formally *assigns* his Joint Ownership Note and Deed of Trust/Mortgage to his living trust by executing two documents – Assignment of Note and Assignment of Deed of Trust/Mortgage. These assignment documents do not require the Occupier's signature – only that of the Investor. Upon assignment of these documents, any foreclosure process will properly commence in the name of the living trust. Remember, these changes are in addition to the new Deed and Memorandum of Joint Ownership Agreement.

Occupier Transfer Documents

The Joint Ownership Agreement states that the Occupier will not transfer his interest without the Investor's consent. Thus, the Occupier must obtain the Investor's consent before transferring his joint ownership interest to his living trust.

The Investor's consent to Occupier trust transfer should be conditioned upon the Occupier signing a new Joint Ownership Note and Deed of Trust/Mortgage in the name of his living trust – and paying the cost of preparing and recording those documents. Other than these conditions, the Investor has no reason to object to Occupier transfer to a living trust.

Upon obtaining Investor consent, the Occupier follows the same process with the Deed and Memorandum of Joint Ownership Agreement as the Investor did when his living trust was established. In addition, a new Joint Ownership Note and Deed of Trust/Mortgage should be prepared naming the Occupier's living trust as the obligated party. This change isn't mandatory, but it will best protect the Investor's interest.

Tax Benefits Flow Through the Living Trust

Your tax deductions do not change when you place your assets in a living trust. The living trust is transparent as far as income and deductions are concerned — they all go to you. With the living trust you continue to file your Form 1040 Individual Income Tax Return and record all trust income and deductions on that form and its supporting schedules.

Investor Tax Benefits Flow Through

Thus, the joint ownership Investor who has taken title in the name of his living trust reports income from the Occupier and takes depreciation and other deductions on Individual Form 1040. He also exchanges out of his investment property reporting the exchange information on Form 4797, just as he would have before establishing the living trust.

Occupier Tax Benefits Flow Through

The same is true for the Occupier's tax benefits when he holds title in the name of his living trust. The mortgage interest and property tax deductions are taken directly on Individual Form 1040. When his joint ownership is over he rolls over into another property and reports that transaction on Form 2119, just as he would have before he set up his living trust.

Long-Term Tax Benefits Flow Through

Along with mortgage interest, depreciation and other ordinary joint ownership tax benefits, your IRC §1034 principal residence roll over and IRC §1031 investment property exchange benefits flow to the trust and back to you. Your 55 and over once-in-a-lifetime $125,000 exemption also flows to the trust and back to you.

Similarly, you can file a homestead exemption on property placed in the name of your trust. So don't be concerned. Since you and your trust are considered one and the same by the powers that be, your tax benefits are preserved with the creation of your living trust.

You Can Have the Best of Both Worlds

It is true, you can have the best of both worlds – joint ownership and your living trust. You can purchase an interest in a property and will it away with one stroke of the pen. And in that perfect process, you've established and preserved all those fabulous joint ownership tax deductions and exemptions for yourself. For your heirs, you've eased the burdens of a difficult time which is, we hope, in the far, far distant future.

Now that we've looked at the living trust as a creative tool to be combined with a joint ownership, let's look at other powerful applications as cutting edge strategies. In Chapter Fifteen we'll examine alternatives to a joint ownership – *seller financing, lease option and loan assumption* – and introduce the *Joint Ownership Lease Option*, a new technique developed especially for this book.

Chapter Fifteen

OTHER CUTTING EDGE STRATEGIES

Realizing that one way does not work for all, in this chapter we present a full array of powerful solutions for the down payment crunch – through sole ownership. The traditional formula – *buyer puts up 20% and lender funds 80%* – has monopolized the market for too long. It's outdated. Modern times require modern solutions. This chapter presents other reliable structures that respond to the market and solve the down payment/loan qualification dilemma now faced by our qualified buyers. Here, we present the lease option, joint ownership lease option, seller financing, wrap around loans, loan assumption and many other solutions to provide greater access to home ownership.

$\mathscr{R}$eal estate is a valuable commodity made readily accessible through easily obtained loans and vigorous marketing. Its permanent and fixed attributes symbolize its value. The amount of land covering this earth was defined a long time ago. There will never be more, and perhaps there will be less. The only true variable is the extent of its development.

Residential real estate is even more valuable than commercial property because of its high demand – a house is one of the top five dreams on every American's wish list, usually as Number Uno. We are discovering more ways to realize the American dream, joint ownership among them. We predict that shared purchases will become more popular during this decade, giving the joint ownership concept increasing influence on our lives.

In this chapter we present more team purchase strategies and a handful of other approaches to solve both down payment and loan dilemmas. There are many ways to buy and sell, but even our more experienced real estate consumers just don't have the hands-on experience to implement these reliable workable methods. With this information, the agreements we've developed, and an attorney-accountant consultation, you will have the resources to move your transaction past the roadblocks currently in your way.

A Wide Variety of Systems Work

Real estate's intrinsic value also lies in the ease with which it can be encumbered and transferred. Recognizing this, society has developed swift and simple systems by which property can be bought, sold, divided, used as security for cash loans, or to purchase more property. Along with these systems, a wide range of financing procedures has evolved to easily buy

and sell property. Joint ownership and other cooperative programs fit particularly well into our existing system.

The housing market has traditionally relied on the
formula where *bank lends 80% to buyer; buyer puts 20% down.*
This structure has monopolized the housing market for decades. In modern times, to respond to skyrocketing home
prices followed by recessionary times, new home buying
structures are needed. In this chapter we present a platter of
other proven solutions for the traditional purchase. These
methods have remained the exception, rather than the rule –
not because they don't work. They do work, and very well.
Very simply, they are not fully understood.

The Lease Option

A lease option is a contract where an owner leases his
property, granting the tenant an exclusive right to buy it
within a certain time at a set price. For example, a party
referred to as the "Occupier" wants to buy his landlord's
house, but doesn't have the 20% down payment. He will offer
to buy the property at a specified price, usually one to three
years down the line, continuing to lease the property in the
interim. His offer is backed by a non-refundable option
deposit – which increases monthly as a portion of each lease
payment goes into the option fund. If the Occupier exercises
his option, the accumulated option funds are applied. If not,
he loses them to the owner.

Example: Randy and Renee Renter want to buy a home but just
don't have the down payment cash yet. They have found the house
they want to purchase, but it will take them another few years to
save up enough cash to buy. They make an offer to lease option the
property. They offer $184,000 as the option price to be exercised in
three years, which they believe is about $5,000 above fair market

value, a lease option deposit of $7360 as 4% of the purchase price, rent of $850.00 per month with $250.00 representing 30% credited toward the option funds. In three years they will have accumulated option credit of $9,000 for the option portion of their monthly payments. Added to the $7360 paid up front, they will have a fund of $16,360 to put toward the 20% down payment of $36,800 they'll need. They anticipated that need and each month they put $600 in a savings account to meet the rest of the option down payment. (See our example under *Joint Ownership Lease Option* for how they handled this without the savings account.)

The cash requirements of the lease option are so low that this structure rivals joint ownership as a means to buy property with little capital. It should be considered as an option by the joint ownership participant – whether a cash-poor first-time buyer or a distressed seller. The lease option may be a better choice for a seller who can't wait out the customary five-year joint ownership period to completely cash out. And for potential buyers who can't qualify for a loan now, a lease option may be the only choice. During the lease term, the buyers can clean up their credit to qualify for the loan they'll need when option exercise time arrives.

Its Cash Requirements

What are the figures involved in the lease option? The non-refundable option deposit can range anywhere from 2% to 7% of the option purchase price. Rent usually approximates or exceeds fair market value. Typically, 25% to 35% of rent is applied to the option deposit.

The specific terms under which the option is to be exercised must be clearly detailed – especially since the intended buyer loses the option deposit if the option goes unexercised. For instance, as part of the option the seller may be required to finance 10% of the purchase price, the option deposit applied to the other 10%, and the balance of 80% financed by the lender. These terms must be clearly stated in the option – so that years later, the Occupier's 10% deposit enables him to exercise his option without question.

Be Creative with Your Terms

Since the lease option is setting up a purchase relatively far in advance, more creative terms can be established. For instance, a seller may not want to finance the loan now, but if he has a few years to plan for it, he may be far more willing to do so. If you feel you won't be able to qualify for the loan or you don't want to pay the high fees associated with obtaining it, structure your lease option offer so that the seller finances the loan. In this scenario, the lease option proceeds as it did above, but at term the seller takes a note and receives monthly payments from you in the position of lender, instead of landlord. When the option is exercised, the seller signs the property over to you, and you sign a Note and Deed of Trust/Mortgage for the purchase price less the option funds he has received – and any additional funds required to meet the down payment. Your seller may even agree to fund 90% of the purchase price. Of course, for a lease option with seller financing, you will want to locate a seller who has cashed out of the property or has a very small loan on it. See our Order Form for sample documents you will need.

Protect Yourself

As soon as the Option Agreement is signed, record it on the property. Take it to the Recorder's Office in the county where the property is located and instruct them to record it. The Option Agreement will give any potential lender or buyer notice that you have a claim to the property. This will protect you in the event that your optionor *forgets* that he has made an agreement with you. When times of financial distress suddenly hit, people sometimes do the unscrupulous and unexpected. In my law practice I have seen the nicest people perform fraudulent acts when faced with stressful situations. Recording your Option Agreement gives you the security you need in every sense of the word.

Tax Benefits: Joint Ownership Wins Over Lease Option

What are the primary differences between the joint ownership and lease option, and why would someone choose one over the other? The cash requirements are substantially the same, with the Occupier depositing about 5% of the purchase price. The joint ownership Occupier makes all payments, while the lease option Occupier makes lease payments approximating monthly expenses. Thus, the monthly expenses are about the same.

The big difference lies in the Occupier's ability to qualify for the loan. The Occupier unable to qualify for a loan selects the lease option over the joint ownership. During the lease option period the Occupier improves his credit profile for lender approval at exercise of the option.

Another big difference lies in the Occupiers' tax deductions – or lack of them. In the joint ownership, the Occupier immediately receives his full spectrum of ownership tax benefits because he is on title. With the lease option he must wait until he exercises his option to go on title – thus delaying his tax benefits. For the lease period the Occupier receives no tax benefits, while the joint ownership co-owner claims all. This is a big tax loss for the lease optionee, since he is still being treated as a renter for tax purposes. While the lease option results in no tax shelter for the Occupier, he is building up his home buying fund – a real financial plus when compared with the renter.

Don't Lose Your Option Deposits

The Occupier should carefully evaluate the lease option to ensure that he will be able to exercise it at term. He should also review his credit profile with his friendly banker – and assure himself that he will be able to qualify for the loan he will need to exercise the option. Otherwise, he'll be throwing valuable money at an option he can't exercise. A better idea would be to contribute his hard earned money to a charity – at least he'd get a tax deduction and personal reward in return.

One way to hedge against this eventuality is to clearly provide for *assignment* in the lease-option agreement. This provision will state that the Option Agreement can be assigned to someone of your choosing, along with all option proceeds. With this provision, as long as it is worded correctly, you will have the best chance to either exercise your option or, if you can't, to recoup your option funds. Your solution will be to locate someone to whom you assign your Option Agreement for cash.

Occupier's Benefits

Does the Occupier benefit from the lease option? For the cash-short buyer with blemished credit, the lease option allows him to access the real estate market. It gives him a key to the property of his dreams at a time when he lacks the resources to buy. It grants him occupancy of the home of his dreams, an exclusive right to buy the property, and time to gather the necessary resources. The lease option also encourages a hesitant buyer with more digestible terms, allowing him to preview the property before unconditionally committing to the purchase – in effect, to speculate on the property for somewhat more than the cost of rent. Although he receives no

tax benefits during the term of the lease option, the Occupier
has a valuable opportunity to buy his first home.

Seller's Benefits

What are the lease option seller's benefits? The lease
option expands the seller's pool of buyers to include those
without down payment funds, and those unable to qualify for
a loan, as well. During the lease period, the seller retains his
full array of ownership tax deductions while having his
expenses paid by his lessee. Last but not least, if the Occupier
reneges, the seller retains all of the option funds to compensate for lost marketing time. Actually, he receives a windfall to
which he is legally entitled. In the example above, the seller
will keep $16,360 if Randy and Ranee can't exercise the
option.

A New Technique: Joint Ownership Lease Option

We are proud to present a valuable variation of the
joint ownership – the joint ownership lease option. Combining
lease option features with a joint ownership transaction, it
eases the Occupier's purchase requirements and retains a 40%
to 50% ownership interest for the seller.

The Occupier who would like a lease option, but may
be unable to exercise the *full* purchase option at term, should
consider the *joint ownership lease option* instead. The joint
ownership lease option takes on the same structure as the
traditional lease option, except deposit and purchase requirements are substantially less. The option exercised isn't an
outright purchase by the Occupier – it's a joint ownership with
the seller. The joint ownership requires a cash commitment of
less than the 20% required by the lease option. Upon exercise
of the joint ownership option, the seller becomes a 20% to

40% owner of his property and the Occupier takes the remaining interest in the jointly owned property.

Example: Refer to the example with Randy and Renee lease optioning, above. At the end of the three year lease they have deposited $16,360 in option funds. They add $1,640 to that for a 10% down payment of $18,000. Now, they exercise their joint ownership option, coming on title with the sellers at an appropriate ownership split to reflect seller's deferral of the other 10% down payment. These parties agreed upon a 24% interest to Sellers and a 76% interest to Occupiers (projecting 4% annual appreciation and a 10% annual return to the Sellers).

The joint ownership lease option offer should be made contingent upon the parties entering into mutually agreeable joint ownership terms. The most desirable vehicle for accomplishing this would be the long-form Joint Ownership Agreement. Their joint ownership will not commence until the lease option period is up, but the co-owners will have agreed upon all terms in advance. A less desirable form of agreement would be the Joint Ownership Preliminary Commitment specifying basic essential terms, including the all-important ownership splits. To determine your terms, calculate how much the option deposit will be when you are to exercise the joint ownership option. Here it was $18,000. The parties agreed on their joint ownership split based on a 10% contribution by Occupiers and 10% contribution in retained equity by sellers.

These Options Compared

Let's see how the straight purchase, joint ownership, lease option, and joint ownership lease option stack up. The next chart involves a $200,000 property, calculating and comparing cash requirements for each purchase technique.

- **Straight Purchase:** Requires **$46,000** to close – $40,000 as 20% down and $6,000 in closing costs. Occupier's monthly ownership expenses are $1400.

- **Joint Ownership:** Requires **$10,000** as Occupier's 5% contribution to close, which covers closing costs and a small portion of the down payment. His monthly ownership expenses are $1400.

- **Lease Option:** Requires **$44,200** to close out the option – $25,400 more than the option reserve of $18,800. Based on a $200,000 option price exercisable in 3 years, the initial option deposit is $8,000, slightly more than 4% of the option price. Monthly rent is $950, $300 of which is allocated to the option deposit fund over the 3 year option period. In 3 years the option reserve contains the original $8,000 deposit plus $10,800 in rent reserves, for a total of $18,800. With 80% financing ($160,000) and $4,200 in closing costs the optionee needs a total of $44,200 to close out the option – $25,400 more than the option reserve.

- **Joint Ownership Lease Option:** Requires no funds beyond the deposit reserve to exercise the joint ownership lease option in 3 years. $13,000 is a little over 6% of the $200,000 joint ownership option price, which is expected to cover closing costs with about $8,000 toward the down payment. As with the lease option, this Occupier pays $950 in monthly rent with $300 deposited to the option account. At the end of 3 years the account will contain $10,800. Thus, an up front deposit of $2,200 is set – the difference between the $13,000 required to exercise the joint ownership option and the proposed accrued $10,800 rent allocation.

As you can see, the cash and time requirements of each purchase technique are different. These options should all be compared by anyone considering joint ownership.

Straight Seller Financing

Many compare joint ownership with seller financing. They ask, "Why not avoid the complexities of joint ownership by using simple seller financing?" Yes, seller financing is a choice – but the seller gives up potential profits and tax breaks of joint ownership for a mere monthly payment or low interest balloon payment. For the Occupier, there is no difference between seller financing and the seller joint ownership.

With seller financing, the seller does just that. He becomes his buyer's bank. He takes the place of the lender. The buyer makes an agreed upon down payment and seller transfers the property to the buyer with a Deed of Trust/Mortgage for the unpaid amount. Here, this seller is financing the entire transaction, aside from the down payment.

The seller involved in this transaction is not your typical seller, but he's not far from it. Statistics currently show that 46% of single family homes nationwide are owned free and clear. In the 65 and older owner market, 60% are free and clear. The rest of the home sellers have what is typically a large loan on his home, which he needs to pay off to buy another property. Thus, the seller able to serve as the bank generally represents half of the home seller population. That's a lot of room to negotiate seller financing.

Example: Mr. and Mrs. Free and Clear have owned their property for 15 years. They paid off their mortgage in the first ten years. They moved to a new home a year ago and are financially set with that new home. They don't need the money from their old home for the new purchase. Tammy and Tim are their buyers – who offered to buy with a 12% down payment, seller to provide financing for the remainder. Mr. and Mrs. Free and Clear have reviewed their buyers' credit history and financial condition. They have decided that 12% down and seller financing will work as long as the buyers agree to a 3% increase to the purchase price offered. Buyers have agreed. The purchase price is $203,000, the buyers are putting $24,000 down, sellers are financing $179,000 at 9% annual interest amortized over 30 years with a balloon pay-off due in seven years.

If the seller is only partially free of debt on the property, partial seller financing can fill in the down payment gap or provide additional funds, if you have a risky history and your lender will only give you a 50% or 60% loan.

Convincing the Seller to Finance

How can you convince your seller to finance the transaction? First, you don't want to spend the time, unless the seller has little or no loan on the property. Assuming you have a qualified seller, these are your strong points.

It's a Very Good Investment

First, for investment purposes. The seller providing financing will receive a return on investment far greater than he would receive in the general marketplace. Buyers offer their financing sellers a higher return than traditional lenders charge. There are many reasons for this. This buyer probably can't qualify for a conventional loan. It's likely that he doesn't have the full down payment. He will be saving loan fees of about 3% of the loan amount. For these reasons, we usually offer sellers 1% to 1.5% more than the conventional lender would charge. Work up a loan projection. Show him exactly how much he'll be raking in per month and per year. About 90% of that will be pure interest, meaning he'll receive the full loan amount on top of the monthly payments you make.

Calculate exactly how much he'll be making if he seller finances – and what he loses if he doesn't. Work it up for him and present it. Dollars are worth so much more on paper. Ask yourself, "Why are so many banks in existence?" Lending money pays very well. Your seller will earn more than most lenders on this transaction – while you save on the expensive loan origination fees.

Installment Reporting Saves Taxes

Second, payment in installments instead of lump sum will defer the seller's capital gain taxes, if he is not otherwise sheltering his tax. This can be a real savings by entitling the seller to use the installment method of reporting gain for tax purposes. The installment method allows the seller to defer paying tax on profit realized on the sale until the seller actually receives the payment. With a lump sum payment, the seller would have to pay all gain in the year he received the lump sum cashout. Many sellers face a substantial capital gains tax, which your seller can intentionally defer by selecting the installment sale process. If you find a seller who will be facing gain on sale, you will have found someone who should be a willing participant in seller financing.

Give the Seller More Security

If you want the seller to lend you more than 80% of value, he might be concerned that a down market may deplete his security – the property. If this is his concern, you should offer him more security for the loan. Stocks can be pledged; the jewelry you inherited can too. Even an assignment of a promissory note that is due you down the line can qualify as security. Just the fact that you have offered this additional security will impress the seller. If you do give the additional security, also include a provision in the security agreement for its release. You will want this additional security to be released as you pay down the principal on the loan in an amount commensurate with the value of the additional security.

Seller Financing on Paper

The seller-financed sale can be structured in two ways. Forms for both methods can be ordered through the Order Form at the back of the book. First, the seller deeds the property to the buyer and takes back a Deed of Trust/Mortgage for the amount due. In this manner, the buyer is on title and the seller has to foreclose if the buyer defaults. The buyer prefers this process, while the seller does not.

Second, the seller sells to the buyer by an Installment Sale Contract whereby title is not transferred until the amount due is paid off to the seller. With the Installment Sale Contract the seller does not have to go through expensive foreclosure proceedings to get back title to the property – he still has it. Sellers prefer this process, while buyers do not.

Using the second method, the buyers should make sure the Contract of Sale is recorded on the property to protect their potential ownership interest – by prohibiting the seller from selling the property to someone else or obtaining a loan on the property. While buyer and seller may prefer different methods, tax-wise, either method is the same to all parties.

Note: With the installment method, although the buyer is not on title, the Internal Revenue Service treats him as an owner since he is responsible for all payments on the property. This transaction is treated differently from the lease option since the lease optionor does not become an owner until he exercises the option.

Seller Co-Ownership vs. Seller Financing

There are a few disadvantages to seller financing when compared with seller joint ownership. The lending seller gives up all interest in the property and its future appreciation. He leaves title and the loan and gives up ownership. In the process, he no longer shares in the property's appreciation.

What's more, he is *guaranteed* a return – making him a *lender*. When converted into a lender, the seller promptly loses all ownership tax benefits. Most significantly, he loses his right to defer tax on profit. The lending seller potentially earns much less than his joint ownership counterpart. He pays taxes on *profit from his note*, whereas the joint ownership defers all tax on *profit from his ownership* under Internal Revenue Code §1031. The difference is only apparent when examined with the tax eye.

For these reasons, the seller considering seller financing should very carefully evaluate joint ownership with his buyer as a more lucrative alternative. The seller considering straight seller financing should review Chapter Two at *Joint Ownership vs. Seller Financing*.

Assume the Seller's Loan

Since 1976, most loans with savings and loans or banks have not been assumable. So, if the seller's loan with a conventional lender was obtained after 1976, it generally won't be assumable. Always inquire, though. The seller's Deed of Trust/Mortgage will identify its assumability. If it is assumable, you will still have to qualify, but since the loan is already placed with them, the existing lender will usually cooperate more than a new lender. In addition to easier qualification, assumption packages are considerably less expensive than new loans. If the seller has a favorable interest rate, you'll assume that too. So, assumption can be very attractive to the buyer.

FHA and VA mortgages are always assumable. In earlier years they were assumable practically as a matter of right. But times have changed. If the FHA/VA mortgage was obtained in the past few years, you will have to obtain approval. With an adjustable rate loan you probably won't have a problem with assumption, as long as you qualify. Many adjustable loans don't allow assumption in the first two to three years of the loan. If you assume the adjustable loan when it has fully adjusted or is near its cap, you may inherit a very attractive loan. Always look at assumption before you look at a new loan with a new lender.

Wrap the Seller's Loan

There are a few situations where a wrap around loan package should be considered. If the seller has decided to finance the transaction, he can keep his existing loan in place while you pay for it. In essence, the seller *wraps* his existing loan into the debt you will owe him. A new Note and Deed of Trust/Mortgage are created which states that the amount you owe the seller consists of (1) the principal due on his existing loan and (2) the difference between the existing loan amount and the purchase price. The seller wraps his existing loan as a cost-saving to you, and as a money maker to him. He ends up charging you more interest than his lender charged him, and makes a profit on wrapping his loan.

Example: Sanford Seller sells his house to Brenda Buyer. The house is worth $160,000, Brenda puts up $8,000 as a 5% down payment and Sanford's existing loan is in the amount of $100,000 bearing interest at 7.5% per annum. The remaining amount due, the difference between the down payment and the existing loan, is $52,000. A Note and Deed of Trust/Mortgage is prepared in the amount of $152,000, and these parties agreed upon interest at 9% per annum. Brenda pays the amount due on this note each month to the seller. The seller in turn pays his existing mortgage out of that amount.

This is a good way for the seller to provide seller financing and make a profit on his existing mortgage – the difference between the interest he is charged by the bank and the interest he is charging his buyer. In the example above, the seller is making 1.5% more each month than his lender is charging him.

The buyer in this situation would be wise to ensure that the seller's mortgage is *actually* paid each month. There are two ways of doing this. The preference would be for the buyer to make out two checks each month, one to the seller's lender for the amount of the seller's mortgage payment and the second check payable to the seller for the remaining amount due seller each month. The bank is not concerned with who makes the payment, and will typically just credit the payment in the normal course of receivables. They rarely even notice that the payment is coming from someone other than their borrower.

Often, buyers are concerned that if they make the payments instead of the borrower, the lender will call a violation of their "due on sale" prohibition. In actuality, the lender does not take any such action unless the loan is in default. Their policy is, if it's not broken, don't fix it – or more appropriately, if the payments are being made, don't call the loan due. The wise buyer ensures against his seller's loan de-fault by making payment directly to seller's lender himself. The second way for the buyer to insure that payment is being made by the seller is to require proof of payment of the mortgage from seller each month. It is essential that the buyer confirms the loan "he is paying" does indeed get paid. In some situations, we've seen the seller get lost shopping on the way to the bank.

Buy "For Sale by Owner"

The seller saves 6% of the sale price when selling the property without an agent. That could amount to a substantial reduction in sales price. The seller may argue that it was through his efforts that the 6% was saved, and you should not share in this saving. You should counter that the buyer's agent receives half of that 6% commission; thus, you are contributing equally to this saving by not hiring an agent. For this reason, both seller and buyer should share equally in this saving.

To locate sellers selling without an agent, investigate the classified ads, the real estate open house section and drive around looking for signs posting "For Sale by Owner." If you are successful in finding this seller and coming to terms, you should hire a lawyer or real estate agent as consultant to assist you with the transaction. The agent will be less expensive and more qualified than the lawyer. If you ask your agent of choice to review the documents instead of signing them in the agent capacity, they will typically charge you a reasonable hourly rate for consultation only. By consulting with a real estate agent you will be directed to take all the very important steps required by your purchase.

Since your home is the biggest single purchase of your life, you do not want to cut any corners evaluating its condition or putting the transaction together. With a qualified real estate agent by your side you will take these steps with confidence and ease. You may incur a bill for numerous hours of the agent's time, but it will be well worth your while, especially considering the significant savings you and the seller have reaped by finding one another without agent involvement.

Buy in the Slow Season

Spring is high season for sellers. It's their market. During the spring season it's difficult to get a deal. The best time for bargain hunting is late November and December. Due to the holidays and inclement weather, the buyer market dries up. This is the time to scoop up a deal. Sellers are sitting there, probably left over from last spring without a sale. They realize that they probably won't sell until next spring. Are they ready to make a deal? Probably. It all depends on their unique circumstances. Has the seller already bought another house and moved out? Is he paying on a mortgage without a tenant? Has he been relocated for business and can't sell his home here? Is there financial stress of divorce? Is foreclosure just around the corner? Must the sale close in this tax year? During the low season in winter you will find deals that are unheard of in high season. Some sellers need to sell in the current tax year. These sellers are against the wall.

For all these reasons November and December are ideal months to buy. You'll find the real estate agents are more available since they are experiencing the same slow season as the sellers. Ask your agent to search the listings for deals that read "Seller highly motivated," "Creative financing available," "Bring any offer," "Lease option available." Concentrate on these properties. Take advantage of this time of year which may bring you a fabulous deal.

First-Time Buyer Programs

Most states have programs for first-time buyers to assist them in obtaining loans with 5% down. These programs have many limitations, including a cap on the mortgage and on the amount of money you make. You'll have to pay for mortgage insurance with these loans, which can be between 1% and 4% of the mortgage amount, in addition to a monthly surcharge. Often the benefits of a low down are quickly eaten up by mortgage insurance. Look in your local yellow pages under state government listings for these home buying programs. For purposes of these programs, a first-time buyer is someone who has not owned an interest in a principal residence for the past three years. So, you do not actually have to be a first-time buyer to apply.

Get an Adjustable Rate Mortgage (ARM)

An adjustable rate mortgage (ARM) can be the answer for the buyer without a down payment. These mortgage packages provide a lot of leeway, and buyer qualification is a bit more flexible than for fixed rate loans. Down payment requirements, too, are more flexible. See if you can cut the down payment to 10%. Again, you'll probably have to pay for mortgage insurance if your down payment is less than 20%.

The ARM's initial low rates provide cash surplus for the first few years, when compared with the fixed rate loan. Since your payments will be substantially less than they would be with a fixed rate loan, you will have extra funds. Borrow the down payment you don't have and promise to pay it back on a monthly basis. With the ARM, you will have the extra funds for at least the first two or three years.

Obtain Early Inheritance from Your Family

Each individual can gift $10,000 a year to anyone without a tax consequence to gifter or beneficiary. Gather your family members, including aunts, uncles, grandparents, and parents. Tell them you want to buy a home but you don't have the down payment.

Example: Jeff and Linda have been married for two years. They have just had their first child and need a larger home. They are renting. They have located a property within their budget but they don't have the down payment. The house is worth $220,000 and they need a 20% down payment of $44,000. They have $10,000, most of which they will need for closing costs and moving. They both spoke with their pool of relatives. Jeff's parents each gave him $10,000, for a total of $20,000. No one in Linda's family had a large amount, but each parent and grandparent was able to scoop $3,000 together, for $12,000. That brought the down fund to $32,000. For the remaining $12,000 Jeff talked to his grandmother, with whom he had not previously approached the gift idea. His grandmother said that her dearly beloved husband had left his estate in trust, a portion of which was to be distributed to Jeff at her death. As trustee of the trust, she could distribute some gifts early. She was willing to do that, and gave Jeff $10,000 as an early distribution from the trust and $2,000 as her own gift.

Tradition Gives Way to Practicality

Traditionally, gifts are not given until death. This concept is outdated, especially considering the joy of giving while you're alive. You can assist your loved one at a critical time and sit back and watch the benefits of your gift take hold. Why wait until you die, if you have it now? Tax-wise, as long as any gift to any one individual is no more than $10,000 per year, there is no tax consequence, *ever.* The gift receives a full exemption and is not reported anywhere. You are only required to report a gift if it exceeds $10,000 per year to one person. In that event, you file a Gift Tax Return listing the gift amount. At your death the gift amount stated on the Gift Tax Return is offset against a $600,000 credit afforded to each decedent. As long as you don't exceed $600,000 in lifetime gifts (not including $10,000 exemption gifts) and gifts at death, there will be no gift tax due.

If you plan to buy close to the beginning of the new year you can receive, tax free, $10,000 each for the current taxable year – and on January 1 $10,000 more. Not only is the beginning of the year a good time to buy due to lack of buyers, it is also a good time to receive double tax-free gifts staggered from one calendar year to the next.

Example: If Jeff and Linda talk to their relatives and obtain cash gift pledges in advance, they can time their purchase so as to receive down payment gifts over time. If they had begun coordination with relatives when they were married, they could have received $10,000 per year each, tax-free, thereby allowing individual relatives to collectively gift more than $10,000 each. If they closed in the beginning of the year they could receive a $10,000 tax free gift on December 31 and another $10,000 on January 1, one day later, each receiving the annual exemption.

A Loan of the Down Payment

By planning your purchase well, you will identify your needs early on. If your problem lies with the down payment funds, you can begin tapping friendship and family loan sources well in advance. The earlier the better, for many reasons.

First, the lender making the purchase loan will review your bank account history for three months back to insure that your down payment funds were not borrowed. (By contrast, your relative's *gift* is treated as a gift not requiring early deposit in your account.) The lender wants to know that the down payment came from your own savings. Thus, you will need to have the down payment funds in your account at least three months before you apply for the loan.

Second, if you've already performed a loan analysis, you will be able to budget for repayment of the down payment loans. If you've decided on an ARM, you'll have more money each month than if you selected a fixed rate loan – at least for the first two to three years. If your down payment is less than 20%, you'll have to factor in an extra cost for mortgage insurance. With careful analysis and planning, you will not be caught by surprise. More importantly, you will be able to make loan repayment commitments by which you will abide. Be realistic. You don't want to jeopardize any of these important relationships by making promises you can't keep.

If a parent is lending you money, find out if they can wait a few years before you pay it back. For this loan a balloon payment of all principal and interest in five years may be acceptable. If a friend is lending and needs some repayment each month, propose payment of interest only with the principal due in a couple of years. Make sure you realistically project your repayment schedule. Remember that your ARM payment will likely increase over time, so account for that. It might be wise to pay off as much of the down payment loans as you can when your ARM has its initial teaser rate, and you are making very low monthly payments.

You will want to give a note secured by a Deed of Trust/Mortgage to each down payment source. The promissory note will come first when they advance you the loan funds before escrow closes. The Deed of Trust/Mortgage will be signed and recorded after escrow closes. Forms for these documents can be ordered by the Order Form at the back of the book.

Foreclosure Buying

The inventory of foreclosure properties is very high. In fact, the foreclosure rate is now the highest it has been since 1929. A good source of real estate values is obtained by tracking foreclosures. Someone else's bad news becomes your good news. See Chapter Thirteen for more on foreclosure properties. There are many ways to locate a property in foreclosure. The best way to track foreclosure sales is through the legal notices section in your local newspaper.

Buying from the Borrower Before Foreclosure Sale

You want to catch the foreclosure when it is first recorded. In this way you can locate the owner and work with him to solve his problem and yours. He wants to keep his property or at least preserve his credit. You want to get a good deal. Many states have laws regulating contact with debtors in foreclosure, to prevent outsiders from taking advantage at a difficult time. Some states also require any sales contract to contain rescission rights granting the distressed owner a five day cancellation period. Check the laws in your state to make sure these laws are followed in taking these steps. Through the Order Form at the back of the book, you can obtain the purchase agreement used in California.

By matching up the published Notice of Default with information obtained at the Recorder's Office, you can usually come up with the owner's name and address. The best way to contact this person is by mail. Let them know you are an independent person not associated with any creditor or mortgage company. Advise that you are interested in obtaining a property for less than fair market value, and it may be possible for the two of you to join together to solve his financial problem and yours. Give him your telephone number.

If you receive a call back, which is likely 50% of the time if your letter has been opened, ask to meet or discuss options on the phone. There usually is a bargaining range between the amount the defaulted borrower owes on the mortgage and the fair market value of the property. The closer the sale date, the more reasonable your offer may sound. You can either enter into a joint ownership with the borrower or buy him out by assuming the loan and saving his credit. He may require a little walking money on top of that, which you should seriously consider paying. Joining with the defaulted borrower can solve your problem and his if the structure is right. And, you can get a very good deal in the process.

Buying at the Foreclosure Sale

This section deals with buying a property at its foreclosure sale. Legal notices posted in the newspaper provide the date of sale, the minimum bid amount, and the address of the property. At the sale you will have to pay the full amount of your bid in cash or by cashier's check, or at the least you will have to post an earnest money cash deposit with a lender set up for the loan. The foreclosing lender will probably be on hand to lend if you are qualified. Although you can get some good deals on these foreclosed properties, often they are in bad shape. Although you have the address, you won't have a chance to have any inspections performed on the property before you buy at foreclosure sale. Also, the defaulted borrower may still be living in the property you buy. Read books on buying foreclosed properties and take your steps slowly.

Buying After the Foreclosure Sale

You can find properties that have already been foreclosed upon and are now for sale at your local lender's "REO" (real estate owned) department. Ask for a list of properties for sale. You can typically get a good deal if the lender has not yet signed a listing agreement with a real estate agent.

When dealing with the lender's REO department, ask if you can see their appraisal. Lenders are required to appraise a property when they foreclose upon it. So, if they tell you they don't have an appraisal, tell them you know otherwise. These lenders may act like they are firm on their suggested sale prices, but they will negotiate. They are not in the business of selling properties and they sustain big losses each day they hold a property as REO. For tax reasons too, they do not want to keep a high inventory of properties. So, make this lender's headache work for you if you are interested in the property at all. You could walk away with a very good deal.

. . . And now, some very important tips and insider information about loans. Your home buying arsenal wouldn't be complete without a good loan strategy. In Chapter Sixteen you'll receive a generous helping of what you need to know to get a home loan, and lots more.

Chapter Sixteen

ALL ABOUT LOANS

In this chapter we wind up the Home Buying Epic with a Bonus: Everything You'll Ever Need to Know About Loans. We begin by revealing the Lenders' Rules of Thumb for Home Loans. How much can you afford? How can they tell? Then, we look at the loan market. What loans are available, and how do they stack up? What do they *really* cost? What is private mortgage insurance, and when will you need it? Which loan is better: fixed rate or adjustable rate? And finally, how do VA and FHA loan packages work? This chapter locks in on loans – to demystify an unnecessarily stressful process.

$\mathscr{T}$he loan process is, at the very least, challenging. Usually, it is the one facet of home buying that causes the most stress. Why? Because it involves the most regulations. Actually, it need not be a stressful process. To qualify, a few standards apply. Beyond that, locking in a rate depends solely on market conditions. This chapter is about simplifying the loan process and removing the cloud of misunderstanding surrounding it.

How Much Can You Afford?

The answer to this question depends upon the down payment you make and your income. The higher your down payment, the lower your loan will be. The lower the loan amount, the lower your income requirements will be. For purposes of establishing norms, we will utilize the standard 20% down payment, 30-year fully amortized fixed rate loan.

Down Payment Requirements

This chart is based on the traditional 20% down, 80% financed structure.

Down Payment Required	Home Price
$16,000	$80,000
$20,000	$100,000
$24,000	$120,000
$28,000	$140,000
$32,000	$160,000
$40,000	$200,000

Traditional 20% Down Payment

Income Requirements

The chart below supports the current rule of thumb that take-home income must be three times the property's primary expenses – loan, property taxes and insurance. If you will also be paying mortgage insurance (see *Mortgage Insurance*, below) that expense will be factored in here, as well. This chart converts the formula into monthly requirements.

This chart is based on a 20% down payment and a 30-year fully amortized loan at 8.5% annual interest. 15% of housing expense is for insurance and property taxes; 85% is for loan payment.

Net Income Per Month	Housing Expenses	Home Price
$1,740	$ 580	$ 80,000
$2,175	$ 725	$100,000
$2,604	$ 868	$120,000
$3,036	$1,012	$140,000
$3,471	$1,157	$160,000
$4,338	$1,446	$200,000

Income Requirements for a Home Loan

The above charts illustrate that in order to purchase a $120,000 home, your cash requirements will be $24,000 for down payment and monthly after-tax income of $2604, computed yearly at $31,248. Again, the above chart represents a standard rule of thumb. Requirements may differ with differing loan packages, but generally the lenders use this rule.

The amount of your other debts will also be considered by the lender, who wants all debt, including these housing expenses, to be less than 75% of your take-home income.

Mortgage Insurance: Less Down at a Cost

If you have found a loan that does not require a 20% down payment, you must factor mortgage insurance into your expense log. This is not always true, but it is the norm for all types of loans. The following chart presents guidelines to determine the amount of your mortgage insurance expense if your down payment is less than 20%.

Down Payment	Mortgage Insurance	
	First Year	Subsequent
5 to 9%	1.0% of mortgage	.5%
10 to 14%	.4% of mortgage	.35%
15 to 19%	.3% of mortgage	.3%

Mortgage Insurance Formula

Applying these percentages to two sample homes follows:

Home Price	Down Payment Percentage	Mortgage Insurance	
		First Year	Subsequent
$100,000	5%	$ 950	$475
$100,000	10%	$ 360	$315
$100,000	15%	$ 255	$255
$200,000	5%	$ 1,900	$950
$200,000	10%	$ 720	$630
$200,000	15%	$ 510	$510

Mortgage Insurance Calculation

The borrower who does not provide the full 20% down will need to factor this additional cost into the formula *Income Requirements,* on the previous page.

The Standard 30-Year Loan

You will probably want a 30-year loan, which is generally the longest term available for a loan. Some lenders infrequently provide 40-year loans, but 30 years is the norm. The 30-year loan is amortized over its 30-year term. The term of the loan is the period of time you have to pay off the loan. If you pay the loan to term it will be fully paid off. This is the process called *full amortization,* meaning interest and principal are fully apportioned over the term of the loan. The 30-year fully amortized loan is the most popular because its payments are lower than shorter term loans.

Fixed Rate Loans

The fixed rate loan is the standard in the home lending industry. Although the adjustable rate mortgage (ARM) has become increasingly more popular over the years, a fixed rate remains the most desirable loan. The fixed rate loan is dependable and allows for future planning, since it bears the same fixed rate of interest for each payment over its term. The payment always stays the same. The fixed rate loan is the answer for the buyer who wants to define exactly how much he'll be paying on the loan for the foreseeable future. Remember to factor mortgage insurance into your loan expense if your down payment is less than 20%.

Buying Down the Interest Rate

When you are obtaining a fixed rate loan, you can generally buy the interest rate down to a target rate. For instance, your lender is quoting an 8.75% fixed rate loan. You want to get that loan down to 8%. You can buy it down by paying points, which are a percentage of the loan amount. Generally, 1% of the loan amount will buy you a ⅛ of 1% interest rate reduction. If you want a 1% reduction you'll pay eight points – meaning 8% of the loan. Here, you want to buy the interest rate down ¾ of 1%, which will cost six points. If your loan is $150,000 you'll pay $9,000 to get the loan down ¾ of 1%. Only you can determine if interest buy down is worth it. Calculate it out and ascertain your savings. Compare that with your up front costs. This is the only way you can determine whether you should buy down the interest rate.

Balloon Payments

Some fixed rate loans are fully amortized for 30 years but are payable earlier in a balloon payment. When the balloon payment is due you'll have to pay off the entire loan amount, which is usually accomplished by a refinance. Typically it is best to choose a balloon payment loan only if you are fairly certain you will be selling before the balloon payment is due. Otherwise, you will again incur loan costs for the refinance.

Adjustable Rate Mortgage (ARM)

In the innovative 80s the ARM was introduced. The typical ARM carries a 30-year term. Its interest rate is different from the fixed rate loan. The ARM is not fixed and goes up or down as general interest rates fluctuate. In essence, the adjustable feature shifts the risk of climbing interest rates to the borrower. But these loans also set a cap on how much the interest rate can go up. Often, the ARM begins with a very low teaser rate which adjusts in six months to a rate that is about 2.5% less than what is being charged for fixed rate loans.

Again, remember to add your mortgage insurance expense to this type of loan if your down payment is less than 20%.

Review the ARM's Index

The ARM's adjustable interest rate is linked to a certain index – a category of general interest rates. As the index rate fluctuates, the ARM follows. There are many indexes to which the ARM is tied. Treasury bills are common, as is the 11th District Cost of Funds, commonly used in the West. We have found the 11th District to be particularly stable. If your ARM is linked to treasury bills, we find that the longer the maturity of the treasury note, the better.

Review the ARM's Cap and Adjustment Intervals

Each ARM has a cap that needs to be analyzed. What is the cap for each interest rate adjustment? What is the overall cap for the life of the loan? A five or six percent cap over the life of the loan is acceptable, as long as it began low enough. It's not ideal, but it is acceptable. Be the devil's advocate and project your loan using the worst case scenario. You will be projecting the worst result, but you should be aware of the ultimate down side of your loan.

How many times can your interest rate change? Every year? It is best to look for an ARM that seldom adjusts. The most undefined ARM, which you should probably avoid, adjusts every month. Some adjust every six months. Some adjust every three years. Every year is probably acceptable. The longer the adjustment period, the more consistent your interest rate.

Other ARM Factors to Consider

The best way to determine which loan is better for you is to calculate it out and compare it with its fixed rate competitor. If you need to keep your payment down for the first few years, the ARM is best. Usually, for the first few years of the ARM the payments remain lower than its fixed rate rival. For the average individual in the process of gradually increasing his income, this loan is a plus since its payments graduate more along the lines of your salary. If you have individual loans to pay back for your purchase, low initial payments may allow for co-payments to those generous people who lent you funds to close. Finally, the ARM may give you an initial window in which to recover from the shocking expense of buying your home.

With an ARM your lender's criteria may also be more flexible. Down payment requirements may be more lenient. You may choose an ARM because you do not plan to own the property much longer than the loan's initial low payment term of two to three years. If this is the case, review the pre-payment penalty features of your ARM. Some ARMs charge a pre-payment fee if you sell the property too early. Loan assumption, too, may have to be delayed until after the first few years.

Which Is Better – ARM or Fixed Rate?

Since the ARM depends upon interest rates in the future, it cannot be calculated with certainty – nor can it be accurately compared to the fixed rate. Speculation is required. The fixed rate will always be the same. Those who find certainty important will lean in favor of a fixed rate loan. Those who need initial low payments will lean toward the ARM. Those who predict that interest rate indexes will remain consistent over the course of their ownership will opt for the

ARM. Those who are concerned that they may be caught up in rising interest rates will choose fixed rate. The decision is as individual as the choice of a doctor.

In summary, the fixed rate will be the answer when interest rates rise. The ARM borrower will be subject to upward interest rate adjustments while you sit back assured that your fixed interest rate cannot change – despite the market. The fixed rate provides a certain peace of mind that the ARM cannot equal. On the other hand, the ARM can provide substantial savings in the absence of skyrocketing interest rates.

The Annual Percentage Rate Is Important

Don't just focus on interest rates. Look at the *annual percentage rate (APR)* which gives a clearer picture of how much actual interest you will be paying for the loan. The APR consists of the interest rate plus other loan charges – usually points. A point is a special charge assessed by the lender to keep the interest rate down. One point is equal to 1% of the loan amount. The APR includes points that are charged for the loan and not paid up front. When comparing mortgages, compare APR's – not just basic interest rates. The APR provides the more accurate cost for your loan.

Pre-Payment and Assumption Features

Review your loan to determine its assumption and pre-payment features. Some loans do not allow pre-payment before the loan has matured. Some lenders define maturity as two years, while others use five. During this period when the loan is considered immature, the lender charges a pre-payment penalty for early pay-off. These penalties can be stiff.

Some loans are assumable, while others are not. Assumability of a loan is a strong selling point when you put your house on the market, especially if you have a competitive fixed rate loan. An ARM can also be a plus, especially if you've reached the lifetime adjustment cap.

Negative Amortization

Make sure the loan you get does not negatively amortize. This means that the principal gets bigger instead of smaller. These mortgages are not very popular, but they do come along every so often. Carefully analyze this loan and make sure you fully understand it. The best policy with negative amortization is to stay away from it.

More on Private Mortgage Insurance (PMI)

Private mortgage insurance (PMI) can enable you to buy a home with far less down than the standard 20%. VA and FHA loans fall into this category. But PMI differs in that its loan limits are far higher. While FHA and VA loans limit the loan amount to $45,000 and $151,725, respectively, PMI extends to loans up to $500,000.

Lenders are more inclined to offer loans with down payments less than 20% if buyers pay for mortgage insurance. The insurance protects the lender if the buyer defaults on payments. The guidelines set forth at the beginning of this chapter are general, but give you a good idea of the premium you'll be paying for your low down payment.

To qualify for PMI your major housing expenses – loan repayment, taxes and insurance – should make up no more than one-third of your net income. In addition, the rest of your regular debts should not exceed 26% of your income.

Typically, you must occupy the property as your principal residence. Your employment history should show consistent employment for the last two years. Your credit record should be clear or close to it.

FHA-Backed Loans

FHA loans are insured by the U. S. Department of Housing and Urban Development. Thus, the FHA does not lend money; it insures loans. There are several good things about these loans. First, they are generally 1% below market. Although you'll end up paying about ½% in mortgage insurance, you'll still come out ½% ahead. Second, because of the FHA's agreement to insure, a lender will be far more inclined to give you a mortgage with a small down payment. Often the down payment can be as low as 3 to 5%. Although FHA-backed loans allow low down payments, you still have to pay mortgage insurance.

One important thing to remember with your mortgage insurance is that once the loan is paid off, the mortgage insurance is refunded. So, it is a temporary cost. If you are the original borrower, the refund is automatically made to you. If you are not and you assumed the loan, you must apply for the refund within two years of pay off. Remember to think of your mortgage insurance as a fund being held for you; otherwise, you may lose out on getting back what could be a hefty amount. If you are allowing someone to assume your loan, make sure you notify your buyer of this fact and get his agreement to return your proportionate share of the refunded payments. It's not guaranteed you'll get them back, but clarifying this early on will increase your chances of reimbursement.

The highest priced loan insured by the FHA is $67,500, but in high priced areas they are willing to insure a loan up to

$151,725. There is no cap on the value of the home; the cap only applies to the loan amount. The down payment amount depends on the value of the house, and typically does not exceed 5%.

Call the FHA office closest to your area and obtain their requirements. The lender deals with the FHA, making sure you meet their requirements. But you should know exactly what the requirements are for planning your FHA-insured mortgage. To locate a lender who makes FHA-insured loans, look in the yellow pages under "Loans" and check for lenders that specify "FHA." Your local FHA office will also have a list of lenders who write loans backed by them.

A full range of FHA-insured loans is available, including fixed rate and ARM. FHA mortgages are assumable. Assumption was formerly a matter of right. In the last few years, the buyer has to qualify with the lender for assumption.

VA-Guaranteed Loans

The VA loan guarantee amount is not as simple to understand as FHA-backed loans. The bottom line is that the VA guarantees between 25% and 50% of value. The higher the property value, the lower the percentage guaranteed by the VA. The maximum guarantee for a loan is $46,000 for purchases over $144,000. The maximum loan amount for which a guarantee will be given is $184,000, but again recall that the guarantee is for no more than $46,000. For example, you can buy a house valued at $184,000 with no down payment with the VA guaranteeing $46,000, which is 25% of value. The VA guarantee takes the place of a down payment for a lender who will loan on 100% of value.

Some states have additional VA backed loans. For instance, California has a Cal-Vet loan that has been increased to $250,000 to reflect high California prices. Under this package, the state actually sells the property to the veteran. Call the Veterans' Administration office in your area and ask if there are any state-sponsored Veterans' programs to purchase homes. If you strike out there, go to the State Government pages and call numbers for house purchase assistance.

The Quick Qualifier

If you are unable to qualify for a loan, consider the quick qualifier method. Your application, along with two years of tax returns, goes a long way with one of these loan packages. These packages are often referred to as "non-qualifiers" because the criteria for traditional loans is suspended. So, what do you have to do to obtain one of these loan packages? Pay at least 35% of the purchase price down. If credit is your problem and you have extra cash, this is the way to go.

A Closing Comment

This book is a testament to democratic access to home ownership – so you will have the best chance to achieve the American dream. Using the information you have gained from this book – armed with the software, forms, and other aids available through the Order Form – you, too can claim expertise in acquiring real estate, and with it, claim your own piece of the rock.

Appendix

This Appendix is provided for you to have at your fingertips all samples, forms, charts, checklists, and references necessary to put your transaction together. If you get stuck, give us a call. You can consult with the author by phone with your credit card deposit by calling 415-461-2311. If you need more copies of forms or additional documents, please see the Order Form at the back of the book.

Sample Forms (see more at Order Form):

. Memorandum of Joint Ownership Agreement
· Joint Ownership Agreement
. Joint Ownership Promissory Note
. Joint Ownership Deed of Trust/Mortgage
. Joint Ownership Lease Agreement

Blank Charts (see more at Order Form):

· Joint Ownership Preliminary Commitment
· Joint Ownership Worksheet
· Rent Calculation
· Depreciation Calculation
· Occupier Gain Calculation
· Occupier IRC §1034 roll over with IRC §121 exemption
· Investor Gain Calculation
· Investor Exchange Profile
· Investor Exchange Calculation

Internal Revenue Code Sections:

· Internal Revenue Code §121
· Internal Revenue Code §280A
· Internal Revenue Code §1031
· Internal Revenue Code §1034

SAMPLE FORMS

The sample forms which follow reflect the sample transaction in Chapter 9. These sample documents and many more may be ordered as hard copy forms, on software, on line, or by fax-on-demand through the Order Form at the back of the book.

Caution – The sample documents are intended as guides. They are not substitutes for legal or other necessary professional advice. Each transaction is unique, as are the relevant laws of different states. You are urged to consult with competent counsel when putting together a transaction. We caution against merely filling in the blanks without consultation.

Sample Memorandum of Joint Ownership Agreement

Recording Requested By
Harold Investor and Ingrid Investor
After Recording Return To
Harold Investor and Ingrid Investor
(Address)
(City) (State) (Zip)

MEMORANDUM OF JOINT OWNERSHIP AGREEMENT

This memorandum has been recorded to give constructive notice as to the existence of a Joint Ownership Agreement dated Sept. 2, (year) by and between:

Joint Ownership Co-owners:

Investors: Harold Investor and Ingrid Investor, husband and wife.
Occupiers: Orville Occupier and Margie Occupier, husband and wife.

Joint Ownership Title:

Orville Occupier and Margie Occupier, husband and wife, as joint tenants, as to an undivided 45% interest, and Harold Investor and Ingrid Investor, husband and wife, as community property, as to an undivided 55% interest, all as Tenants in Common.

Joint Ownership Property:

[Property address], which legal description is attached hereto as Exhibit A.

Ownership Split: Occupier: 45%
                              Investor: 55%

_____   _____
Orville Occupier   Harold Investor

_____   _____
Margie Occupier   Ingrid Investor

[Notary acknowledgment]

Joint Ownership Agreement

The sample Joint Ownership Agreement which follows is the standard model. There are many variations which are available through the Order Form at the back of the book. The variations are described below.

Family Joint Ownership

Because of IRS presumptions when family members are involved in transactions, we feel it is even more important to fully secure the transaction and preserve Investors' foreclosure rights. However, some families have been unable to conceive of including foreclosure rights against their family members. The family joint ownership available through the Order Form excludes foreclosure remedies. With this type of agreement, a deed of trust/mortgage and note will not be required.

Investor Uninterested in Tax Benefits

The Investor who claims any tax benefits must comply with Internal Revenue Code §280A. If your tax advisor finds that compliance with §280A is not required because the Investor does not claim tax benefits in the transaction, the Agreement excluding compliance with IRC §280A, available through the Order Form, will be your choice. With this type of agreement, the lease agreement will not be necessary.

Joint Occupancy

A purchase involving joint occupancy by the co-owners will require joint duties and obligations throughout the Joint Ownership Agreement. This variety of Agreement is available through the Order Form along with notes and trust deeds/mortgages which become reciprocal, binding each of the co-owners to secure their respective obligations. Since this structure differs substantially, the package available through the Order Form includes the Grant Deed, the Agreement, Memorandum, and the reciprocal notes and deeds of trust/mortgage.

Gifting by Relatives

This Agreement gifts $10,000 per Investor each year to each Occupier, allowing tax-free transfer of the joint owner-ship property to the Occupier over time. Since this structure differs substantially from the standard agreement, the package available through the Order Form includes the Grant Deed, the Agreement, Memorandum, and the note and deeds of trust/mortgage which automatically annually adjust to reflect ownership shifting.

WARNING: The obligations undertaken by Occupiers in
this Agreement are secured by a Deed of Trust/
Mortgage with a Power of Sale.

JOINT OWNERSHIP AGREEMENT

Joint Ownership Co-owners:

As Occupiers: **Orville Occupier and Margie Occupier**

As Investors: **Harold Investor and Ingrid Investor**

Joint Ownership Title: **Orville Occupier and Margie Occupier**, husband
and wife, as joint tenants, as to an undivided 45%
interest, and **Harold Investor and Ingrid Investor**,
husband and wife, as community property, as to
an undivided 55% interest, all as Tenants in
Common.

Ownership Split:	Occupiers:	45%
	Investors:	55%

Joint Ownership Property:

1 Wave Drive, Sausalito, CA 94965

This Agreement is entered into this 2nd Day of September, (year) by and between **Orville Occupier and Margie Occupier** and **Harold Investor and Ingrid Investor**. The parties hereto have agreed to associate themselves as joint ownership Co-owners on the following terms and conditions:

1. Purpose of Joint Ownership

The purpose of this joint ownership shall be the [purchase and] joint ownership of a single family dwelling bearing an address of 1 Wave Drive, Sausalito, CA 94965, and being the real property in the County of Marin, State of California, more particularly described in **Exhibit A** hereto.

2. Joint Ownership of Property

Legal title shall be acquired by this joint ownership and maintained thereafter during the term of this joint ownership in the names of the individual joint ownership co-owners, as tenants in common, each owning undivided interests, as follows:

> **Orville Occupier and Margie Occupier, husband and wife, as joint tenants, as to an undivided 45% interest, and Harold Investor and Ingrid Investor, husband and wife, as community property, as to an undivided 55% interest, all as Tenants in Common.**

3. Designation of Parties

Orville Occupier and Margie Occupier are designated as joint ownership Occupiers and all references to Occupiers shall pertain to them. **Harold Investor and Ingrid Investor** are designated as joint ownership Investors and all references to Investors shall pertain to them.

4. Duration of Joint Ownership

This joint ownership shall commence on execution of this Agreement by the parties and shall continue until dissolved by mutual consent of the parties or terminated as provided for in this Agreement.

5. Name of Joint Ownership

The name of this joint ownership shall be "1 Wave Drive, Sausalito, CA 94965, a Joint Ownership."

6. Joint Ownership Address

The joint ownership's mailing address shall be:

1 Wave Drive, Joint Ownership
Orville Occupier and Margie Occupier
1 Wave Drive, Sausalito, CA 94965

and

1 Wave Drive, Joint Ownership
Harold Investor and Ingrid Investor
(Address)
(City, State)

7. Initial Capital

The purchase price of the joint ownership property is the sum of **One Hundred Thirty Five Thousand Dollars ($135,000.00).** The initial capital of this joint ownership is the sum of **Twenty Seven Thousand Dollars ($27,000.00)**, which has been contributed to the joint ownership by the parties as follows:

a. Investors have contributed the sum of **Twenty Seven Thousand Dollars ($27,000.00)** in the form of retained equity ["cash" if Investor is not seller] toward purchase and ownership of the joint ownership property. Said amount shall be reimbursed to Investors in accordance with the terms of this Agreement.

b. The Occupiers have contributed the sum of **Zero** in the form of cash toward purchase and ownership of the joint ownership property. Said amount shall be reimbursed to Occupiers in accordance with the terms of this Agreement.

8. Purchase of Real Property

This joint ownership [shall purchase said real property and] shall own, maintain and sell the real property in accordance with the terms of this Agreement.

9. Waiver of Right to Partition

The parties hereto have agreed to take title to the subject property as tenants in common. The co-tenancy interests in the property of each of the co-owners are shown on the attached cover page as "Ownership Split." The parties hereby waive any right they may have to partition the property during the duration of this Agreement.

10. Occupiers Exclusive Occupancy

Occupancy of the joint ownership property shall proceed as follows:

a. **Orville Occupier and Margie Occupier** are designated as the Occupiers to this joint ownership.

b. Occupiers agree to occupy the joint ownership property at all times during the term of this joint ownership.

c. In the event that the parties hereto desire to have the joint ownership property occupied by someone other than the Occupiers, written consent of Investors is required, which consent shall not be unreasonably withheld.

d. Occupiers' agreement to occupy the joint ownership property is a material inducement to Investor's decision to participate in the joint ownership transaction. Therefore, in the event that Occupiers cease occupancy of the joint ownership property without written consent of Investor, Investors shall be entitled to the remedies set forth in Paragraph 34 hereof, entitled "Primary Obligations Default."

11. Investors Inspection Rights

In consideration of exclusive occupancy of the property being granted to Occupiers, Investors are granted a reasonable right of inspection which may be exercised upon giving three days' written notice to Occupiers.

12. Duty of Maintenance and Repair

Maintenance and repair shall proceed as follows:

a. Occupiers agree to individually manage, occupy, maintain, and repair the subject property, in as good as or better condition as when this joint ownership commenced, less reasonable wear and tear.

b. All costs of ordinary improvements, maintenance, and repairs shall be borne solely by the Occupiers and shall not be reimbursed to them, unless agreed to in writing by Investor.

c. It is specifically agreed that under no circumstance are Investors responsible in any sum or manner for maintenance or repair of the joint ownership property, except as to necessary capital expenditures specifically set forth under Paragraph 19 entitled "Necessary Capital Improvements."

d. Occupiers' agreement to repair and maintain the joint ownership property is a material inducement to Investor's decision to participate in the joint ownership transaction. Therefore, in the event that Occupiers fail to repair and maintain the joint ownership property in accordance with this provision, Investors shall be entitled to foreclose under the terms of their Deed of Trust/Mortgage in accordance with the provisions of Paragraph 34 hereof, entitled "Primary Obligations Default." Said Deed of Trust/Mortgage contains a specific maintenance and repair requirement.

13. Rental by Occupiers

In order to comply with Internal Revenue Code §280A, the co-owners agree:

a. Occupiers agree to rent the subject property from Investors for a rental of $240.00 per month. Said rent constitutes consideration for Occupiers' exclusive right to occupy the joint ownership property. The rental charged herein represents the fair market rental value of the property in the amount of $540.00 in accordance with the provisions of Internal Revenue Code §280A times Investors' 55% ownership interest in the property, less a 20% good tenant discount.

b. As and for rental reimbursement, Investors agree to contribute this rent payment in its entirety in the annual amount of $2880 to the joint ownership property as follows:

Insurance:	$ 350.00 annually
Condominium/Assn. dues:	$1260.00 annually
Property Taxes:	$1270.00 annually
[Alternate options: management fees, mortgage payments]	

c. Occupiers agree to pay said rent to Investors on a monthly basis. Investors' duty to make payments designated herein is contingent upon Investors' receipt of the rent specified herein. Investors shall reimburse paid rental amounts to insurance, condominium or association dues and property taxes in the amounts set forth above when due commencing with the first day of this ownership.

[Alternate option: $ (blank) shall be paid toward the mortgage on a monthly basis. Said payment shall be forwarded to Occupiers and made payable to the lender.]

14. Insurance/Association Dues

[Insurance may be paid by either party depending on rental reimbursement calculations.]

Insurance and association dues shall be paid as follows:

a. As rental reimbursement Investors shall maintain such insurance as may be required to protect and hold this Joint Ownership and its co-owners harmless from all liability.

b. Insurance requirements are as follows: A comprehensive general liability policy with limits of not less than $500,000.00 per occurrence, excluding earthquake coverage [Optional: including earthquake coverage]

c. The parties maintaining said insurance agree to list the remaining joint ownership co-owners as additional named insureds on the policy of insurance.

d. As rental reimbursement Investors shall pay all association dues assessed to the property.

e. Investors' duties hereunder are contingent upon receipt of rental payments from Occupiers in accordance with this Agreement. If Occupiers fail to make rental payments to Investors in accordance with Paragraph 13 entitled "Rental by Occupiers," then these obligations shall pass to the Occupiers.

[Alternate option: Occupiers shall maintain, at their sole cost and expense, insurance and association dues described herein.]

15. Property Tax Payments

[Property tax payments may be made by either party depending on rental reimbursement calculations.]

Property taxes shall be paid as follows:

a. Occupiers shall be individually and separately responsible for payment of all property taxes not paid by Investors as rental reimbursement payable to the County of Marin during the term of this Agreement.

b. As reimbursement of rental income Investors shall be individually and separately responsible for payment of $1270 of property taxes annually to the County of Marin during the term of this Agreement. Investors' duty to make property tax payments is contingent upon receipt of rental payments from Occupiers. If Occupiers fail to make rental payments to Investors in accordance with the provisions of Paragraph 13 entitled "Rental By Occupiers," then the obligation to make property tax payments shall pass to Occupiers.

[Alternate: Occupiers shall be exclusively, individually and separately responsible for payment of all property taxes to the County of Marin during the term of this Agreement.]

        c. Occupiers' agreement to pay property taxes is a material inducement to Investors' decision to enter into this joint ownership. Accordingly, if Occupiers fail to make property tax payments in accordance with this provision, Investors shall be entitled to foreclose on their Deed of Trust/ Mortgage in accordance with the provisions of Paragraph 33 entitled "Notice of Money Default – Investor's Deed of Trust/Mortgage." Said Deed of Trust/Mortgage contains a specific property tax payment requirement.

16. Loan Repayment
The purchase money loan shall be paid as follows:

        a. Occupiers shall be individually and separately responsible for repayment of the loan acquired to finance this purchase in the amount of **One Hundred Eight Thousand Dollars ($108,000.00)**, except for the nominal amount which may be paid by Investors as rental reimbursement if so specified in Paragraph 13 entitled "Rental by Occupiers," upon all terms and conditions set forth in the loan documents.

        b. Occupiers' agreement to make loan payments is a material inducement to Investors' decision to enter into this joint ownership. Accordingly, if Occupiers fail to make loan payments in accordance with this provision, Investors shall be entitled to foreclose on their Deed of Trust/Mortgage in accordance with the provisions of Paragraph 33 hereof, entitled "Notice of Money Default – Investor's Deed of Trust/Mortgage." Said Deed of Trust/Mortgage is all-inclusive and specifically includes Occupiers' obligations under the purchase loan.

17. Loan Negative Amortization - Principal Reductions
Negative Amortization: In the event that the subject purchase loan is one involving negative amortization, Occupiers agree to be responsible for all additional sums incurred by the application of negative amortization. Therefore, when the underlying loan is deducted from property value upon buyout or sale hereunder, sums incurred as a result of negative amortization shall be borne solely by Occupiers and those sums shall be separately assessed to Occupiers upon buyout or sale.

Principal Reductions: Principal reduction is any reduction of the principal balance of said loan beyond the original loan principal amount. Any party making such a principal reduction shall be credited with said reduction out of the equity of the property or on buyout as set forth herein.

18. Labor Contribution by Occupier
Occupiers labor shall be contributed in accordance with the following provisions:

        a. Occupiers agree that there will be no charge for their first 10 hours of labor, per any singular property improvement. [Optional]

b. Thereafter, when any improvement is undertaken by Occupiers, after the first 10 hours they will charge no more than $20.00 per hour for their own personal labor.

c. Said labor contribution by Occupiers shall be approved in advance in writing by Investors upon presentation of an estimate by Occupiers to Investors setting forth the reasonable estimate of the labor contributions they intend to make for which they seek reimbursement. Investors shall approve or disapprove of said labor charges; however, Investors' consent will not be unreasonably withheld.

d. Written approval of said labor expenditure and the amount thereof is a condition precedent to reimbursement to Occupiers of said labor charges at sale or buyout.

e. All reasonable and approved labor charges in conformity with this paragraph will be credited to Occupiers at sale or buyout, first returning said reasonable and authorized labor charges to Occupiers without interest before the net equity is determined and split between the parties.

19. Necessary Capital Improvements

Necessary capital improvements shall be defined and paid for as follows:

a. Necessary capital improvements include necessary roof replacement, sewer and septic replacement, structural integrity replacement, and furnace replacement.

b. Occupiers agree to solely bear the cost of necessary capital expenditures, receiving reimbursement for each improvement and any contribution they have made for materials and outside labor.

[Alternate: Investors and Occupiers agree to share the cost of necessary capital expenditures in accordance with their joint ownership interests as set forth herein, the cost of which shall be recovered in proportion to amounts paid by Investors and Occupiers at cost.]

c. Necessary capital improvements shall require three estimates from qualified professionals to confirm that the expenditure is necessary and reasonable.

d. Written consent to select a contractor and proceed with these repairs must be obtained from all co-owners before commencing work. Such consent shall not be unreasonably withheld.

e. Credit shall be calculated at sale or buyout first crediting said capital expenditure amount without interest to the party making it before the net equity is determined and split between the parties.

20. Unnecessary Capital and Other Improvements

Unnecessary capital improvements shall be defined and paid for as follows:

a. An unnecessary capital improvement is any improvement other than those defined herein as necessary capital improvements which add to the value of the dwelling, such as remodeling and other aesthetic improvement.

b. If any of the co-owners desire to make such improvements, such improvement may be made without consultation with the remaining co-owners and at each party's expense without expectation of reimbursement as long as the improvement costs **$750.00** or less.

c. If the anticipated unnecessary improvement costs more than **$750.00** or if reimbursement is requested, the parties agree to consult with one another and the improving co-owner shall obtain the written consent of the remaining co-owners to such improvement and its reimbursement amount, without interest, which consent shall not be unreasonably withheld.

d. The parties agree that in maintaining, repairing, and improving the joint ownership property, each party will exercise good faith to insure that any improvement will increase the value of the joint ownership property as a whole.

e. Any party who makes improvements in violation of this Agreement shall not be entitled to reimbursement for the improvement made.

21. Responsibility for Joint Ownership Expenses Not Allocated

As occupying co-owners, Occupiers agree to be responsible for all joint ownership expenses, duties and obligations not otherwise allocated in this Agreement.

22. Books of Account

The joint ownership co-owners shall keep their own books of account for accounting, tax and other purposes. However, since Occupiers have exclusive occupancy of the property and all duties of ordinary repair and maintenance, Occupiers shall, during the term of this Agreement, keep accurate books of account in which all matters relating to ordinary and capital expenditures to the property, and other property information relative to tax and resale, shall be entered. The books of account shall be kept on a cash basis and shall be open to examination by any party to this Agreement upon reasonable notice.

23. Assignment of Interest

Assignment of the joint ownership co-owners' property interests shall proceed as follows:

a. **Occupiers Assignment**:

(1) Occupiers shall not sell, assign, mortgage, borrow against, transfer or encumber their respective interest in the joint ownership without first receiving the written consent to such transfer by Investors, which consent shall not be unreasonably withheld.

(2) The parties herein acknowledge that the Occupiers' ownership capacity as the exclusive property occupants and primary loan obligors is sufficiently personal and unique that any purported transfer or assignment of Occupiers' ownership interest would inherently cause a material failure of consideration unless their assignees possess substantially comparable financial and personal characteristics.

(3) Occupiers may lease out the property as long as the lessees are first approved by Investors, which consent shall not be unreasonably withheld.

(4) Occupiers' agreement to refrain from assigning their property interest or any portion thereof without Investors' written consent is a material inducement to Investor's decision to enter into this joint ownership. Accordingly, if Occupiers violate this provision by assigning their interest without Investors' written consent, Investors shall be entitled to foreclose on their Deed of Trust/Mortgage in accordance with the provisions of Paragraph 34 hereof, entitled "Primary Obligations Default." Said Deed of Trust/Mortgage contains a prohibition against assignment or encumbrance.

b. **Investors Assignment**: Since Investors' involvement in the property's ongoing obligations is limited, Investors may freely assign and transfer their interest in the joint ownership property, which interest shall be subject to all terms of this Agreement.

c. **Buyout Options**: Both Investors and Occupiers are granted a first option to buy out one another before assignment of interest may be made to any third party in accordance with applicable provisions of this paragraph. Said buyout if exercised shall proceed in conformity with applicable provisions of this Agreement and be valued in accordance with Paragraph 43 entitled "Appraisal."

24. Management of and Liability for Remainder

None of the co-owners hereto shall have authority to bind the joint ownership property or the co-owners in making contracts or incurring obligations in the joint ownership name or on its own credit or account in the ordinary course of the joint ownership, or otherwise. Any Owner who incurs any obligation in the name of the joint ownership shall be in violation of this provision and shall be personally liable to both the creditor and the other co-owners for the entire amount of the obligation so incurred.

25. No Partnership Existence

The parties specifically agree and represent to one another that a partnership does not exist with respect to their joint ownership of the subject property within the meaning of the Internal Revenue Code, and more specifically, §280, §761 and §1031, or for any other non-tax purpose. Instead, the parties have joined for the sole purpose of owning the subject property as tenants in common. The parties hereto represent that they do not and will not carry on a trade, business or financial venture together with respect to the subject property in which they shall divide income and profits during ownership. Accordingly, no party to this Agreement shall be entitled to any compensation other than specifically stated herein for its services in connection with ownership of the joint ownership property.

26. Restriction on Authority of Owners

The individual joint ownership co-owners shall have no authority with respect to the joint ownership and this Agreement to:

a. Do any act in contravention of this Agreement;

b. Do any act which would make it impossible to carry on the joint ownership;

c. Make, execute, or deliver any general assignments for the benefit of creditors, or any bond, guaranty, indemnity bond, or surety bond;

d. Assign, transfer, pledge, compromise, or release any joint ownership claim except for full payment;

e. Incur any debt or obligation in the name of the joint ownership property or a co-owner;

f. Do any of the following without unanimous consent of the co-owners:

(1) Confess a judgment;

(2) Make, execute, or deliver for the joint ownership any bond, mortgage, deed of trust, guaranty, indemnity bond, surety bond, or accommodation paper or accommodation endorsement;

(3) Amend or otherwise change this Agreement so as to modify the rights or obligations of the co-owners as set forth; or

(4) Create any personal liability for any co-owner other than liability to which such co-owner may agree in writing.

27. Tax Allocations and Declarations

Tax allocations are agreed to as follows:

a. Principal Residence Deductions to Occupiers:

The parties acknowledge that Occupiers may claim all tax benefits for deductible payments made by them consisting of mortgage interest and property taxes as allocated in Paragraph 13 entitled "Rental by Occupiers."

b. Occupiers are occupying this property pursuant to Internal Revenue Code §1034:

Occupiers acknowledge that they intend to occupy this property during the term of this Agreement as their principal residence. At term, Occupiers intend to defer tax on their gain on the subject property by rolling into another principal residence pursuant to Internal Revenue Code §1034.

c. Investment property tax deductions to Investors:

Investors are holding the subject property as their investment. The parties acknowledge that Investors may claim depreciation on their property interest and all tax benefits for deductible payments made by them associated with their investment ownership of said property, including insurance, condominium dues, property tax, [optional: and a portion of mortgage interest] in the amounts paid by Investors itemized in Paragraph 13 entitled "Rental by Occupiers."

d. Investors are holding this property pursuant to Internal Revenue Code §1031:

Investors acknowledge that this property is and will be held as investment property pursuant to Internal Revenue Code §1031. Investors intend to have any tax on gain on the subject property treated as deferred and nontaxable pursuant to Internal Revenue Code §1031.

28. Tax Disclosure

The co-owners hereto acknowledge that there has not yet been a test case setting forth specific Internal Revenue Service interpretations and regulations relating to joint ownership as set forth herein and tax treatment by the tenant-in-common owners. The parties hereto are declaring their tax-related intentions and no guarantees with respect to Internal Revenue Service acceptance of these deductions have been given.

29. Promissory Note to Investor

Occupiers agree to execute to Investors a joint ownership Promissory Note secured by a Deed of Trust/Mortgage on their interest in the subject property under the following terms:

a. The face amount of the Note and Deed of Trust/Mortgage shall include all of the principal amount of the purchase money note secured by a first Deed of Trust/Mortgage in addition to Occupiers' equity ownership interest as defined herein multiplied by initial reimbursable capital contribution of Investors as set forth in Paragraph 7 entitled "Initial Capital."

b. Occupiers acknowledge that the sum set forth in the Promissory Note and Deed of Trust/Mortgage is a true and accurate valuation of the amounts Occupiers owe Investors in the event of default entitling Investors to foreclose under the Deed of Trust/Mortgage as defined herein. Said valuation takes into account the fact that Occupiers' material contribution to Investors and the joint ownership was payment of the mortgage, property taxes, insurance and other primary obligations as defined herein, for which Investors shall become responsible upon Occupiers's default.

c. The parties hereto expressly agree that it would be extremely difficult and impracticable to fix the actual loss, damage, and extra expense of the Investor/beneficiary under the Deed of Trust/Mortgage securing the joint ownership Note upon Occupiers's default in money payment as required by Paragraphs 14, 15, and 16 entitled "Insurance/AssociationDues," "Property Tax Payments" and "Loan Repayment" or performance of the Primary Obligations as required by Paragraph 34 entitled "Primary Obligations Default" and all paragraphs incorporated therein, and the money amount set forth in the joint ownership Promissory Note as calculated in provision a., above, and set forth in the Deed of Trust/Mortgage of same date is a reasonable estimate of such loss, damage and expense.

Occupier	Investor
Occupier	Investor

d. Investors acknowledge that any demand for sale made by Investors upon the foreclosure trustee shall be reduced by the amount of the first note and Deed of Trust/Mortgage at purchase, plus negative amortization accrued.

30. Deed of Trust/Mortgage to Investors

The following provisions govern the Deed of Trust/Mortgage from Occupiers to Investor:

a. Occupiers agree to execute a Deed of Trust/Mortgage on the subject property to Investors to secure the Promissory Note as well as Occupiers' payment of all monetary obligations and performance of all other duties and obligations undertaken by them in this Agreement.

b. It is specifically agreed that the Deed of Trust/Mortgage will be subordinated to and shall include the purchase money loan on the property, which loan is secured by a First Deed of Trust/Mortgage.

c. Occupiers acknowledge that the Deed of Trust/Mortgage contains a Power of Sale which entitles Investors to sell Occupiers' property interest if Occupiers default on obligations undertaken herein.

d. Investors agree that any demand for sale upon the foreclosure trustee under the Deed of Trust/Mortgage shall be reduced by the amount of the first note and trust deed at purchase, plus negative amortization accrued.

e. Investors agree that its Deed of Trust/Mortgage shall be reconveyed in full at such time as the joint ownership is terminated under the terms of this Agreement without breach or default by Occupiers.

31. Foreclosure Under Deed of Trust/Mortgage

Occupiers agree to pay Investors reasonable attorney's fees and costs incurred in foreclosure under its Deed of Trust/Mortgage.

32. Occupiers As Tenants Upon Default

Upon the occurrence of the following events Occupiers agree to immediately become month-to-month tenants obligated to pay Investors as rent an amount equal to all principal, interest, insurance, property tax, dues and assessment payments due on the subject property and further acknowledge that if they are unable to pay the rent called for herein, they will be subject to eviction in an unlawful detainer proceeding or by way of a writ of ejectment:

a. Upon default on any payment obligation as defined herein.

b. Upon Occupiers' failure to remedy any default requiring written notice of breach within 30 days following Investor's notice.

33. Notice of Money Default – Investor's Deed of Trust/Mortgage

Investors are entitled to file and record a Notice of Default under its Deed of Trust/Mortgage upon thirty days' delinquency in loan payment, property tax payment or insurance payment by Occupiers. Delinquency occurs the day after a payment is deemed due by the creditor, except for property tax payments which are delinquent when deemed delinquent.

34. Primary Obligations Default

The co-owners shall have the following remedies upon co-owner's default of the primary obligations under this Agreement:

a. The primary performance obligations are defined as follows: the duty to pay for insurance, property tax and the purchase money loan as defined respectively in Paragraphs 14, 15 and 16, the Occupiers' duty to occupy the property as defined in Paragraph 10 entitled "Occupiers Exclusive Occupancy," to repair and maintain the property as defined in Paragraph 12 entitled "Duty of Maintenance and Repair" and to refrain from assigning or encumbering their interest as defined in Paragraph 23 entitled "Assignment of Interest."

b. As for non-monetary defaults relating to these primary obligations, the non-defaulting co-owners agree to provide written notice of said breach to the defaulting co-owners specifying the condition of default.

c. After giving notice of breach as provided in b., above, non-defaulting co-owners shall allow a 30 day period to lapse within which to allow defaulting co-owners to cure said default.

d. If said default is not cured within the discretion of the non-defaulting party within that thirty-day period, non-defaulting party shall be entitled to exercise any of the following remedies:

(1) Foreclosure by filing its Notice of Default under its Deed of Trust/Mortgage, and proceeding thereunder, or

(2) Buyout as provided for in Paragraph 35 entitled "Buyout Upon Primary Obligations Default," or

(3) Sale of the property as provided for in Paragraph 57 entitled "Sale Upon Default."

35. Buyout Upon Primary Obligations Default

In accordance with the provisions of Paragraph 34 entitled "Primary Obligations Default" the non-defaulting co-owners shall be entitled to buy out the defaulting co-owners as follows:

a. Buyout shall be calculated at seventy-five percent (75%) of appraised value.

b. Buyout under this provision shall be performed in escrow in accordance with the provisions of Paragraph 36 entitled "Method of Buyout."

c. Buyout under this provision shall be paid in accordance with Paragraph 53 entitled "Payment of Buyout – Installments."

36. Method of Buyout

The method of buyout by a co-owner shall proceed as follows:

a. Each co-owner shall exercise all options to buyout as described in this Agreement by serving written notice of intent to so exercise within 30 days after occurrence of the event triggering said option. Said notice shall be served by personal delivery or mail delivery on the remaining Owners at their addresses specified in this agreement or on the personal or legal representative entitled thereto.

b. Said Notice of Intent to Buy Out shall calculate the amounts proposed upon buyout in accordance with Paragraph 43 entitled "Appraisal" and shall designate the escrow company to be used for the buyout.

c. If appraisal is required, appraisal shall proceed according to provisions of Paragraph 43 entitled "Appraisal."

d. The amount of buyout shall be determined according to Paragraph 44 entitled "Interest Valuation on Buyout."

e. Unless otherwise specified, buyout shall be payable in accordance with Provision 52 entitled "Payment of Buyout - Lump Sum."

f. In the event that the party being bought out fails to convey title to the property as described herein or by other conveyance acceptable to the buying out party, all buyout funds on deposit shall be returned to depositor, the party refusing to complete buyout shall pay all escrow charges incurred in the escrow process, and buying out party shall be free to pursue his legal remedies.

37. Five-Year Term

At five years, the parties may extend this Agreement, and at each anniversary thereafter this Agreement may be extended, by all co-owners executing a written extension hereof so extending this agreement, as is more fully scheduled in Provision 39 entitled "Extension of Agreement at Term." If all co-owners do not agree to extend after the initial five-year period, the parties hereby agree to terminate the joint ownership five years from September 2, (year) by sale of the joint ownership property or buyout of one another's interests, whichever method is elected according to the terms of this agreement, unless the parties all agree to extend this agreement or unless the required appreciation rate has not been met, as defined in Provision 40, "Automatic Extension of Agreement if Required Appreciation not Met."

38. Buyout - Mutual Agreement - Before Term

The parties hereto may buy out one another upon mutual agreement at any time. If the parties so mutually agree, buyout shall proceed according to the provisions of Paragraph No. 36 entitled "Method of Buyout" and Paragraph No. 43 entitled "Appraisal."

39. Extension of Agreement at Term

Commencing 150 days before termination of this agreement, the parties hereto may extend this agreement for a period of time upon mutual agreement by all parties to this agreement in accordance with the schedule set forth in Paragraph 54 entitled "Five-Year Termination of Joint Ownership." Said extension shall be in writing signed by all parties, shall specify the extension term, shall set a new Termination schedule and shall adopt all other provisions of this agreement.

40. Automatic Extension of Agreement if Required Appreciation not Met

The parties agree that annual simple appreciation of 1.5% is required for the joint ownership to terminate without a loss at sale. Thus, the co-owners agree that if this agreement is not extended at term and if buyout at term fails to occur, sale at term shall only proceed if the within required appreciation is reached. Value of the property shall be determined in accordance with Provision 43 hereof entitled "Appraisal." If said required appreciation is not met, yearly extensions shall be entered into by the co-owners until such date as the required appreciation rate is achieved, at which time termination shall proceed according to the time frame set in Paragraph 54 entitled "Five-Year Termination of Joint Ownership."

41. Termination of Joint Ownership

The joint ownership shall commence on execution of this Agreement and shall continue until the first of any of the following events occur:

a. Sale of the joint ownership property in accordance with the terms of this Agreement.

b. Five years from September 2, (year) hereof, unless all co-owners agree to extension hereof in writing.

c. Upon buyout by co-owners.

d. Following an extension as set forth in Provision 40 entitled "Automatic Extension of Agreement if Required Appreciation not Met," when the value of the joint ownership property reaches the required appreciation rate.

e. Mutual agreement of all of the parties hereto;

f. Substantial default or breach of this Agreement by any party hereto.

42. Buyout Options at Term

At term, which is five years after commencement, the parties may elect to buy out one another in accordance with Paragraph 36 entitled "Method of Buyout" and Paragraph 43 entitled "Appraisal" instead of selling the joint ownership property, on the following terms:

a. The Occupiers are first granted an option to buy out the Investors.

b. If the Occupiers fail to exercise their option to buy out Investors, Investors are then given an option to buy out the Occupiers.

c. Timing of buyout options shall proceed in accordance with Paragraph 54 entitled "Five-Year Termination of Joint Ownership."

43. Appraisal

On exercise of an option to purchase an outgoing Owner's joint ownership interest, or in order to determine if the required appreciation rate has been met, or for any valuation purpose hereunder, value shall be determined as follows:

a. Fair market value shall be determined as agreed upon by unanimous mutual consent of all co-owners.

b. In the event that the co-owners are unable to agree upon a fair market value between themselves, the co-owners hereto shall jointly select an MAI certified appraiser actively engaged in business in the county in which the joint ownership property is located.

c. Said appraiser so selected shall perform an appraisal of the property and the value established by the appraiser shall be binding and conclusive on the parties hereto and on any person legally entitled to receive the value of any co-owner's interest.

d. In the event that the parties are unable to agree upon selection of a single appraiser, and only in that event, the exiting joint ownership co-owner or representative shall appoint an MAI certified appraiser actively engaged in business in the county in which the joint ownership property is located. The remaining Joint ownership co-owners shall appoint an appraiser of equal designation. The average of the two appraisals shall conclusively constitute the fair market value of the property.

e. All fees and expenses of each appraiser above described shall be paid by the party ordering the appraisal.

44. Interest Valuation on Buyout

The co-owners' interests on buyout shall be calculated as follows:

a. **Buyout of Investor**:

FIRST: From fair market value, the balance due on the purchase money loan as evidenced by the First Deed of Trust/Mortgage shall first be deducted less amounts which have been incurred due to negative amortization, which amounts shall be borne solely by Occupiers. The remaining amount represents gross equity in the property

SECOND: To the extent of equity remaining, Investors shall receive a return of its initial capital contribution in the amount of **Twenty Seven Thousand Dollars ($27,000.00).**

THIRD: Deducted next is the amount of Occupiers' initial capital contribution in the amount of **Zero**.

FOURTH: To the extent of equity remaining, Investors contributing principal loan reductions shall receive the amount of said contribution.

FIFTH: Deducted next is any principal loan reduction contributed by Occupiers.

SIXTH: To the extent of equity remaining, Investors shall be reimbursed for improvement contributions and interest thereon, if provided, in accordance with Paragraphs 19 and 20 hereof, respectively entitled "Necessary Capital Improvements" and "Unnecessary Capital and Other Improvements."

SEVENTH: Deducted next is the amount for which Occupiers are entitled to reimbursement for improvement contributions and interest thereon, if provided, per Paragraphs 18, 19 and 20 hereof, respectively entitled "Labor Contribution by Occupiers," "Necessary Capital Improvements," and "Unnecessary Capital and Other Improvements."

EIGHTH: Remaining amount is net equity. Investors shall receive 55% of net equity.

NINTH: Value shall be reduced, if so provided, in accordance with the applicable buyout provision.

TENTH: Investors shall be reimbursed by Occupiers for all amounts Investors have advanced for mortgage, property tax, insurance, repairs and deferred maintenance, for which expenses Occupiers are responsible under this Agreement.

ELEVENTH: Closing costs on buyout shall be shared by the parties in accordance with their ownership split. However, if buyout is triggered by default, the defaulting party shall pay all closing costs.

b. **Buyout of Occupiers**:

FIRST: From fair market value, the balance due on the purchase money loan as evidenced by the First Deed of Trust/Mortgage shall first be deducted less amounts which have been incurred due to negative amortization, which amounts shall be borne solely by Occupiers. The remaining amount represents gross equity in the property.

SECOND: Deducted from gross equity is the initial capital contribution by Investors in the amount of **Twenty Seven Thousand Dollars ($27,000.00)**.

THIRD: To the extent of equity remaining, Occupiers shall receive a return of its initial capital contribution in the amount of **Zero**.

FOURTH: Deducted next is principal loan reduction contributed by Investors.

FIFTH: To the extent of equity remaining, Occupiers contributing principal loan reductions shall receive the amount of said contribution.

SIXTH: Deducted next is the amount by which Investors are entitled to reimbursement for improvement contributions and interest, if provided, per Paragraphs 19 and 20 hereof, respectively entitled "Necessary Capital Improvements" and "Unnecessary Capital and Other Improvements."

SEVENTH: To the extent of equity remaining, Occupiers shall be reimbursed for improvement contributions and interest thereon, if provided, in accordance with Paragraphs 18, 19 and 20 hereof, respectively entitled "Labor Contribution by Occupiers," "Necessary Capital Improvements," and "Unnecessary Capital and other Improvements."

EIGHTH: Remaining amount is net equity. Occupiers shall receive 45% of net equity less amounts which have been incurred due to negative amortization of the purchase money loan described in FIRST above.

NINTH: Value shall be reduced, if so provided, in accordance with the applicable buyout provisions.

TENTH: Occupiers shall be reimbursed by Investors for all amounts Occupiers have advanced for mortgage, property tax, insurance, repairs and deferred maintenance, for which expenses Investors are responsible under this Agreement.

ELEVENTH: Closing costs on buyout shall be shared by the parties in accordance with their ownership split. However, if buyout is triggered by default, the defaulting party shall pay all closing costs.

45. Default by Death

Death of the joint ownership co-owners may constitute a material default entitling the co-owners to buy out the interest of the decedent or sell the joint ownership property as follows:

a. Upon the death of all joint ownership Investors or joint ownership Occupiers, the surviving co-owners shall have a first option to purchase the deceased co-owners' interest in the joint ownership property.

b. Buyout shall proceed according to the provisions of Paragraph 49 entitled "Buyout Upon Default by Death, Bankruptcy, Conservatorship and Creditor Recording."

c. If non-defaulting parties do not exercise their buyout option, the property shall be sold in accordance with Paragraph 57 entitled "Sale Upon Default."

46. Default by Bankruptcy

The filing of a Chapter 7 or Chapter 13 petition in bankruptcy of a joint ownership co-owner shall constitute a material default entitling the remaining co-owners to buyout or sale of the joint ownership property as follows:

a. The bankruptcy estate shall sell and the remaining co-owners shall have a first option to purchase the bankrupt co-owner's interest in the joint ownership in accordance with the provisions of Paragraph 49 entitled "Buyout Upon Default by Death, Bankruptcy, Conservatorship and Creditor Recording."

b. If non-defaulting parties do not exercise their buyout option, the property shall be sold in accordance with Paragraph 57 entitled "Sale Upon Default."

47. Default by Conservatorship

Appointment of a general conservator for any of the co-owners shall constitute a material default entitling the remaining co-owners to buyout or sale of the joint ownership property as follows:

a. The conservatorship estate shall sell and the remaining co-owners shall have a first option to purchase the ownership interest of the co-owner for whom the conservator has been appointed in accordance with the provisions of Paragraph 49 entitled "Buyout Upon Default by Death, Bankruptcy, Conservatorship and Creditor Recording."

b. If non-defaulting parties do not exercise their buyout option, the property shall be sold in accordance with Paragraph 57 entitled "Sale Upon Default."

48. Default by Creditor Lien Recording

A material default entitling the remaining co-owners to buyout or sale of the joint ownership property shall occur if a creditor of a party records a lien or abstract of judgment on the joint ownership property and the lien remains unsatisfied for a period of 90 days, as follows:

a. The co-owners who are not debtors of said creditor shall have a first option to purchase the ownership interest of the debtor co-owner in accordance with the provisions of Paragraph 49 entitled "Buyout Upon Default by Death, Bankruptcy, Conservatorship and Creditor Recording."

b. If non-defaulting parties do not exercise their buyout option, the property shall be sold in accordance with Paragraph 57 entitled "Sale Upon Default."

49. Buyout Upon Default by Death, Bankruptcy, Conservatorship, Creditor Filing

In accordance with the provisions of Paragraphs 45 through 48, inclusive, respectively entitled "Default by Death," "Default by Bankruptcy," "Default by Conservatorship," and "Default by Creditor Lien Recording," the parties shall be entitled to buy out one another as follows:

a. Buyout shall be valued at eighty percent (80%) of appraised value.

b. Buyout under this provision shall be performed in escrow in accordance with the provisions of Paragraph 36 entitled "Method of Buyout."

c. Buyout under this provision shall be paid in accordance with Paragraph 52 entitled "Payment of Buyout – Lump Sum."

50. Buyout on General Default

The non-defaulting co-owners shall have a first option to buy out the defaulting owners or by sale of the joint ownership property upon default for any substantial breach of this agreement not otherwise specifically described by any other provision herein as follows:

a. Buyout shall be valued at seventy-five (75%) of appraised value.

b. Buyout under this provision shall be performed in escrow in accordance with the provisions of Paragraph 36 entitled "Method of Buyout."

c. Buyout under this provision shall be paid in accordance with Paragraph 53 entitled "Payment of Buyout – Installments."

d. If non-defaulting parties do not exercise their buyout option, the property shall be sold in accordance with Paragraph 57 entitled "Sale Upon Default."

51. Buyout if More Than One Provision Applies

If more than one buyout provision applies to a defaulting party's act or omission or series thereof, the buyout provision providing the lowest amount to the defaulting party shall prevail.

52. Payment of Buyout – Lump Sum

Payment of buyout under this provision shall proceed as follows:

a. No later than sixty (60) days after value is determined, payment by certified or cashier's check of the entire amount of the co-owner's interest shall be deposited in escrow.

b. Concurrent with the deposit referred to in Paragraph a., above being made, the party being bought out shall deposit into escrow a fully executed Grant Deed to that co-owner's interest in the subject property.

53. Payment of Buyout – Installments

Payment of buyout under this provision shall proceed as follows:

a. No later than sixty (60) days after value is determined one half of the buyout amount in the form of a certified or cashier's check shall be deposited in escrow, along with a promissory note for the remaining buyout amount payable in six equal installments over six months after close of escrow without interest.

b. A Deed of Trust/Mortgage on the subject property securing payment of said promissory note shall be executed in favor of the party being bought out and deposited in escrow and recorded.

c. Concurrent with the deposit referred to in Paragraph a., above, being made, the party being bought out shall deposit into escrow a fully executed Grant Deed to that co-owner's interest in the subject property.

54. Five-Year Termination of Joint Ownership

The method to be followed by the parties in terminating the joint ownership in five years is as follows:

a. On or before **April 5, (year)**, which is 150 days before the five-year expiration of this joint ownership, the parties may execute an Extension of Joint Ownership Agreement in writing pursuant to Provision 39, "Extension of Agreement at Term," which document shall be fully executed within 30 days. If said extension is executed, the remaining paragraphs hereunder will become void.

b. On or before **May 6, (year)**, which is 120 days before the five-year expiration of this joint ownership, Occupiers shall be granted an exclusive 30-day option to buy out Investor, exercisable by providing written Notice of Intent to Buy Out to Investors within said option period.

c. In the event that Occupiers do not exercise their buyout option pursuant to b., above, on or before **June 5, (year)**, which is 90 days before the five-year expiration of this Joint Ownership Agreement, Investors shall be granted an exclusive 30-day option to buy out Occupiers, exercisable by providing written Notice of Intent to Buy Out to Occupiers within said option period.

d. If buyout is selected by the parties as set forth herein, the buyout shall proceed according to Paragraph 36 entitled "Method of Buyout."

e. Buyout under this provision shall be paid in accordance with the provisions of Paragraph 52 entitled "Payment of Buyout – Lump Sum."

f. On or before **July 5, (year)**, which is 60 days before the five-year expiration of this Joint Ownership Agreement, if no party elects to buy out the other per the schedule above and if this agreement has not otherwise been extended, this agreement shall automatically be extended for a one year period in the event the Required Appreciation Rate specified in Provision 40 entitled "Automatic Extension of Agreement if Required Appreciation Not Met" has not been met. The dates herein shall automatically be extended one year in said event and all terms of this Agreement and the accompanying documents shall remain in full force and effect.

g. If no provision above operates to terminate or extend this Agreement and if neither party elects to buy out the other per Paragraphs b. and c., above, on **August 4, (year),** which is 30 days before the five-year expiration of this joint ownership, the parties agree to jointly list the property for sale with the listing agent specified herein. If no listing agent is specified, the property shall be listed with the agent selected by Investors.

h. If the joint ownership is terminated by sale of the joint ownership property, distribution shall proceed according to Paragraph 56 entitled "Sale at Term."

55. Listing Price – Designation of Listing Agent
At term, the property listing shall proceed as follows:

a. The parties hereto irrevocably designate Rebecca Realtor, currently with Rebecca's Realty, (address), as listing agent for the sale of the joint ownership property at term. In the event that listing agent is no longer employed by Rebecca's Realty, the listing agreement will be placed with Rebecca Realtor at her address then listed with the Department of Real Estate.

b. The parties agree to cooperate fully to facilitate sale of the joint ownership property at term at the highest reasonable price.

56. Sale at Term
Sale proceeds shall be distributed in the following order as proceeds permit according to this provision when sale occurs at term without default.

FIRST: From the unadjusted sales price, the balance due on the purchase money loan as evidenced by the First Deed of Trust/Mortgage shall first be deducted less amounts which have been incurred due to negative amortization, which amounts shall be borne solely by Occupiers.

SECOND: Less seller closing costs.

THIRD: To the extent of remaining proceeds, Investors shall be reimbursed for its initial capital contribution in the amount of **Twenty Seven Thousand Dollars ($27,000.00)**.

FOURTH: To the extent of remaining proceeds, Occupiers shall be reimbursed for its initial capital contribution in the amount of **Zero.** However, any unpaid negative amortization as described in Provision FIRST above, shall first be deducted.

FIFTH: To the extent of remaining proceeds, amounts that have been paid as loan principal reductions as defined in Provision 17 entitled "Loan Negative Amortization - Principal Reductions" shall be repaid to the contributing party.

SIXTH: To the extent of remaining proceeds, Investors shall be reimbursed for improvement contributions and interest thereon, if provided, in accordance with Paragraphs 19 and 20 hereof, respectively entitled "Necessary Capital Improvements" and "Unnecessary Capital and Other Improvements."

SEVENTH: To the extent of remaining proceeds and to the extent that Occupiers have repaid all negative amortization as described in Provision **FIRST**, above, Occupiers shall be reimbursed for improvement contributions and interest thereon, if provided, in accordance with Paragraphs 18, 19 and 20 hereof, respectively entitled "Labor Contribution by Occupiers," "Necessary Capital Improvements," and "Unnecessary Capital and Other Improvements." Remaining amount is net equity.

EIGHTH: Investors shall receive 55% of any remaining net equity.

NINTH: Occupiers shall receive the remaining 45% of net equity less any unpaid amounts incurred due to negative amortization of the purchase loan at Provision FIRST above.

57. Sale Upon Default

Sale proceeds shall be distributed in the same manner as "Sale At Term" at Paragraph 56, with the following exceptions:

a. The closing costs are solely borne by the party causing the default from any proceeds the defaulting party receives from the sale.

b. The non-defaulting party shall be reimbursed for payments advanced on behalf of the defaulting party for mortgage, property taxes, insurance, deferred maintenance and repairs from any proceeds the defaulting party receives from the sale.

c. Thus, any amounts due defaulting party will first be repaid to non-defaulting party as specified in a. and b. above, before non-defaulting party receives any proceeds. Each party's obligation is limited to his equity in the subject property; thus no party shall owe more than is received from the sale proceeds.

58. Co-owner Obligations Limited to Equity

Each co-owners' obligation hereunder is limited to his equity in the joint ownership property. Thus, no Party shall owe more than his equity in the joint ownership property.

59. Cooperation in Internal Revenue Code §1031 Exchange/§1034 Rollover

The parties agree to cooperate to all extents required in each other's facilitating an Internal Revenue Code §1031 exchange or §1034 rollover upon buyout of Investors or upon sale of the joint ownership property.

60. Termination if Options Unexercised

In the event that the remaining Owners fail to exercise buyout options conferred herein, the affairs of the joint ownership shall be wound up, the assets liquidated, the debts paid and the remaining funds divided among the joint ownership co-owners in accordance with this Agreement.

61. Assumption of Obligations Upon Buyout

On buyout of a joint ownership interest under this Agreement, the remaining Owners shall assume all ownership obligations and shall protect and indemnify the withdrawing or terminated joint ownership co-owner, the personal representative and estate of a deceased, insane, bankrupt or incompetent owner, and the property of any withdrawing, deceased or terminated owner from liability for any such obligations.

62. Notices

All notices between the joint ownership co-owners shall be in writing and shall be deemed duly served when deposited in the United States mail, certified, first-class postage prepaid, return receipt requested, addressed to the owners at the address of each individual owner as follows:

Occupiers:
Orville Occupier and Margie Occupier
1 Wave Drive
Sausalito CA 94965
and
Investors:
Harold and Ingrid Investor
(Address)
(City, State)

63. Consents and Agreements

Any and all consents and agreements provided for or permitted by this Agreement shall be in writing. Signed copies of all such consents and agreements shall be filed and kept with the books of the joint ownership.

64. Each Party's Independent Analysis/Conflict of Interest

The parties agree that their interests are in conflict with one another and that the preparer of this Agreement has disclosed that he or she is unable to adequately represent the interests of any co-owner individually. The parties acknowledge this conflict of interest. The parties acknowledge that the legal and tax aspects of joint ownership have not yet been fully tested through litigation in the court or tax system; thus, no guarantees have been given as to whether the tax benefits or advantages claimed herein would be upheld in such litigation or review. The parties acknowledge that they have been advised to independently hire economic, tax and legal counsel to evaluate and review the financial, tax and legal consequences of this transaction and this Agreement. The parties acknowledge that they have either conducted their own independent tax and legal analysis of each of the terms herein or hereby knowingly waive their right to do so. The parties acknowledge that the joint ownership transaction has been reviewed in a purely hypothetical manner and they have not relied upon the figures and percentages used in such projections. No guarantees as to amounts to be earned by any party have been made.

Occupier	Investor
Occupier	Investor

65. Mediation – Arbitration

Any dispute or claim in law or equity arising out of this Agreement, concerning the joint ownership property, sale of said property, or the rights and duties of any party under this Agreement shall be first submitted to non-binding mediation under the Residential Real Estate Dispute Resolution Rules of the American Arbitration Association. If after a full mediation hearing the matter has not been resolved, said dispute shall be decided by neutral binding arbitration with the arbitrator paid from day one in accordance with the Residential Real Estate Dispute Resolution Rules of the American Arbitration Association. Judgment upon the award rendered by the arbitrator(s) may be entered in any court having jurisdiction thereof.

The following matters are excluded from mediation – arbitration hereunder:

(a) Judicial or nonjudicial foreclosure or other action or proceedings to enforce the accompanying Deed of Trust/Mortgage, or underlying real property sales contract; (b) An unlawful detainer or ejectment action; (c) The filing or enforcement of a mechanics lien; or (d) any matter which is within the jurisdiction of a probate court.

NOTICE: BY INITIALLING IN THE SPACE BELOW YOU ARE AGREEING TO HAVE ANY DISPUTE ARISING OUT OF THE MATTERS INCLUDED IN THE MEDIATION – ARBITRATION PROVISION DECIDED BY BINDING ARBITRATION PRECEDED BY MEDIATION AND YOU ARE GIVING UP ANY RIGHTS YOU MIGHT POSSESS TO HAVE THE DISPUTE LITIGATED IN COURT OR JURY TRIAL. BY INITIALLING IN THE SPACE BELOW YOU ARE GIVING UP YOUR JUDICIAL RIGHTS TO DISCOVERY AND APPEAL, EXCEPT FOR THE FOLLOWING: [Reference the specific discovery you want or the code section in your area that pertains to non-judicial arbitration/Reference the appeal rights you may want to retain]. IF YOU REFUSE TO SUBMIT TO MEDIATION – ARBITRATION AFTER AGREEING TO THIS PROVISION, YOU MAY BE COMPELLED TO MEDIATE – ARBITRATE. YOUR AGREEMENT TO THIS ARBITRATION PROVISION IS VOLUNTARY. WE HAVE READ AND UNDERSTAND THE FOREGOING AND AGREE TO SUBMIT DISPUTES ARISING OUT OF THE MATTERS INCLUDED IN THE MEDIATION – ARBITRATION PROVISION TO BINDING ARBITRATION PRECEDED BY MEDIATION.

_____   _____
Occupier   Investor

_____   _____
Occupier   Investor

66. Attorneys' Fees

If any arbitration or litigation is commenced between the co-owners herein or their personal representatives concerning any provision of this Agreement or the rights and duties of any person in relation thereto, the prevailing party or parties shall be entitled, in addition to such other relief as may be granted, to a reasonable sum for their actual attorneys' fees and costs incurred in mediation, arbitration or litigation.

67. State Law to Apply

This Agreement shall be construed under and in accordance with the laws of the State of (insert). All obligations created under this Agreement are performable in (state).

68. Parties Bound

This Agreement is binding on and shall inure to the benefit of the parties and their respective heirs, executors, administrators, legal representatives, successors, and assigns when permitted by this Agreement.

69. Legal Construction

If one or more of the provisions contained in this Agreement shall, for any reason, be held unenforceable in any respect, its unenforceability shall not affect any other provision and the Agreement shall be construed as if the unenforceable provision had never been included.

70. This Agreement Supersedes Purchase Agreement

Any and all terms of the within Joint Ownership Agreement that conflict with any terms of the Purchase Agreement and Deposit Receipt or any other prior agreement between the parties hereto shall supersede and prevail over any other agreement between the parties hereto.

71. Sole Agreement

This instrument contains the sole agreement of the parties relating to this joint ownership and correctly sets forth the rights, duties, and obligations of each to the other as of its date. Any prior agreements, promises, negotiations, or representations not expressly set forth in this Agreement are of no force or effect. Any agreement changing any of the terms of this Agreement must be in writing and signed by the parties hereto in order to be binding.

72. Counterparts
This Agreement may be executed in any number of counterparts and each counterpart shall be deemed an original for all purposes.

Executed at _____, (state) on the date herein-above set forth on the title page.

_____
Orville Occupier

_____
Margie Occupier

_____
Harold Investor

_____
Ingrid Investor

[Exhibit A consisting of legal description attached]

Sample Joint Ownership Promissory Note

Joint Ownership Promissory Note
Secured by Deed of Trust/Mortgage [Select one]

$120,150 (City) (State) September 2, (year)

This Note is secured by a Deed of Trust/Mortgage ("Joint Ownership Deed of Trust/Mortgage") of even date. This note and its Deed of Trust/Mortgage is junior and subordinate to a deed of trust recorded concurrently with, but immediately prior to, the Joint Ownership Deed of Trust/Mortgage, in Official Records of Marin County, California ("First Deed of Trust/Mortgage") securing a certain promissory note of even date with this Note, given by **Orville Occupier, Margie Occupier, Ingrid Investor and Harold Investor** in favor of **International Bank** in the original principal amount of **One Hundred Eight Thousand Dollars [$108,000] (First Note).**

Affirming Occupiers/Trustors' agreement to assume all obligations under the First Note and Deed of Trust/Mortgage as contained in the Joint Ownership Agreement of even date herewith, the original principal amount of this Note of **One Hundred Twenty Thousand One Hundred Fifty Dollars [$120,150]** includes the original principal balance of the First Note in the amount of **One Hundred Eight Thousand Dollars [$108,000]** as of the recording date of the Deed of Trust/Mortgage securing this Note and the sum amount of all other amounts due to holder of the First Note in addition to any and all sums Investors have advanced for payment due by Occupiers under the Joint Ownership Agreement of same date. The original principal amount of this note also includes the sum of **Twelve Thousand One Hundred Fifty Dollars [$12,150]** representing Forty-five percent [45%] of the original reimbursable contribution of $27,000 in retained equity [optional: cash] contributed by Investors to acquire the joint ownership property. Forty-five percent [45%] is utilized to value Occupiers' interest in Investor existing equity in the subject property.

In installments as described in the First Note, **Orville Occupier and Margie Occupier**, Occupier, promise to pay to **Ingrid Investor and Harold Investor**, Investors, payable to and at **International Bank**, the principal sum of **One Hundred Eight Thousand Dollars [$108,000]**, with interest from the date hereof as hereafter provided, payable in installments as called for in said First Note until said First Note is paid in full or natural termination of the Joint Ownership Agreement of even date, whichever occurs first.

This Note amount is a true and accurate valuation of the amounts Trustors owe Investors in the event of default entitling Investors to foreclose under their Deed of Trust/Mortgage securing this Note as defined herein. Said valuation takes into account the fact that Occupiers' material contribution to Investors and the joint ownership is payment of the mortgage, property taxes, insurance and other primary obligations as defined in the Joint Ownership Agreement, less Investor rental reimbursement, for which Investors shall become responsible upon Occupier default.

Trustors expressly agree that it would be extremely difficult and impracticable to fix the actual loss, damage and extra expense of the Investor/Beneficiary under the Deed of Trust/Mortgage securing this Note upon Trustor's default in money payment as required by Paragraphs 14, 15 and 16 entitled "Insurance/Association Dues", "Property Tax Payments" and "Loan Repayment" or performance of the Primary Obligations as defined by and required in Paragraph 34 entitled "Primary Obligations Default" and all paragraphs incorporated therein of the Joint Ownership Agreement of even date, as attested to in Paragraph 29 thereof entitled "Promissory Note to Investors", and the money amounts set forth herein and in the Deed of Trust/Mortgage securing this note of same date is a reasonable estimate of such loss, damage and expense.

Initial Here: _____   _____
                  O. O.   M. O.

Should Occupiers default in the payment of any installment when due or in the performance of any other obligation called for in this Note, the Joint Ownership Agreement of same date, or in the Deed of Trust/Mortgage securing this Note, all amounts due under this Note plus all amounts deemed due by the first lender described herein and amounts advanced by Investors for payment due by Occupiers under the Joint Ownership Agreement shall become due excluding only the first note amount stated herein.

If any action is instituted to enforce payment of this Note or the Joint Ownership Agreement of same date, or if any proceeding is commenced to foreclose the Deed of Trust/Mortgage securing the Note through exercise of the power of sale, judicial foreclosure, or otherwise, Occupiers promise to pay all costs incurred in the action or proceeding, including without limitation all reasonable attorneys' fees.

This Note is secured by the Joint Ownership Deed of Trust/Mortgage executed on this date.

_____   _____
Orville Occupier   Margie Occupier

Sample Joint Ownership Deed of Trust/Mortgage

Warning

Laws relating to trust deeds and mortgages differ. We have included in these sample documents only a Trust Deed. If you are in a state that uses mortgages instead of trust deeds, please obtain the proper mortgage form by using the Order Form at the end of this book. Do not use this Deed of Trust.

Joint Ownership Deed of Trust

Recording Requested By
Harold Investor and Ingrid Investor

After Recording Return To
Harold Investor and Ingrid Investor
(Address)
(City) (State) (Zip)

JOINT OWNERSHIP DEED OF TRUST
AND ASSIGNMENT OF RENTS

THIS DEED OF TRUST AND ASSIGNMENT OF RENTS is made this 2nd day of September, (year), by and between **Orville Occupier and Margie Occupier**, whose address during the term of this instrument shall be 1 Wave Drive, Sausalito, CA. 94965, hereinafter TRUSTORS; **Ingrid Investor and Harold Investor**, whose address during the term of this instrument shall be:_____ hereinafter BENEFICIARY; and **International Bank Title Company**, whose address during the term of this instrument shall be:_____ hereinafter TRUSTEE.

TRUSTORS HEREBY irrevocably grant, transfer, and assign to TRUSTEE, in trust, with power of sale, TRUSTORS' forty-five percent (45%) tenancy in common interest in that property in the City of Sausalito, County of Marin, State of California, described as:

[Property description]

hereafter the "property", together with buildings and improvements of every nature and kind now or hereafter erected or placed thereon including fixtures and equipment affixed thereto and all rents, issues, and profits of the property, subject, however, to the right, power, and authority given to and conferred upon BENEFICIARY to collect and apply these rents, issues, and profits.

FOR THE PURPOSE OF SECURING:

(1) Payment of the indebtedness evidenced by a Joint Ownership Promissory Note executed by Trustors on the same date as this Deed of Trust in the principal sum of **One Hundred Twenty Thousand One Hundred Fifty Dollars [$120,150]**, which amount represents the sum of **One Hundred Eight Thousand Dollars [$108,000]** as the "all-included" note and first Deed of Trust recorded concurrent herewith, but prior hereto, and executed by **Orville Occupier and Margie Occupier, Harold Investor and Ingrid Investor**, as Trustors, in favor of **International Bank**, as Beneficiary and **International Bank Title Company, Inc.**, as Trustee, and **Twelve Thousand One Hundred Fifty Dollars ($12,150)** representing the "unincluded" amount of the joint ownership all-inclusive note, and any renewal, extension or modification of the promissory note (Joint Ownership Note).

(2) Beneficiary's demand at trustee sale shall specifically exclude the current amount of the First Note (the "included amount").

(3) All amounts authorized under this Deed of Trust, its Note and the Joint Ownership Agreement between the parties.

(4) Any additional sums above the current loan amount due under the "all-included" first note and all amounts advanced by Beneficiaries for payment due by Trustors/Occupiers under the Joint Ownership Agreement of same date.

(5) The performance of each agreement contained in this Deed of Trust, the Joint Ownership Promissory Note and Joint Ownership Agreement of even date, the provisions of which are hereby incorporated by reference.

A. SUBORDINATION TO FIRST DEED OF TRUST AND NOTE. Trustors and Beneficiary agree that this is an all-inclusive Deed of Trust and is subject and subordinate to the deed of trust executed by **Orville Occupier and Margie Occupier, Harold Investor and Ingrid Investor**, as Trustors, in favor of International Bank, as Beneficiary and **International Bank Title Company, Inc.**, as Trustee in the principal amount of **One Hundred Eight Thousand Dollars [$108,000]** recorded concurrently herewith but prior hereto in the official records of the County of Marin, State of California and referred to as the First Deed of Trust.

B. INCLUSION OF FIRST DEED OF TRUST AND NOTE. This Deed of Trust and the Note it secures include the indebtedness evidenced by the First Note and Deed of Trust described in Paragraph A, above, executed by **Orville Occupier and Margie Occupier, Harold Investor and Ingrid Investor**, as Trustors, in favor of **International Bank**, as Beneficiary and **International Bank Title Company, Inc.**, as Trustee, in the principal amount of **One Hundred Eight Thousand Dollars [$108,000]**.

C. TO PROTECT THE SECURITY OF THIS ALL-INCLUSIVE DEED OF TRUST: TRUSTORS AGREE TO THE FOLLOWING:

(1) **Repair and Maintenance Requirement.** TRUSTORS will: (a) keep the property in good condition and repair; (b) not substantially alter, remove, or demolish the property or any building on the property, except when incident to the replacement of fixtures, equipment, machinery, or appliances with items of like kind; (c) restore and repair promptly and in good and workmanlike manner no less than the equivalent of its original condition, all or any part of the property that may be damaged or destroyed, including, but not limited to, damage from termites and dry rot, whether or not insurance proceeds are available to cover any part of the cost of such restoration and repair; (d) pay when due all claims for labor performed and materials furnished in connection with the property and not permit any mechanic's or materialman's lien to arise against the property; (e) comply with all laws affecting the property or requiring that any alterations or improvements be made to the property; (f) not commit or permit waste on or to the property, or commit, suffer, or permit any act or violation of law to occur upon the property; (g) not abandon the property; (h) cultivate, irrigate, fertilize, fumigate, and prune; (i) if required by BENEFICIARY, provide for the management of the property by a professional rental property manager satisfactory to BENEFICIARY under a management contract approved by BENEFICIARY; and (j) if the property is rental property, generally operate and maintain the property in such manner as to realize the maximum rental potential of the property and do all other things that the character or use of the property may reasonably render necessary to maintain the property in the same condition (reasonable wear and tear excepted) as it was at the date of this Deed of Trust.

(2) **Occupancy Requirement.** Unless otherwise agreed to by written document signed by Trustors and Beneficiaries, as an inducement to BENEFICIARY to jointly acquire the subject property secured by this Deed of Trust, TRUSTORS have represented to BENEFICIARY that the real property security will be occupied, within thirty (30) days following recordation of the within Deed of Trust and continuously for the term of the Joint Ownership Agreement of same date as the primary residence of the TRUSTORS.

TRUSTORS acknowledge that BENEFICIARY would not have agreed to acquire the joint ownership property if the real property security was not to be occupied by TRUSTORS and that the other terms of the joint ownership acquisition were determined as a result of TRUSTORS' representation that the real property security would be occupied by the TRUSTORS. TRUSTORS further acknowledge that, among other things, joint ownership Investors typically require the properties securing Occupier's interest in the joint ownership property be occupied by Occupier party; and will reject such joint ownership participation unless Occupiers have agreed to occupy the joint ownership property; Investor's ability to assign its interest in the joint ownership property, which it often does in the ordinary course of dealings, will be impaired where a real property security is not occupied by the Occupier party; the risks involved and the costs associated with owning the subject property are higher in the case of a joint ownership acquisition where the property is not occupied as the primary residence of the Occupiers; and, if and when Investors acquire joint ownership property, the Investors typically acquire such property on terms different from and requiring a higher return than for acquisitions which are secured by owner-occupied interests.

Accordingly, if the real property security is not occupied continuously for the term of the Joint Ownership Agreement of same date within thirty (30) days following recordation of the Deed of Trust of same date as the primary residence of the TRUSTORS herein who are the persons jointly holding title to the subject property and its security, BENEFICIARY may, at its option, declare all sums and obligations as set forth in the Joint Ownership Agreement and secured by the Deed of Trust to be due and payable. BENEFICIARY and TRUSTORS expressly agree that it would be extremely difficult and impracticable to fix the actual loss, damage, and extra expense of the BENEFICIARY if it could not assign or sell all or a part of its interest in the joint ownership property in the primary or secondary market because the TRUSTORS did not occupy the real property as their principal residence, and the money amounts set forth in the underlying note and Joint Ownership Agreement of same date is a reasonable estimate of such loss, damage and expense.

(3) **Due on Sale/Encumbrance.** In the event that all or any of the property described in this Deed of Trust, or any interest in that property, is sold, agreed to be sold, conveyed, encumbered, or alienated by TRUSTORS, or by the operation of law or otherwise, without the prior written consent of BENEFICIARY, all sums secured by this Deed of Trust shall, at the option of BENEFICIARY, immediately become due and payable. Consent to one such transaction shall not be deemed to be a waiver of the right to require consent to future or successive transactions.

(4) **Defense of Security.** TRUSTORS shall appear in and defend any action or proceeding purporting to affect the security of this Deed of Trust or the rights or powers of BENEFICIARY, or TRUSTEE; and to pay all costs and expenses, including cost of evidence of title and attorney's fees in a reasonable sum, in any such action or proceeding in which BENEFICIARY or TRUSTEE may appear, and in any suit brought by BENEFICIARY to foreclose upon this Deed of Trust.

(5) **Payment of Liens and Taxes.** TRUSTORS shall pay when due all taxes, assessments, and other liens on the property as required under the Joint Ownership Agreement or First Note. If TRUSTORS fail to make any payment or to do any act as provided in this Deed of Trust or the Joint Ownership Agreement of same date, then BENEFICIARY or TRUSTEE may (but is not obligated to) make the payment or do the act in the required manner and to the extent deemed necessary by BENEFICIARY or TRUSTEE to protect the security of this Deed of Trust. The performance by BENEFICIARY or TRUSTEE of such an act shall not require notice to or demand upon TRUSTORS and shall not release TRUSTORS from any obligation under this Deed of Trust or the underlying Joint Ownership Agreement. BENEFICIARY or TRUSTEE shall also have the following related rights and powers: to enter upon the property for the foregoing purposes; to appear in and defend any action or proceeding purporting to affect the security of this Deed of Trust or the rights or powers of BENEFICIARY or TRUSTEE; to pay, purchase, contest, or compromise any encumbrance, charge, or lien that in the judgment of either appears to be prior or superior to this Deed of Trust; to employ counsel; and to pay necessary expenses and costs, including attorney's fees.

(6) **Reimbursement of Costs.** TRUSTORS shall pay immediately and without demand all sums expended by BENEFICIARY or TRUSTEE pursuant to this Deed of Trust, with interest from date of expenditure at the amount allowed by law in effect at the date of this Deed of Trust, and shall pay any amount demanded by BENEFICIARY (up to the maximum allowed by law at the time of the demand) for any statement regarding the obligation secured by this Deed of Trust. TRUSTORS further agree to pay BENEFICIARY the cost of any penalty or other charge imposed by the holder of the First Note and First Deed

of Trust for BENEFICIARY's default under either, when the default was caused by TRUSTORS' failure to promptly pay any sum required under this Deed of Trust.

D.   IT IS MUTUALLY AGREED THAT:

(1)   **Insurance/payment**. Any insurance proceeds or condemnation award recovered in connection with said property or any part thereof is hereby assigned and shall be paid to BENEFICIARY in accordance with buyout provisions of the Joint Ownership Agreement of same date.

(2)   **Non-Waiver of Late Payments**. By accepting payment of any sum secured hereby after its due date, BENEFICIARY does not waive his right either to require prompt payment when due of all other sums so secured or to declare default for failure so to pay.

(3)   **Trustee's Power of Sale**. At any time or from time to time, without liability therefor and without notice, upon written request of BENEFICIARY and presentation of this Deed of Trust and its note for endorsement, and without affecting the personal liability of any person for payment of the indebtedness secured hereby, Trustee may reconvey all or any part of said property; consent to the making of any map or plat thereof; join in granting any easement thereon; or join in any extension agreement or any agreement subordinating the lien or charge hereof.

(4)   **Full Reconveyance**. Upon written request of BENEFICIARY stating that all sums secured hereby have been paid, upon surrender of this Deed of Trust and said note to Trustee for cancellation and retention, and upon payment of its fees, Trustee shall reconvey, without warranty, the property then held hereunder. The recitals in any reconveyance executed under this Deed of Trust of any matters or facts shall be conclusive proof of the truthfulness thereof. The grantee in such reconveyance may be described as "the person or persons legally entitled thereto."

(5)   **Assignment of Rents**. As additional security, TRUSTORS hereby give to and confer upon BENEFICIARY the right, power, and authority, during the continuance of these Trusts, to collect the rents, issues, and profits of said property, reserving unto TRUSTORS the right, prior to any default by TRUSTORS in payment of any indebtedness secured hereby or in performance of any agreement hereunder, to collect and retain such rents, issues, and profits as they become due and payable. Upon any such default, BENEFICIARY may at any time without notice, either in person, by agent, or by a receiver to be appointed by a court, and without regard to the adequacy of any security for the indebtedness hereby secured, enter upon and take possession of said property or any part thereof, in his own name sue for or otherwise collect such rents, issues, and profits, including those past due and unpaid, and apply the same, less costs and expenses of operation and collection, including reasonable attorneys' fees, upon any indebtedness secured hereby, and in such order as BENEFICIARY may determine. The entering upon and taking possession of said property, the collection of such rents, issues, and profits, and the application thereof as aforesaid, shall not cure or waive any default or notice of default hereunder or invalidate any act done pursuant to such notice.

(6)   **Default in Foreclosure**. Upon default by TRUSTORS in payment of any indebtedness secured hereby or in performance of any agreement hereunder, all sums secured hereby shall immediately become due and payable at the option of the BENEFICIARY. In the

event of default, BENEFICIARY may employ counsel to enforce payment of the obligations secured hereby, and shall execute or cause the Trustee to execute a written notice of such default and of his election to cause to be sold the herein described property to satisfy the obligations hereof, and shall cause such notice to be recorded in the office of the Recorder of each county wherein said real property or some part thereof is situated.

Prior to publication of the notice of sale, BENEFICIARY shall deliver to Trustee this Deed of Trust and the Note or other evidence of indebtedness which is secured hereby, together with a written request for the Trustee to proceed with a sale of the property described herein, pursuant to the provisions of law and this Deed of Trust.

Notice of sale having been given as then required by law, and not less than the time then required by law having elapsed after recordation of such notice of default, Trustee, without demand on TRUSTORS, shall sell the portion of said property pledged herein at the time and place fixed by it in said notice of sale, either as a whole or in separate parcels and in such order as it may determine, at public auction to the highest bidder for cash in lawful money of the United States, payable at time of sale. Trustee may postpone sale of all or any portion of said property by public announcement at such time and place of sale, and from time to time thereafter may postpone such sale by public announcement at the time and place fixed by the preceding postponement. Trustee shall deliver to the purchaser its deed conveying the interest in the property so sold, but without any covenant or warranty, express or implied. The recitals in such deed of any matters or facts shall be conclusive proof of the truthfulness thereof. Any person, including TRUSTORS, Trustee, or BENEFICIARY, may purchase at such sale.

After deducting all costs, fees, and expenses of Trustee and of this Trust, including cost of evidence of title and reasonable counsel fees in connection with sale, Trustee shall apply the proceeds of sale to payment of all sums due BENEFICIARY under the terms of the Joint Ownership Promissory Note Secured by this Deed of Trust and the Joint Ownership Agreement of same date and all sums expended by BENEFICIARY under the terms hereof, not then repaid, with accrued interest at ten percent (10%) per annum; all other sums then secured hereby; and the remainder, if any, to the person or persons legally entitled thereto.

(7)   **Offset of First Note**. Notwithstanding any other provision of this Deed of Trust or Note, any demand for sale delivered to the TRUSTEE for the foreclosure of this Deed of Trust shall be reduced by the amount at purchase of the all included First Note Described in B, above.

BENEFICIARY agrees that, in the event of foreclosure on this Deed of Trust, BENEFICIARY shall, at any TRUSTEE's sale, bid an amount not in excess of the amount then due upon the obligation secured by this Deed of Trust, including late charges, penalties, and/or advances, minus the balance then due on the First Note, including late charges, interest penalties, advances, and/or impounds as described herein.

(8)   **General Provisions**. This Deed of Trust applies to, inures to the benefit of, and binds all parties hereto, their heirs, legatees, devisees, administrators, executors, successors, and assigns. The term BENEFICIARY shall mean the holder and owner of the note secured hereby; or, if the note has been pledged, the pledgee thereof. In this Deed of Trust, whenever the context so requires, the masculine gender includes the feminine and/or neuter, and the singular number includes the plural.

(9)   **Acceptance by Trustee**. Trustee is not obligated to notify any party hereto of pending sale under any other Deed of Trust or of any action or proceeding in which THRUSTORS, BENEFICIARY, or Trustee shall be a party unless brought by Trustee.

(10)   **Substitution of Trustees**. BENEFICIARY may from time to time or at any time substitute a Trustee or Trustees to execute the trust hereby created, and when any such substitution has been filed for record in the office of the Recorder of the county in which the property herein described is situated, it shall be conclusive evidence of the appointment of such Trustee or Trustees, and such new Trustee or Trustees shall succeed to all of the powers and duties of the Trustee or Trustees named herein.

(11)   **Cumulative Powers and Remedies**. The powers and remedies conferred in this Deed of Trust are concurrent and cumulative to all other rights and remedies provided in this Deed of Trust or given by law. These powers and remedies may be exercised singly, successively, or together, and as often as deemed necessary.

(12)   **Conclusiveness of Recitals**. The recitals contained in any reconveyance, trustee's deed, or any other instrument executed by the TRUSTEE from time to time under the authority of this Deed of Trust in the exercise of its powers or the performance of its duties under this Deed of Trust, shall be conclusive evidence of their truth, whether stated as specified and particular facts, or in general statements or conclusions. Further, the recitals shall be binding and conclusive upon the THRUSTORS, their heirs, executors, administrators, successors, and assigns, and all other persons.

(13)   **Attorneys' Fees**. If any action is brought for the foreclosure of this Deed of Trust or for the enforcement of any provision of this Deed of Trust (whether or not suit is filed), THRUSTORS agree to pay all costs and expenses of BENEFICIARY and TRUSTEE, including reasonable attorneys' fees; and these sums shall be secured by this Deed of Trust.

(14)   **Co-trustees**. If two or more persons are designated as TRUSTEE in this Deed of Trust, any, or all, power granted by this Deed of Trust to the TRUSTEE may be exercised by any of those persons, if the other person or persons are unable, for any reason, to act. Any recital of this inability in any instrument executed by any of those persons shall be conclusive against THRUSTORS and their assigns.

(15)   **Purchase Money Encumbrance**. The promissory note secured by this Deed of Trust is given as a part of the purchase price of the property.

(16)   **Request for Notice of Default and Sale**. Request is hereby made that a copy of any Notice of Default and a copy of any Notice of Sale under that Deed of Trust executed by **Orville Occupier and Margie Occupier and Harold Investor and Ingrid Investor** as THRUSTORS, and recorded concurrent herewith but immediately prior hereto in the Official Records of Marin County, State of California, in which **International Bank** is named as BENEFICIARY be mailed to:

Harold Investor and Ingrid Investor
(Address)
(City) (State) (Zip)

(17)   **Notice Provisions.** A copy of any notice of default and of any notice of sale will be sent only to the address contained in this document. If Trustor or Beneficiaries' address changes, notice must be recorded. Otherwise notice to the address stated is herein deemed sufficient notice.

Orville Occupier and Margie Occupier   Harold Investor and Ingrid Investor
(Address)   (Address)
(City) (State) (Zip)   (City) (State) (Zip)

TRUSTOR/OCCUPIER

_____
Orville Occupier

_____
Margie Occupier

Sample Lease

JOINT OWNERSHIP LEASE AGREEMENT

WHEREAS **Ingrid Investor and Harold Investor**, hereinafter called "Lessor," and **Orville Occupier and Margie Occupier**, hereinafter called "Lessee," have entered into a Joint Ownership Agreement dated September 2, (year) whereby each party is the owner of an undivided interest in the real property located at 1 Wave Drive, Sausalito, California herein called the "demised premises," and,

NOW THEREFORE, Lessor leases his interest in the demised premises to Lessee in accordance with Internal Revenue Code Section §280A under the terms set forth in said Joint Ownership Agreement and on the following terms and conditions:

Term

1. The term of this Lease is five years from the date hereof.

Amount

2. Rental payments for said term shall be in the amount of $240.00 per month.

Use

3. The demised premises shall be used only for a single family residence and Lessee shall not permit the demised premises or any part thereof to be used for:

a. any offensive, noisy, or dangerous activity that would increase the premiums for fire insurance on the demised premises;

b. the creation or maintenance of a public nuisance;

c. anything which is against any laws or rules or any other provisions or regulations of any public authority at any time applicable to the demised premises.

Utilities

4. Lessee shall pay promptly as they become due all charges for the furnishing of water, electricity, garbage service, and other public utilities to the demised premises during the term of this Lease (including any water tax or water rate imposed on the demised premises for the furnishing of water to such premises during the term of this Lease).

Indemnity Agreement

5. Lessee agrees to indemnify and hold Lessor and the property interest of Lessor, including the demised premises, free and harmless from any and all

liability for injury to or death of any person, including Lessee and employees of Lessee, or for damage to property arising from the use and occupancy of the demised premises by Lessee or from the act or omission of any act by any person or persons, including Lessee and employees of Lessee, in or about the demised premises with the express or implied consent of Lessee.

Assignment and Subletting

6. Lessee shall not abandon the premises nor shall he assign this Lease or sublet the demised premises or any interest therein without the written consent of Lessor first had and obtained, which consent shall not be unreasonably withheld. Any assignment, subletting or abandonment without the written consent of Lessor or an assignment or subletting by operation of law, shall be void and shall, at the option of Lessor, terminate this lease.

Default by Lessee

7. Should Lessee be in default in the payment of any rent under this Lease or the performance of any other provisions of this Lease, Lessor shall have all rights and remedies available under the terms of the Joint Ownership Agreement dated September 2, (year) and under the laws of the State of _____ in effect on the date of default, including unlawful detainer. The prevailing party shall be awarded costs and reasonable attorneys' fees incurred in said proceedings to enforce default.

Lessee Breach of Joint Ownership Agreement

8. Should Lessee breach the underlying Joint Ownership Agreement between the parties hereto dated September 2, (year), Lessor's duties and obligations under this Lease shall automatically terminate.

Holdover by Lessee

9. Should Lessee remain in possession of the demised premises with the consent of Lessor after the natural expiration of this Lease, a new tenancy from month-to-month shall be created between Lessor and Lessee which shall be subject to all the terms and conditions of this Lease and the Joint Ownership Agreement, until the property is sold or transferred as called for in said Agreement.

Integrated Agreement

10. Lessor and Lessee agree that this instrument is and shall be incorporated into and become a part of the Joint Ownership Agreement dated September 2, (year) executed by them, and further agree that this instrument and said Joint Ownership Agreement shall be deemed to collectively set forth their rights and obligations to each other concerning the demised premises. Any agreement or representation respecting the demised premises or the duties of either Lessor or Lessee in relation thereto not expressly set forth in this Lease, the Joint Ownership Agreement, note and security instrument is null and void.

Non-Ownership Status

11. Lessee confirms that while Lessee may be an owner of his interest in the subject property, he is not an owner of the portion of the property he is leasing pursuant to this lease. Lessee confirms that his ownership interest extends only to his percentage interest in the subject property which is not subject to this lease.

Dated: September 2, (year).

LESSOR:_____
         Ingrid Investor

LESSOR:_____
         Harold Investor

LESSEE:_____
         Orville Occupier

LESSEE:_____
         Margie Occupier

BLANK CHARTS

Caution – These blank charts are intended as guides. They are not substitutes for legal or other necessary professional advice. Each transaction is unique, as are the relevant laws of different states. You are urged to consult with competent counsel when putting together a transaction. We caution against merely filling in the blanks without consultation.

Joint Ownership Preliminary Commitment

Investors:
Occupiers:

We, Occupiers and Investors, enter into this Preliminary Commitment prior to preparation of a Joint Ownership Agreement. Occupiers and Investors agree to the following terms which shall be incorporated into the Joint Ownership Agreement. The parties agree to be bound by the following terms until such time as the Joint Ownership Agreement is entered into:

1. The parties shall acquire property to be held by them as tenants in common.

2. Investors shall contribute _____% of the purchase price / $_____ as their initial capital contribution.

3. Occupiers shall contribute _____% of the purchase price/ $_____ as their initial capital contribution.

4. Acquisitional closing costs are not reimbursable and shall be paid _____% / $_____ by Occupiers and _____% / $_____ by Investors.

5. With Seller as Investor, Occupier shall advance, subject to Seller reimbursement, $_____ of the real estate commission.

6. Ownership split shall be _____% to Investors and _____% to Occupiers.

7. The Agreement term will be:
    ☐ 3 years   ☐ 5 years   ☐ 7 years   ☐ 10 years

8. Occupier shall be granted exclusive occupancy during term.

9. Purchase price shall be [in the range of] $_____.

10. Additional terms:

      Executed this ___ day of _____, (year)

              Investors: Occupiers:
        _____   _____

Joint Ownership Worksheet

Initial purchase
Purchase price _____

Down payment - Investor paid _____

Down payment - Occupier paid _____

Loan _____

Term: _____ Years

Projected annual appreciation rate: _____%

Investor projected annual simple return: _____%

Ownership split: Occupier____%/Investor____%

280A rental: _____

Payments/Rent reimbursement
Occupiers:

	Yearly	Term
Mortgage/Interest	_____	_____
Property taxes	_____	_____
Total	_____	_____

Investors:

	Yearly	Term
Rental income	_____	_____
Deductions		
[equal to rental income]		
Insurance	_____	_____
Association dues	_____	_____
Property taxes	_____	_____
Mortgage/Interest	_____	_____
Total:	_____	_____
Depreciation	_____	_____

Joint Ownership Worksheet — 2 —

Projected Buyout of Investor

Appraisal (_____% annual appreciation)   _____
Loan pay off   _____
Equity   _____
Return of investment to Investor   _____
Return of investment to Occupier   _____
Return of loan principal reduction to _____   _____
Net equity   _____
Times Investor interest   _____
Investor share of equity   _____
Plus Investor down payment   _____
Plus Investor loan principal reduction   _____
Buyout of Investor   _____

Projected Buyout of Occupier

Appraisal - (_____% annual appreciation)   _____
Loan pay off   _____
Equity   _____
Return of investment to Investor   _____
Return of investment to Occupier   _____
Return of loan principal reduction to _____   _____
Net equity   _____
Times Occupier interest   _____
Occupier share of equity   _____
Plus Occupier down payment   _____
Plus Occupier loan principal reduction   _____
Buyout of Occupier   _____

Joint Ownership Worksheet – 3 –

Projected Refinance by Occupier

Appraised value - (___%) assumed appreciation: _____
Times refinance percentage _____
Loan proceeds [_____ equity] _____
Loan Pay off _____
Net proceeds _____
Investor buyout _____
Net/Deficit to Occupier _____

Projected Refinance by Investor

Appraised value - (___%) assumed appreciation _____
Times refinance percentage _____
Loan proceeds [_____ equity] _____
Loan Pay off _____
Net proceeds _____
Occupier buyout _____
Net/Deficit to Investor _____

Joint Ownership Worksheet — 4 —

Projected Sale at Term

Sale price - (___%) assumed appreciation   _____
Loan pay off   _____
Less negative amortization paid by Occupier   _____
Less sale expenses   _____
Gross proceeds   _____
Return of investment to Investor   _____
Return of investment to Occupier   _____
Return of loan principal reduction to _____   _____
Net equity   _____
Times Investor interest   _____
Investor share of equity   _____

Recap – Investor down payment   _____
Recap – Investor loan principal reduction   _____
Investor Proceeds   _____

Gross proceeds recap   _____
Less Investor proceeds   _____
Occupier Proceeds   _____

IRC §280A Rental Calculation

Fair market value   _____
(x) Rent apportionment (.004)   _____
Fair market rent   _____
(x) Investor's interest   _____
Rent - Investor interest   _____
Less 20% good tenant discount   _____
Fair rent to Occupier   _____

Investor's Depreciation Deduction

Depreciable basis   _____
(x) Improvements allocation (% age)   _____
Value of improvements   _____
(x) Investor interest   _____
Investor interest in improvements   _____
(÷) 27.5 Years - residential depreciation   _____
Investor annual depreciation   _____
(x) Term years   _____
Depreciation over term   _____

Basis and Gain Calculations - Occupier
To Compute Gain Recognized Without Roll Over

1. Relinquished property acquisition cost   _____
2. Capital expenditures   _____
3. Adjusted basis - relinquished property   _____
      (Line 1 plus Line 2)
4. Relinquished property sales price   _____
5. Selling fix-up expenses   _____
6. Selling closing expenses   _____
7. Adjusted sales price on   _____
      relinquished property
      (Line 4 minus Line 5 minus Line 6)
8. Gain recognized without roll over   _____
      (Line 7 minus Line 3)

Sections 1034 and 121 Combined

1. Relinquished property sales price   _____
2. Selling fix-up expenses   _____
3. Selling closing expenses   _____
4. Adjusted sales price on   _____
      relinquished property
      (Line 1 minus Line 2 minus Line 3)
5. Fair market value, replacement   _____
      property
6. Gain realized (Line 4 minus Line 5)   _____
7. Less up to $125,000,   _____
      IRC §121 exemption
8. Gain recognized   _____

- Basis and Gain Calculations -
Investor
To Compute Gain Realized Without Exchange

1. Relinquished property acquisition cost _____
2. Capital expenditures _____
3. Balance (Line 1 + Line 2) _____
4. Depreciation adjustment _____
5. Adjusted basis — relinquished property _____
    (Line 3 minus Line 4)
6. Relinquished property sales price _____
7. Selling fix-up expenses _____
8. Selling closing expenses _____
9. Adjusted sales price _____
    on relinquished property
    (Line 6 minus Line 7 minus Line 8)
10. Gain realized without exchange _____
    (Line 9 minus Line 5)

Investor's Exchange Profile

	Relinquished Property	Replacement Property
1. Market value	_____	_____
2. Existing loans	_____	_____
3. New loans	_____	_____
4. Equity (Line 1 less 2 & 3)	_____	_____
5. Cash boot	_____	_____
6. Other (boot) property	_____	_____
7. Loan proceeds	_____	_____
8. **Balance**	_____	_____

EXCHANGE TAX CALCULATION
To Compute Gain Recognized in Exchange

REALIZED GAIN

1. Fair market value of replacement property _____
2. Fair market value of boot replacement property _____
3. Liabilities on relinquished property _____
4. Cash received _____
5. Total (lines 1 + 2 + 3 + 4) _____
6. Adjusted basis of relinquished property _____
7. Adjusted basis of boot relinquished property _____
8. Liabilities on replacement property _____
9. Cash paid out _____
10. Total (Lines 6 + 7 + 8 + 9) _____
11. Gain/loss realized (Line 5 minus Line 10) _____

BOOT RECEIVED

12. Liabilities on relinquished property _____
13. Liabilities on replacement property _____
14. Line 12 minus Line 13 _____
15. Fair market value - boot relinquished property _____
16. Difference (Line 14 minus Line 15) _____
17. Cash received (offset by exchange expense) _____
18. Total (Line 16 + Line 17) _____
19. Cash paid out _____
20. Line 18 minus Line 19 _____
21. Market value - boot replacement property _____
22. Total boot received (Line 20 + Line 21) _____

RECOGNIZED GAIN _____
(the smaller of Line 11 or Line 22)

INTERNAL REVENUE CODE SECTIONS

Internal Revenue Code §121

One-time exclusion of gain from sale of principal residence by individual who has attained age 55.

The following is a synopsis followed by an excerpt from IRC §121.

Synopsis

In the case of a sale or involuntary conversion of his principal residence, a taxpayer is allowed a once-in-a-lifetime election to exclude up to $125,000 ($62,500 on the separate return of a married taxpayer) of gain. The exclusion rule applies to all taxpayers who are age 55 or older prior to the sale. To qualify the seller must have owned the residence and used it as his principal residence for at least three years in the five-year period preceding the sale.

Both husband and wife will be treated as satisfying the age 55 ownership-and-use requirements where (1) one spouse satisfies such requirements in regard to a residence that they own as joint tenants, tenants by the entirety, or as community property, and (2) they file a joint return. However, spouses cannot "divide" the requirements for eligibility between them. That is, if a principal residence is held by a husband and wife as joint tenants, at least one spouse must meet all of the use, age and ownership requirements in order for the couple to qualify for nonrecognition treatment.

Internal Revenue Code §121

Excerpt from Code Section

(a) General rule.

At the election of the taxpayer, gross income does not include gain from the sale or exchange of property if –

(1) the taxpayer has attained the age of 55 before the date of such sale or exchange, and

(2) during the 5-year period ending on the date of the sale or exchange, such property has been owned and used by the taxpayer as his principal residence for periods aggregating 3 years or more.

(b) Limitations.

(1) Dollar limitation. The amount of the gain excluded from gross income under subsection (a) shall not exceed $ 125,000 ($ 62,500 in the case of a separate return by a married individual).

(2) Application to only 1 sale or exchange. Subsection (a) shall not apply to any sale or exchange by the taxpayer if an election by the taxpayer or his spouse under subsection (a) with respect to any other sale or exchange is in effect.

(3) Additional election if prior sale was made on or before July 26, 1978. In the case of any sale or exchange after July 26, 1978, this section shall be applied by not taking into account any election made with respect to a sale or exchange on or before such date.

(c) Election.

An election under subsection (a) may be made or revoked at any time before the expiration of the period for making a claim for credit or refund of the tax imposed by this chapter for the taxable year in which the sale or exchange occurred, and shall be made or revoked in such manner as the Secretary shall by regulations prescribe. In the case of a taxpayer who is married, an election under subsection (a) or a revocation thereof may be made only if his spouse joins in such election or revocation.

Internal Revenue Code §280A

Disallowance of certain expenses in connection with business use of home, rental of vacation homes, etc.

The following is a synopsis of the relevant section, followed by an excerpt from IRC §280A.

Synopsis

One of the latest innovations in creative real estate financing techniques is the Shared Equity Financing Agreement (SEFA). The SEFA permits one individual to assist another in the purchase of a principal residence and obtain substantial tax benefits at the same time. While SEFAs have been part of the Code since 1981, their use has been retarded by the lack of financial regulations. However, SEFAs offer the participants the dual advantages of making home ownership possible in otherwise difficult situations and of permitting one of the owners to claim expenses that are associated with rental property.

The term "Shared Equity Financing Agreement" means an agreement under which two or more persons acquire a qualified ownership interest in a dwelling unit, and one of the persons is entitled to occupy the unit as a principal residence. The agreement must further provide that the person occupying the unit as a principal residence pay rent to the other person or persons holding an ownership interest in the unit.

In order to be an ownership interest that qualifies under the SEFA provisions, each of the co-owners must acquire an undivided interest for more than 50 years in the entire dwelling unit and any appurtenant land that is acquired in the transaction to which the SEFA relates.

The co-owner who occupies the unit as a principal residence must pay "fair rental" to the other co-owner, and such rent is to be determined by taking into account the occupant's ownership interest in the unit.

An arrangement of co-ownership that satisfies the SEFA requirements offers significant non-tax and tax advantages to all the co-owners. For example, a SEFA provides a means by which a parent may help a child purchase a home that would otherwise be unaffordable, while protecting the parent's investment through acquisition of an ownership interest in the property. Under a SEFA, the non-occupant and occupant co-owners are each able to claim deductions for the amount of mortgage interest and real estate taxes each pays on the property.

Internal Revenue Code §280A

Excerpt from Code Section

(6)(3) Rental to family member, etc., for use as principal residence.

(A) In general. A taxpayer shall not be treated as using a dwelling unit for personal purposes by reason of a rental arrangement for any period if for such period such dwelling unit is rented, at a fair rental, to any person for use as such person's principal residence.

(B) Special rules for rental to person having interest in unit.

(i) Rental must be pursuant to shared equity financing agreement*. Subparagraph (A) shall apply to a rental to a person who has an interest in the dwelling unit only if such rental is pursuant to a shared equity financing agreement.

(ii) Determination of fair rental. In the case of a rental pursuant to a shared equity financing agreement, fair rental shall be determined as of the time the agreement is entered into and by taking into account the occupant's qualified ownership interest.

(C) Shared equity financing agreement. For purposes of this paragraph, the term "shared equity financing agreement" means an agreement under which –

(i) 2 or more persons acquire qualified ownership interests in a dwelling unit, and

(ii) the person (or persons) holding 1 or more of such interests –

(I) is entitled to occupy the dwelling unit for use as a principal residence, and

(II) is required to pay rent to 1 or more other persons holding qualified ownership interests in the dwelling unit.

(D) Qualified ownership interest. For purposes of this paragraph, the term "qualified ownership interest" means an undivided interest for more than 50 years in the entire dwelling unit and appurtenant land being acquired in the transaction to which the shared equity financing agreement relates.

*Note: The Joint Ownership Agreement constitutes a Shared Equity financing agreement.

Internal Revenue Code §1031

Code Section in its Entirety

Exchange of property held for productive use or investment.

(a) Nonrecognition of gain or loss from exchanges solely in kind.

(1) In general. No gain or loss shall be recognized on the exchange of property held for productive use in a trade or business or for investment if such property is exchanged solely for property of like kind which is to be held either for productive use in a trade or business or for investment.

(2) Exception. This subsection shall not apply to any exchange of –

(A) stock in trade or other property held primarily for sale,

(B) stocks, bonds, or notes,

(C) other securities or evidences of indebtedness or interest,

(D) interests in a partnership,

(E) certificates of trust or beneficial interests, or

(F) choses in action.

For purposes of this section, an interest in a partnership which has in effect a valid election under section 761(a) to be excluded from the application of all of subchapter K shall be treated as an interest in each of the assets of such partnership and not as an interest in a partnership.

(3) Requirement that property be identified and that exchange be completed not more than 180 days after transfer of exchanged property. For purposes of this subsection, any property received by the taxpayer shall be treated as property which is not like-kind property if –

(A) such property is not identified as property to be received in the exchange on or before the day which is 45 days after the date on which the taxpayer transfers the property relinquished in the exchange, or

(B) such property is received after the earlier of –

(i) the day which is 180 days after the date on which the taxpayer transfers the property relinquished in the exchange, or

(ii) the due date (determined with regard to extension) for the transferor's return of the tax imposed by this chapter for the taxable year in which the transfer of the relinquished property occurs.

(b) Gain from exchanges not solely in kind.

If an exchange would be within the provisions of subsection (a), of section 1035(a), of section 1036(a), or of section 1037(a), if it were not for the fact that the property received in exchange consists not only of property permitted by such provisions to be received without the recognition of gain, but also of other property or money, then the gain, if any, to the recipient shall be recognized, but in an amount not in excess of the sum of such money and the fair market value of such other property.

(c) Loss from exchanges not solely in kind.

If an exchange would be within the provisions of subsection (a), of section 1035(a), of section 1036(a), or of section 1037(a), if it were not for the fact that the property received in exchange consists not only of property permitted by such provisions to be received without the recognition of gain or loss, but also of other property or money, then no loss from the exchange shall be recognized.

(d) Basis.

If property was acquired in an exchange described in this section, section 1035(a), section 1036(a), or section 1037(a), then the basis shall be the same as that of the property exchanged, decreased in the amount of any money received by the taxpayer and increased in the amount of gain or decreased in the amount of loss to the taxpayer that was recognized on such exchange. If the property so acquired consisted in part of the type of property permitted by this section, section 1035(a), section 1036(a), or section 1037(a), to be received without the recognition of gain or loss, and in part of other property, the basis provided in this subsection shall be allocated between the properties (other than money) received, and for the purpose of the allocation there shall be assigned to such other property an amount equivalent to its fair market value at the date of the exchange. For purposes of this section, section 1035(a), and section 1036(a), where as part of the consideration to the taxpayer another party to the exchange assumed a liability of the taxpayer or acquired from the taxpayer property subject to a liability, such assumption or acquisition (in the amount of the liability) shall be considered as money received by the taxpayer on the exchange.

(e) Exchanges of livestock of different sexes.

For purposes of this section, livestock of different sexes are not property of a like kind.

(f) Special rules for exchanges between related persons.

(1) In general. If –

(A) a taxpayer exchanges property with a related person,

(B) there is nonrecognition of gain or loss to the taxpayer under this section with respect to the exchange of such property (determined without regard to this subsection), and

(C) before the date 2 years after the date of the last transfer which was part of such exchange–

(i) the related person disposes of such property, or

(ii) the taxpayer disposes of the property received in the exchange from the related person which was of like kind to the property transferred by taxpayer, there shall be no nonrecognition of gain or loss under this section to the taxpayer with respect to such exchange; except that any gain or loss recognized by the taxpayer by reason of this subsection shall be taken into account as of the date on which the disposition referred to in subparagraph (C) occurs.

(2) Certain dispositions not taken into account. For purposes of paragraph (1)(C), there shall not be taken into account any disposition –

(A) after the earlier of the death of the taxpayer or the death of the related person,

(B) in a compulsory or involuntary conversion (within the meaning of section 1033) if the exchange occurred before the threat or imminence of such conversion, or

(C) with respect to which it is established to the satisfaction of the Secretary that neither the exchange nor such disposition had as one of its principal purposes the avoidance of Federal income tax.

(3) Related person. For purposes of this subsection, the term "related person" means any person bearing a relationship to the taxpayer described in section 267(b) or 707(b)(1).

(4) Treatment of certain transactions. This section shall not apply to any exchange which is part of a transaction (or series of transactions) structured to avoid the purposes of this subsection.

(g) Special rule where substantial diminution of risk.

(1) In general. If paragraph (2) applies to any property for any period, the running of the period set forth in subsection (f)(1)(C) with respect to such property shall be suspended during such period.

(2) Property to which subsection applies. This paragraph shall apply to any property for any period during which the holder's risk of loss with respect to the property is substantially diminished by –
    (A) the holding of a put with respect to such property,
    (B) the holding by another person of a right to acquire such property, or
    (C) a short sale or any other transaction.

(h) Special rule for foreign real property.
    For purposes of this section, real property located in the United States and real property located outside the United States are not property of a like kind.

Internal Revenue Code §1034

Rollover of gain on sale of principal residence.

The following is an excerpt from this Code Section:

(a) Nonrecognition of gain.
    If property (in this section called "old residence") used by the taxpayer as his principal residence is sold by him and, within a period beginning 2 years before the date of such sale and ending 2 years after such date, property (in this section called "new residence") is purchased and used by the taxpayer as his principal residence, gain (if any) from such sale shall be recognized only to the extent that the taxpayer's adjusted sales price (as defined in subsection (b)) of the old residence exceeds the taxpayer's cost of purchasing the new residence.
(b) Adjusted sales price defined.
    (1) In general. For purposes of this section, the term "adjusted sales price" means the amount realized, reduced by the aggregate of expenses for work performed on the old residence in order to assist in its sale.
    (2) Limitations. The reduction provided in paragraph (1) applies only to expenses –
        (A) for work performed during the 90-day period ending on the day on which the contract to sell the old residence is entered into;
        (B) which are paid on or before the 30th day after the date of the sale of the old residence; and
        (C) which are –
            (i) not allowable as deductions in computing taxable income under section 63 (defining taxable income), and
            (ii) not taken into account in computing the amount realized from the sale of the old residence.
(c) Rules for application of section.

For purposes of this section:

(1) An exchange by the taxpayer of his residence for other property shall be treated as a sale of such residence, and the acquisition of a residence on the exchange of property shall be treated as a purchase of such residence.

(2) A residence any part of which was constructed or reconstructed by the taxpayer shall be treated as purchased by the taxpayer. In determining the taxpayer's cost of purchasing a residence, there shall be included only so much of his cost as is attributable to the acquisition, construction, reconstruction, and improvements made which are properly chargeable to capital account, during the period specified in subsection (a).

(3) If a residence is purchased by the taxpayer before the date of his sale of the old residence, the purchased residence shall not be treated as his new residence if sold or otherwise disposed of by him before the date of the sale of the old residence.

(4) If the taxpayer, during the period described in subsection (a), purchases more than one residence which is used by him as his principal residence at some time within 2 years after the date of the sale of the old residence, only the last of such residences so used by him after the date of such sale shall constitute the new residence. If a principal residence is sold in a sale to which subsection (d)(2) applies within 2 years after the sale of the old residence, for purposes of applying the preceding sentence with respect to the old residence, the principal residence so sold shall be treated as the last residence used during such 2-year period.

(d) Limitation.

(1) In general. Subsection (a) shall not apply with respect to the sale of the taxpayer's residence if within 2 years before the date of such sale the taxpayer sold at a gain other property used by him as his principal residence, and any part of such gain was not recognized by reason of subsection (a).

(2) Subsequent sale connected with commencing work at new place. Paragraph (1) shall not apply with respect to the sale of the taxpayer's residence if –

(A) such sale was in connection with the commencement of work by the taxpayer as an employee or as a self-employed individual at a new principal place of work, and

(B) if the residence so sold is treated as the former residence for purposes of section 217 (relating to moving expenses), the taxpayer would satisfy the conditions of subsection (c) of section 217 (as modified by other subsections of such section).

(e) Basis of new residence.

Where the purchase of a new residence results, under subsection (a) or under section 112(n) of the Internal Revenue Code of 1939, in the nonrecognition of gain on the sale of an old residence, in determining the adjusted basis of the new residence as of any time following the sale of the old residence, the adjustments to basis shall include a reduction by an amount equal to the amount of the gain not so recognized on the sale of the old residence. For this purpose, the amount of the gain not so recognized on the sale of the old residence includes only so much of such gain as is not recognized by reason of the cost, up to such time, of purchasing the new residence.

Glossary

A

acquisition costs: The loan fees, title insurance, inspection fees, and escrow charges applied to a property sale.

adjustable rate mortgage (ARM): A mortgage with an interest rate that may fluctuate during the term of the loan, that may or may not be predetermined.

adjusted basis: The original cost of a property which is increased by improvements and capital expenditures and decreased by depreciation deductions.

adjusted sales price: The selling price of a property minus expenses such as a broker's commission, established for tax purposes.

amortization: The repayment of a loan by installments which includes interest and gradual reduction of principal.

annual appreciation rate: The increase in value of a property during a one-year period, expressed as a percentage.

annual percentage rate (APR): The loan interest rate adjusted for the loan term to include loan fees and points, required by the Federal Truth in Lending Act.

annual simple interest: Interest calculated per year on loan principal only, distinguished from compound interest.

appreciation: An increase in the value or price of a property.

arbitration: The process by which a qualified person decides a dispute. Binding arbitration is final and cannot be appealed; non-binding arbitration is advisory only.

381

arms length transaction: A transaction reflecting equal bargaining strength on both sides; transactions between related parties must meet the test of equality to resist IRS challenge.

assumed appreciation: A hypothetical appreciation based on past values.

B

balloon payment: The final payment on a loan which is considerably higher than previous payments and results in loan pay off.

basis: The amount paid for real property.

binding arbitration: Arbitration that results in a final, non-appealable judgment.

boot: The receipt of cash or its equivalent accompanying an IRC §1031 exchange of property.

breach: The failure to complete an obligation.

C

CAM: A realtor designation for a certified commercial investment member.

capital contribution: Initial contribution to the property's equity by cash toward the down payment or by retained equity.

capital improvements: Repairs or additions that add to the value or prolong the life of a property.

capital gains tax rate: The rate at which long-term gains are taxed, expressed as a percentage.

claiming deductions ratably: Claiming deductions based upon one's ownership percentage in real property.

closing costs: The fees attached to a property purchase including real estate commissions, escrow charges, and any other costs a party has agreed to pay.

comparables: The recent selling price of properties similar to the property for sale, used to determine the market price.

compound interest: The interest paid on the original loan principal and on the accumulated unpaid interest.

counter offer: A response to an offer containing new terms.

D

deed of trust/mortgage: A security device created to define and protect the Investor's interest in a joint ownership or a lender's interest in a property.

deferral of gain: A postponement of tax on profit.

deferral options: The opportunity to postpone payment of tax at sale by reinvesting in similar real estate.

deposit receipt: A legal document also known as a real estate purchase agreement.

depreciable basis: The amount paid for real property (basis) allocated to the improvements, as opposed to the land, upon which depreciation is calculated.

depreciate: The decrease of property value caused by aging, deterioration, or economic obsolescence.

depreciation deduction: The amount credited for tax purposes to reflect the loss of property value over time due to age.

due on encumbrance provision: A provision in the Deed of Trust/Mortgage that makes a loan due in full if any interest in the property is transferred or pledged.

E

equity: The value of property over the amount of liens attached to it.

equity interest: Percentage of ownership applied to the equity of the property after return of capital contributions.

escrow: A neutral third party with the responsibility of completing the provisions of a purchase agreement on behalf of the buyers and sellers.

eviction: The dispossession of a tenant by court judgment.

exchange: The trading of equities in two or more properties pursuant to IRC §1031.

exclusive occupancy: The Occupier's privilege of exclusively occupying the joint ownership property.

F

fair market rental: The amount of money that can be charged for occupancy of a property when offered on the open market for a reasonable period of time with all conditions of the property known to both parties.

FHA mortgage: A low interest and/or low down payment loan for residential purchases insured by the Federal Housing Administration and offered by lending institutions.

foreclosure: The legal procedure where property is sold to pay the debt of a mortgagor in default of payment or terms.

G

gain: The difference between the adjusted basis and the adjusted sales price.

gain realized: The net profit resulting when the relinquished and replacement properties are compared in an IRC §1031 exchange.

gain recognized: The lesser of gain realized and net boot received in an IRC §1031 exchange.

good tenant discount: A rental discount afforded to Occupier whose ownership interest in the property should assure a responsible tenancy.

grant deed: A limited warranty deed which assures the grantee that the grantor has not conveyed the land to another party and that the property is free from any unrecorded encumbrances.

gross equity: Sale or buyout price minus loans before return of capital contributions.

I

interest: A portion of ownership. Also, the tax deductible fee for the use of money for a certain time period.

investment holding: An asset held for investment purposes.

Investor: The joint ownership co-owner who typically does not occupy the property or pay its expenses.

J

joint liability: Equal responsibility.

joint ownership: A team strategy for buying residential real estate memorialized by a "Joint Ownership Agreement."

Joint Ownership Agreement: A written agreement memorializing the provisions of a residential joint ownership.

Joint Ownership Lease: The agreement between the Investor as lessor and Occupier as lessee concerning lease of the Investor's interest in the joint ownership property.

Joint Ownership Preliminary Commitment: A statement of intent to jointly own residential real estate, and the fundamental understandings to be memorialized in the subsequent "Joint Ownership Agreement."

L

lease option: An agreement between the property owner and lessee in which the lessee pays an option deposit to purchase the property at an agreed price at a later date with a portion of lease payments credited to the lease option deposit.

lifetime exemption: A once-in-a-lifetime $125,000 capital gain exemption for Occupiers age 55 and over, entitled by IRC §121.

like-kind real property: Real property assets which qualify for preferred tax treatment in an exchange under IRC §1031.

listing agreement: A written contract between the real estate broker and property seller which authorizes the broker to perform the service of securing persons to buy, lease, or rent the property.

living trust: An asset holding entity which operates through its trustee and makes post-death distributions without probate, giving family members control and confidentiality.

loan origination fee: A charge from the lender for processing a mortgage application.

M

Magnet loans: Loan packages designed for employers to assist employees with housing costs, offered by the Federal National Mortgage Association (Fannie Mae).

mediation: A procedure by which a trained mediator facilitates and encourages settlement of a dispute. No judgment is ordered.

mortgage insurance: Amounts paid by borrowers, usually when down payments are less than 20% of purchase price.

mortgage interest deduction: Fully deductible interest subject to certain limitations set by the IRS.

mortgage relief: Release from debt in an IRC §1031 exchange.

multiple listing service: An association of real estate agents who provide a pool of combined listings with established agreements to share commissions.

N

necessary improvements: Improvements which preserve the value and integrity of real property.

negative amortization: Unpaid interest which must be added to the principal when monthly mortgage payments are not enough to pay the full amount of interest accruing on the principal.

net equity: The value of the joint ownership property after deducting capital contributions, loan principal reductions, and mortgage balance.

net boot: The cash or its equivalent which is left after all calculations in an exchange of property.

O

occupancy requirement: The requirement that the Occupier exclusively reside at the joint ownership property.

Occupier: The co-owner who occupies and maintains the joint ownership property.

P

power of sale: A secured party's entitlement to sell the secured property if the buyer defaults on payment or other terms of the contract.

principal: The amount of money provided for in a mortgage or loan, before interest accrues.

property tax deduction: Fully deductible tax paid to the county in which a property is located.

principal residence: The dwelling where an individual intends to permanently reside and lives in the majority of the year, as opposed to a vacation or second home.

R

rate of return: The interest earned on an investment, expressed as a percentage.

reassessment exemption: Exemption from local property tax reassessment, available to homeowners 55 years of age in California (Proposition 60).

refinance: The process of substituting a new mortgage for an old mortgage, or to extend or renew the current mortgage.

relinquished property: The property exchanged out of in an IRC §1031 exchange.

replacement property: The property exchanged into in an IRC §1031 exchange.

retained equity: When a seller becomes Investor, the property's value less the new loan and Occupier's down payment; the value a joint ownership Seller-Investor retains in the joint ownership property.

roll down: Partially taxed replacement of a principal residence of less value within two years of sale per IRC §1034.

roll over: Tax free replacement of a principal residence within two years of sale per IRC §1034.

S

secondary market: The market where mortgages are bought and sold.

security instrument: A contract between lender and borrower where property is offered as collateral for loan repayment as proven by a note and a deed of trust or mortgage.

Seller-Investor: A seller who becomes a joint ownership co-owner in his own property.

statutory process: A legal process mandated by statute.

straight line depreciation: A method of depreciation whereby real estate is depreciated in equal annual amounts over its lifetime.

subordination clause: An agreement by the holder of a lien on real property to take a junior position to another lien on the same property.

supply and demand: In appraisal, the principle which represents property market value as affected by the interaction of supply and demand forces in the market.

sweat equity: The value of property improvement work performed by the Occupier and credited to him as a capital contribution.

T

tenancy in common: Co-ownership of a property by persons who each have undivided interest in the property. If one owner dies, that individual's interest is transferred to the deceased's heirs, not to the co-owner.

third party: In a transaction, someone other than the Seller and Occupier.

title company: A service which insures, guarantees, and records title to real property.

trustee: A person or organization who holds property for another person to secure the completion of contractual obligations; the foreclosing entity under a deed of trust.

U

unlawful detainer: A legal process for achieving eviction.

usury laws: Laws that limit and regulate lenders' return on their loans.

V

VA mortgage: A low interest, low down payment loan guaranteed by the Veteran's Administration.

voluntary improvements: Improvements to real property that are optional or aesthetic in nature, which may or may not affect the life or value of the property.

W

wrap around mortgage: A mortgage which includes the seller's existing loan (the wrapped mortgage).

Index

Sample provisions in the Joint Ownership Agreement are noted in **bold**.

ORDER FORM

Do not include Fax on Demand or E-Mail, which are billed by Invoice.

_____ Payment enclosed (check or money order only): $_____

_____ VISA _____ MC   Acct. No._____-_____-_____-_____

Expiration date _____   Signature _____

Ship to: Name:_____

Address:_____

BOOKS ORDERED: **Quantity: _____ at $24.95** . . . . $_____

shipping   UPS Ground: $ 5 1st item, $2 each addl.   _____

and   UPS 1 Day: $20 1st item, $3 each addl.   _____

handling: UPS 2 Day: $11 1st item, $2 each addl.   _____

DOCUMENTS/SOFTWARE BY MAIL:

(complete back of this form) . . . . $_____

shipping   Regular Mail: 6% of total   _____

and   UPS 1 Day: Greater of $17 or 25% of total   _____

handling: UPS 2 Day: Greater of $12 or 15% of total   _____

SALES TAX: (shipments within California) 7.75% of total . . . . . .   _____

TOTAL OF ORDER . . . . $_____

See Over ⇒

For Software [3¼" disk] - Specify each:

Computer:	**Word Processing:**	**Spreadsheet:**
_____ IBM Compatible	_____ Word	_____ Excel
_____ MacIntosh	_____ WP	_____ Lotus

[Returns on damaged/defective items only.]

☞ **Fax-on-Demand orders: (415) 461-7700.** Many documents are available fax-to-fax dialing from the handset of your fax machine. Follow the prompts to order documents, then press the start button on your fax machine. You will immediately receive the documents requested and an invoice attached for prompt payment. No shipping fees or sales tax.

☎ **Telephone orders: toll free (800) 843-6700.** Provide name, mailing address, Visa or Mastercard number, expiration date, and items requested.

▬ **General fax orders: (415) 461-4509.** Fax Order Form front and back.

✿ **On-line orders: www.venture2K.com.** Visit our site on the World Wide Web to download the documents you need. No shipping fees or sales tax.

✉ **E-Mail Orders: venture2k@worldnet.att.net.** For computer-to-computer orders. Provide information requested by Order Form, front and back, including mailing or E-mail address, and list documents requested. No shipping fees or sales tax.

⌂ **Mail orders:** Venture 2000 Publishers, 100 Larkspur Landing Circle, Suite 112, Larkspur, CA 94939 Send Order Form, front and back. (415) 461-1470

◼ **Trade orders:** National Book Network, 4720 Boston Way, Lanham, MD 20706 Telephone: (800) 462-6420

Document/Software Catalog
[Please circle your choices]

No.	Document Name	Hard Copy	Software	Fax on Demand/ E-Mail
01	Joint Ownership Preliminary Commitment	See 21-22	See 21-22	$1.00
02	Grant Deed	"	"	1.99
03	Memorandum of Joint Ownership	"	"	1.99
04	Joint Ownership Note and Trust Deed	"	"	9.99
05	Joint Ownership Note and Mortgage	"	"	9.99
06	Joint Ownership Lease	"	"	3.99
07	Joint Ownership Agreement - Standard	$29.99	$39.99	n/a
08	Joint Ownership Agreement - Family	29.99	39.99	n/a
09	Joint Ownership Agreement - No Compliance with IRC §280A	29.99	39.99	n/a
10	Joint Ownership Agreement - Joint Occupancy w/ All Necessary Documents	41.50	55.00	n/a
11	Joint Ownership Agreement - Gifting by Relatives, $10,000/yr. w/All NecessaryDocs.	44.99	59.99	n/a
12	Seller Financed Purchase Agreement	14.99	19.99	19.99
13	Seller Financed Promissory Note, Trust Deed	See 23	See 23	9.99
14	Seller Financed Promissory Note, Mortgage	See 23	See 23	9.99
15	Seller Financed Installment Sale Contract with Recordable Memorandum	16.99	21.99	n/a
16	Standard Purchase Agreement - No Joint Ownership	14.99	19.99	19.99
17	Purchase Agreement w/ Rescission Feature [seller in foreclosure] - California	17.99	22.99	n/a
18	Lease Option Agreement	12.99	16.99	16.99
19	Joint Ownership Lease Option Agreement	35.99	47.99	n/a
20	Standard Promissory Notes and Deeds of Trust/Mortgage	10.99	13.99	13.99
21	All documents 01 through 06	18.99	23.99	n/a
22	All documents 01 through 07	41.50	55.00	n/a
23	All documents 02, 12, 13, 14	26.99	35.99	n/a
24	IRC §121	n/a	n/a	1.99
25	IRC §280A	n/a	n/a	1.99
26	IRC §1031	n/a	n/a	2.99
27	IRC §1034	n/a	n/a	2.99
28	All IRC sections 121, 280A, 1031 and 1034	5.00	n/a	7.99
29	Book: *The New Home Buying Strategy*	24.95	n/a	n/a
30	Joint Ownership Calculator	n/a	29.99	n/a

ORDER FORM

Do not include Fax on Demand or E-Mail, which are billed by Invoice.

_____ Payment enclosed (check or money order only): $_____

_____ VISA _____ MC   Acct. No._____-_____-_____-_____

Expiration date _____   Signature _____

Ship to: Name:_____

         Address:_____

BOOKS ORDERED: **Quantity:** _____ **at $24.95**. . . . . $_____

    shipping   UPS Ground: $ 5 1st item, $2 each addl.   _____

    and   UPS 1 Day: $20 1st item, $3 each addl.   _____

    handling: UPS 2 Day: $11 1st item, $2 each addl.   _____

DOCUMENTS/SOFTWARE BY MAIL:

(complete back of this form) . . . . $_____

    shipping   Regular Mail: 6% of total   _____

    and   UPS 1 Day: Greater of $17 or 25% of total   _____

    handling: UPS 2 Day: Greater of $12 or 15% of total   _____

SALES TAX: **(shipments within California)** 7.75% of total . . . . . .   _____

TOTAL OF ORDER . . . . $_____

                                   See Over ⇒

For Software [3¼" disk] - Specify each:

Computer:	**Word Processing:**	**Spreadsheet:**
_____ IBM Compatible	_____ Word	_____ Excel
_____ MacIntosh	_____ WP	_____ Lotus

[Returns on damaged/defective items only.]

☞ **Fax-on-Demand orders: (415) 461-7700.** Many documents are available fax-to-fax dialing from the handset of your fax machine. Follow the prompts to order documents, then press the start button on your fax machine. You will immediately receive the documents requested and an invoice attached for prompt payment. No shipping fees or sales tax.

☎ **Telephone orders: toll free (800) 843-6700.** Provide name, mailing address, Visa or Mastercard number, expiration date, and items requested.

▪ **General fax orders: (415) 461-4509.** Fax Order Form front and back.

✿ **On-line orders: www.venture2K.com.** Visit our site on the World Wide Web to download the documents you need. No shipping fees or sales tax.

✉ **E-Mail Orders: venture2k@worldnet.att.net.** For computer-to-computer orders. Provide information requested by Order Form, front and back, including mailing or E-mail address, and list documents requested. No shipping fees or sales tax.

⌂ **Mail orders:** Venture 2000 Publishers, 100 Larkspur Landing Circle, Suite 112, Larkspur, CA 94939 Send Order Form, front and back. (415) 461-1470

◼ **Trade orders:** National Book Network, 4720 Boston Way, Lanham, MD 20706 Telephone: (800) 462-6420

Document/Software Catalog
[Please circle your choices]

No.	Document Name	Hard Copy	Software	Fax on Demand/ E-Mail
01	Joint Ownership Preliminary Commitment	See 21-22	See 21-22	$1.00
02	Grant Deed	"	"	1.99
03	Memorandum of Joint Ownership	"	"	1.99
04	Joint Ownership Note and Trust Deed	"	"	9.99
05	Joint Ownership Note and Mortgage	"	"	9.99
06	Joint Ownership Lease	"	"	3.99
07	Joint Ownership Agreement - Standard	$29.99	$39.99	n/a
08	Joint Ownership Agreement - Family	29.99	39.99	n/a
09	Joint Ownership Agreement - No Compliance with IRC §280A	29.99	39.99	n/a
10	Joint Ownership Agreement - Joint Occupancy w/ All Necessary Documents	41.50	55.00	n/a
11	Joint Ownership Agreement - Gifting by Relatives, $10,000/yr. w/All NecessaryDocs.	44.99	59.99	n/a
12	Seller Financed Purchase Agreement	14.99	19.99	19.99
13	Seller Financed Promissory Note, Trust Deed	See 23	See 23	9.99
14	Seller Financed Promissory Note, Mortgage	See 23	See 23	9.99
15	Seller Financed Installment Sale Contract with Recordable Memorandum	16.99	21.99	n/a
16	Standard Purchase Agreement - No Joint Ownership	14.99	19.99	19.99
17	Purchase Agreement w/ Rescission Feature [seller in foreclosure] - California	17.99	22.99	n/a
18	Lease Option Agreement	12.99	16.99	16.99
19	Joint Ownership Lease Option Agreement	35.99	47.99	n/a
20	Standard Promissory Notes and Deeds of Trust/Mortgage	10.99	13.99	13.99
21	All documents 01 through 06	18.99	23.99	n/a
22	All documents 01 through 07	41.50	55.00	n/a
23	All documents 02, 12, 13, 14	26.99	35.99	n/a
24	IRC §121	n/a	n/a	1.99
25	IRC §280A	n/a	n/a	1.99
26	IRC §1031	n/a	n/a	2.99
27	IRC §1034	n/a	n/a	2.99
28	All IRC sections 121, 280A, 1031 and 1034	5.00	n/a	7.99
29	Book: *The New Home Buying Strategy*	24.95	n/a	n/a
30	Joint Ownership Calculator	n/a	29.99	n/a

ORDER FORM

Do not include Fax on Demand or E-Mail, which are billed by Invoice.

_____ Payment enclosed (check or money order only): $_____

_____ VISA _____ MC   Acct. No._____-_____-_____-_____

Expiration date _____   Signature _____

Ship to: Name:_____

Address:_____

BOOKS ORDERED:	**Quantity:** _____ **at $24.95**	$_____
shipping	UPS Ground: $ 5 1st item, $2 each addl.	_____
and	UPS 1 Day: $20 1st item, $3 each addl.	_____
handling:	UPS 2 Day: $11 1st item, $2 each addl.	_____

DOCUMENTS/SOFTWARE BY MAIL:

(complete back of this form)		$_____
shipping	Regular Mail: 6% of total	_____
and	UPS 1 Day: Greater of $17 or 25% of total	_____
handling:	UPS 2 Day: Greater of $12 or 15% of total	_____

SALES TAX: (shipments within California) 7.75% of total . . . . . .   _____

TOTAL OF ORDER . . . . $_____

See Over ⇒

For Software [3¼" disk] - Specify each:

Computer:	**Word Processing:**	**Spreadsheet:**
_____ IBM Compatible	_____ Word	_____ Excel
_____ MacIntosh	_____ WP	_____ Lotus

[Returns on damaged/defective items only.]

☞ **Fax-on-Demand orders: (415) 461-7700.** Many documents are available fax-to-fax dialing from the handset of your fax machine. Follow the prompts to order documents, then press the start button on your fax machine. You will immediately receive the documents requested and an invoice attached for prompt payment. No shipping fees or sales tax.

☎ **Telephone orders: toll free (800) 843-6700.** Provide name, mailing address, Visa or Mastercard number, expiration date, and items requested.

▬ **General fax orders: (415) 461-4509.** Fax Order Form front and back.

✿ **On-line orders: www.venture2K.com.** Visit our site on the World Wide Web to download the documents you need. No shipping fees or sales tax.

⊠ **E-Mail Orders: venture2k@worldnet.att.net.** For computer-to-computer orders. Provide information requested by Order Form, front and back, including mailing or E-mail address, and list documents requested. No shipping fees or sales tax.

⌂ **Mail orders:** Venture 2000 Publishers, 100 Larkspur Landing Circle, Suite 112, Larkspur, CA 94939 Send Order Form, front and back. (415) 461-1470

◘ **Trade orders:** National Book Network, 4720 Boston Way, Lanham, MD 20706 Telephone: (800) 462-6420

Document/Software Catalog
[Please circle your choices]

No.	Document Name	Hard Copy	Software	Fax on Demand/ E-Mail
01	Joint Ownership Preliminary Commitment	See 21-22	See 21-22	$1.00
02	Grant Deed	"	"	1.99
03	Memorandum of Joint Ownership	"	"	1.99
04	Joint Ownership Note and Trust Deed	"	"	9.99
05	Joint Ownership Note and Mortgage	"	"	9.99
06	Joint Ownership Lease	"	"	3.99
07	Joint Ownership Agreement - Standard	$29.99	$39.99	n/a
08	Joint Ownership Agreement - Family	29.99	39.99	n/a
09	Joint Ownership Agreement - No Compliance with IRC §280A	29.99	39.99	n/a
10	Joint Ownership Agreement - Joint Occupancy w/ All Necessary Documents	41.50	55.00	n/a
11	Joint Ownership Agreement - Gifting by Relatives, $10,000/yr. w/All NecessaryDocs.	44.99	59.99	n/a
12	Seller Financed Purchase Agreement	14.99	19.99	19.99
13	Seller Financed Promissory Note, Trust Deed	See 23	See 23	9.99
14	Seller Financed Promissory Note, Mortgage	See 23	See 23	9.99
15	Seller Financed Installment Sale Contract with Recordable Memorandum	16.99	21.99	n/a
16	Standard Purchase Agreement - No Joint Ownership	14.99	19.99	19.99
17	Purchase Agreement w/ Rescission Feature [seller in foreclosure] - California	17.99	22.99	n/a
18	Lease Option Agreement	12.99	16.99	16.99
19	Joint Ownership Lease Option Agreement	35.99	47.99	n/a
20	Standard Promissory Notes and Deeds of Trust/Mortgage	10.99	13.99	13.99
21	All documents 01 through 06	18.99	23.99	n/a
22	All documents 01 through 07	41.50	55.00	n/a
23	All documents 02, 12, 13, 14	26.99	35.99	n/a
24	IRC §121	n/a	n/a	1.99
25	IRC §280A	n/a	n/a	1.99
26	IRC §1031	n/a	n/a	2.99
27	IRC §1034	n/a	n/a	2.99
28	All IRC sections 121, 280A, 1031 and 1034	5.00	n/a	7.99
29	Book: *The New Home Buying Strategy*	24.95	n/a	n/a
30	Joint Ownership Calculator	n/a	29.99	n/a